# Taking Shergar

# TAKING
# SHERGAR

*Thoroughbred Racing's*
*Most Famous Cold Case*

MILTON C. TOBY

UNIVERSITY PRESS OF KENTUCKY

Published by The University Press of Kentucky,
scholarly publisher for the Commonwealth,
serving Bellarmine University, Berea College, Centre College of Kentucky,
Eastern Kentucky University, The Filson Historical Society, Georgetown
College, Kentucky Historical Society, Kentucky State University, Morehead
State University, Murray State University, Northern Kentucky University,
Transylvania University, University of Kentucky, University of Louisville,
and Western Kentucky University.
All rights reserved.

*Editorial and Sales Offices:* The University Press of Kentucky
663 South Limestone Street, Lexington, Kentucky 40508-4008
www.kentuckypress.com

Maps by Dick Gilbreath, independent cartographer.

Library of Congress Cataloging-in-Publication Data

Names: Toby, Milton C., author.
Title: Taking Shergar : thoroughbred racing's most famous cold case / Milton
    C. Toby.
Description: Lexington, Kentucky : The University Press of Kentucky, [2018] |
    Series: Horses in history | Includes bibliographical references and index.
Identifiers: LCCN 2018021886| ISBN 9780813176239 (hardcover : alk.
paper) |
    ISBN 9780813176352 (pdf) | ISBN 9780813176369 (epub)
Subjects: LCSH: Horse stealing—Ireland. | Shergar (Race horse)
Classification: LCC HV6665.I73 T63 2018 | DDC
364.16/286361094185—dc23
LC record available at https://lccn.loc.gov/2018021886

This book is printed on acid-free paper meeting
the requirements of the American National Standard
for Permanence in Paper for Printed Library Materials.

Manufactured in the United States of America.

Member of the Association of University Presses

# Contents

Shergar in training as a three-year-old in 1981. (Ed Byrne)

# Author's Note

I met insurance man Julian Lloyd three years ago during a research trip to Ireland and England. We got together in the lobby of an upscale hotel across the road from the Tower of London to talk about Shergar. Julian was in Ireland when the stallion was stolen more than three decades earlier, and he stayed in the country for a few weeks afterward to monitor the search as an unofficial representative for insurance giant Lloyd's of London.[1] The facts of the theft had been widely reported at the time, along with speculation and wild theories, but I was confident that there was more to the story. Julian was a good place to start my research, and the extraordinary tale he told did not disappoint.

Late on a February evening in 1983, the unthinkable happened. A gang of armed men drove onto Ballymany Stud near The Curragh Racecourse, took Epsom Derby winner Shergar from his stall in the stallion barn, loaded him into a horse trailer, and drove off into the night. Ransom was demanded for Shergar but not paid, and neither the horse nor his remains were ever recovered. It is an intriguing puzzle, a cold case that remains unsolved—officially, at least.

When he learned that Shergar was missing, Julian immediately contacted Lloyd's. That telephone call, he said, initiated a series of communications that ended in the offices of the Mobius Group in California. Julian's recollection was that Mobius was a mysterious gathering of psychics who did secret work for clandestine intelligence services in the United States, and that the organization had been hired to search for Shergar. Julian was wrong about the intelligence work but correct that Mobius was an important piece of the Shergar puzzle, a part of the story that remained hidden for thirty-five years.

It took almost two years of on-again, off-again searching, but in March 2017 I found myself on an island located off the coast of Washington State, surrounded by two dozen maps of Ireland spread across a dining table once owned by Robert E. Lee. The table and the maps belonged to Stephan A. Schwartz, founder of the Mobius Group, in reality a research organization that investigated remote viewing.

Among the boxes crammed with files Schwartz presented me with, I came across a padded manila envelope sealed with a row of staples. Inside were a protective shin boot and pieces of thick felt cut from a saddle pad, both worn by Shergar during his racing days. I also found a Polaroid photograph that I believe to be part of the proof supplied by the thieves during ransom negotiations to show that Shergar still was alive. The blurred image, the boot, and the bits of felt were tangible and poignant links to a story that had occupied several years of my life.

The story of Schwartz, Mobius, and the part they played in the final search for Shergar is told here for the first time.

Julian Lloyd was certain that men from the Provisional Irish Republican Army were behind the plot to steal Shergar. The IRA never claimed responsibility for the theft, and some people assumed that no one from Ireland, where people have a centuries-old affinity for horses, would do such a thing. An Garda Síochána, the national police force in the Republic of Ireland, never made any arrests, and as of this writing their files remain unavailable for review.[2] Other official records that might shed light on the theft also remain hidden.[3]

I conducted numerous interviews for this book, both in the United States and during a series of trips to Ireland and England. No one I spoke with doubted that the IRA was responsible for taking Shergar that gloomy February night. There is ample circumstantial evidence pointing toward the IRA, much of it discussed in the following pages, and I agree with that conclusion.

But there's a problem.

"Knowing" and "proving" are very different. The fact that the Irish Republican Army never claimed responsibility for taking Shergar certainly does not absolve the IRA, but it was atypical for an organization with a well-documented record of accepting the blame for bombings, killings, and just about anything else that might help drive British troops

Shergar was one of eight horses featured in the Royal Mail's Racehorse Legends series of postage stamps released in 2017. Other horses in the series were Frankel, Red Rum, Kauto Star, Desert Orchid, Brigadier Gerard, Arkle, and Estimate. (Reproduced with kind permission of Royal Mail Group Limited © Royal Mail Group Limited 2017)

from Northern Ireland. Despite lengthy investigations and a massive countrywide search for Shergar and the people who took him, no one ever has been arrested or charged with the theft.

Officially, the loss of Shergar remains a decidedly cold case. Unofficially, however, there is widespread agreement that the Provos (an Irish slang term for members of the Provisional IRA) were involved in the disappearance of the famous stallion.[4] Perhaps investigations by the Garda were unsuccessful. Or perhaps the authorities gathered sufficient evidence but chose not to pursue the case to conclusion for reasons known only to them. Absent a conviction, or at least a confession under oath in a civil proceeding—both unlikely after the passage of so much time—IRA involvement in the theft of Shergar necessarily will remain speculative.

Alternative theories have been proposed. One connects the death of a French bloodstock agent in Kentucky to the theft, another relates that Shergar was stolen as retribution against his breeder, the Aga Khan, during a long-running legal battle, a third brings Libyan strongman Colonel Muammar al-Qadhafi into the mix. None of these explanations stand up to strict scrutiny, however.

Nonetheless, readers should proceed with the understanding that IRA involvement in the theft of Shergar, no matter how strong the supporting evidence, is a theory that might be wrong. Things become even more problematic when attention focuses on specific individuals, as we will see. For me, though, the lack of any viable alternative solutions to the Shergar puzzle makes a compelling argument that the Provos are the culprits in horse racing's most famous cold case.

Or, as Sherlock Holmes explained to Dr. Watson in *The Sign of Four:* "How often have I said to you that when you have eliminated the impossible, whatever remains, *however improbable,* must be the truth?"

# Missing

Ghislain Drion and Stan Cosgrove stood staring into an empty stall in the stallion barn at Ballymany Stud, unable to believe what they were seeing. Drion had collected Cosgrove after learning that Epsom Derby winner Shergar had been stolen and they had driven together to Ballymany to confirm for themselves that the horse was gone. Drion managed Ballymany and the other Irish farms owned by the Aga Khan IV and Cosgrove was a prominent veterinarian who owned a share in the horse. They realized that they had to do something—but what, exactly?[1]

Time was already running out for Shergar, although hardly anyone knew it then, when the jangling of a telephone woke Captain Sean Berry from a sound sleep. The call came at 3:30 in the morning on Wednesday, February 9, 1983.

The caller was a longtime friend, Kildare veterinarian Stan Cosgrove.[2] Agitated, he asked for the telephone number of Patrick W. McGrath, a prominent Thoroughbred breeder and a member of the syndicate that owned Shergar. Something serious had happened, Cosgrove said, something that Captain Berry would read about in the morning papers.

Soldiers and horsemen are used to interrupted sleep, accustomed by their vocations and their experience to being awakened at all hours of the night. Berry was both: a longtime veteran of infantry service in India, Pakistan, and the Middle East, and at the time, the secretary of the influential Irish Thoroughbred Breeders Association. Now he was being dragged out of a warm bed on one of the coldest, most miserable nights Ireland would experience that year. Serious or not, Berry thought, to hell with it. He asked no questions—simply gave his friend the number, dropped the telephone into its cradle, and went back to bed.

Cosgrove called again a quarter hour later, just as Berry was drifting off to sleep. "Shergar has been stolen," he said bluntly.

This time, Cosgrove had Captain Berry's undivided attention. As he hurriedly dressed and headed for the door, he must have suspected that no member of the Berry family would enjoy a peaceful night again for weeks to come.[3]

It was 4:00 in the morning and sunrise still was hours away when Captain Berry arrived at Stan Cosgrove's home. The place was alive with activity. Ghislain Drion, a Frenchman who managed the Aga Khan IV's Irish farms, was on one telephone trying to reach his boss; a local officer from An Garda Síochána, Inspector Senan Keogh, was on another phone talking with Chief Superintendent James Murphy at the Garda station in Naas, ten miles away.[4]

About eight hours earlier, a gang of masked men, some armed with automatic weapons, had pushed through an unlocked and unguarded gate at the Aga Khan's Ballymany Stud.[5] They kidnapped the stud groom, James Fitzgerald, and hauled Shergar away in a battered horse trailer. Fitzgerald was later released unharmed but badly shaken and fearful for his family's safety. After he made his way back to Ballymany, he notified Drion, who got in touch with Stan Cosgrove, who in turn called Berry for help.

Last to be notified were the authorities. It was an omission that gave the thieves some eight hours of driving time without pursuit and it almost certainly doomed the hunt for Shergar before it even started. Berry immediately recognized the logistical problems caused by those lost eight hours. Even at the pedestrian speed of thirty miles an hour, reasonable considering the wet roads and darkness, in eight hours the thieves could have taken Shergar across the breadth of the republic or traveled across the border into Northern Ireland.

The main Garda stations were linked by radio, and the military was on constant alert because of the Troubles in Northern Ireland.[6] Captain Berry knew that roadblocks could have been put in place and cordon-and-search operations could have been mounted, but only if there had been sufficient time. He also knew that those opportunities were lost forever. The chances of finding Shergar alive and well had plummeted already.

"In my business," Berry later recalled, the telephone calls from Cosgrove were "the equivalent of the director of the Louvre in Paris" being told that "the *Mona Lisa* had been stolen." It was an apt comparison. Shergar was the most important—and the most valuable—Thoroughbred stallion standing at stud in Ireland: European Horse of the Year in 1981, when he won the Epsom Derby by ten lengths for his breeder, the Aga Khan IV.[7]

Captain Berry's analogy was more apropos than he could imagine. An Epsom Derby winner like Shergar and a piece of fine art—the *Mona Lisa,* perhaps, or a Vermeer or a Rembrandt—have much in common. Products of genetics and genius, respectively, they are unique and impossible to replace. In that regard, they are priceless. If stolen, however, a stallion or a painting is worth what the owner or an insurance company will pay to get it back.

Seven years after Shergar went missing and an ocean away in Boston, thieves ransacked the Isabella Stewart Gardner Museum, a castle-like structure not far from Fenway Park. They made off with several paintings from the museum's Dutch Room, including Vermeer's *The Concert* and two works by Rembrandt, *The Storm on the Sea of Galilee* and *A Lady and Gentleman in Black.* The value of the missing paintings was estimated at about $500 million. The Gardner paintings have not been recovered, despite the offer of a multimillion-dollar reward for their return.

Empty frames where the missing paintings once hung, mute reminders of the theft, still greet visitors to the Gardner's Dutch Room. At Ballymany Stud, the brass nameplate that identified Shergar's stall was removed, the farm later was sold, and fading memories of the Epsom Derby winner are all that remain. The Gardner theft generated a number of theories. Most ironic was a supposed link between the missing paint-ings, gangster and FBI informer James J. "Whitey" Bulger, and the Irish Republican Army.[8] Although not specifically addressing the missing Gardner paintings, a subsequent report that dissident members of the IRA had a cache of valuable paintings that could be sold to raise funds or exchanged for weapons lends additional credence to IRA involvement in the theft of Shergar.[9]

That Shergar stayed in Ireland at stud was something of a miracle. A group of American breeders was prepared to pay $28 million to syndi-cate Shergar, and there were unconfirmed offers from the United States that went as high as $40 million.[10] With that much money on the table, it was natural to assume that Shergar was bound for the United States when his racing career was over. The same thing had happened decades earlier when the Aga Khan III sold three Epsom Derby winners to the Americans, in the process drawing the ire of European breeders. Most everyone expected it to happen all over again with Shergar.

The Aga Khan declined those offers, though, and put together a syndicate of his own for substantially less money. There was an impor-tant proviso to the agreement: a requirement that Shergar would stand at Ballymany Stud adjacent to The Curragh Racecourse, located between Kildare and Newbridge.

Although investigations by the Garda into the Shergar mystery were inconclusive, Captain Berry had no doubt then or now about who was behind Shergar's theft: "The IRA certainly did it."

# 1

# Birth of an Empire

His Highness the Aga Khan was a happy man that day, a very happy man. Happier, even, than wildly popular racecourse tout Prince Monolulu, no mean feat at Epsom on Derby Day.

A year earlier, at a press luncheon preceding the 1929 running of the classic race, the Aga Khan speculated that the reporters might find themselves writing about him the following year, as the breeder of his first Derby winner.[1] The Aga Khan apparently did not share with the reporters which among his homebreds he thought would win the 1930 Derby—it was too early in the season for that sort of guessing about untested juveniles—but he seemed confident that it would be one of them.

It was a bold prediction for a man who had been buying and racing horses in England for less than a decade; whether the reporters in attendance that day shared the Aga Khan's optimism is unknown. What should have been clear, however, was that the Aga Khan already had put together a powerful stable that justified the prediction. In 1924, a scant three years after buying his first yearlings at auction, the Aga Khan won English classics with horses purchased on his behalf by George Lambton—Two Thousand Guineas winner Diophon and St. Leger winner Salmon Trout. His goal, though, was to win the Epsom Derby with a homebred. Now, with the sun finally breaking through the heavy mist that had shrouded the grounds at Epsom in the hours leading up to the 1930 Derby, the Aga Khan's prediction of the year before was going to come true—or so it seemed to a man whose vision was suspect.

The Aga Khan wore thick eyeglasses and from his place in the stands he could see a horse with his green and chocolate racing silks challenging for the lead. He was correct about the silks but mistaken about the horse. At that distance the Aga Khan could not distinguish between homebred Rustom Pasha, one of the favorites for the race, and Blenheim, a long shot that the Aga Khan purchased as a yearling. He expected Rustom Pasha to be in the lead, but he was wrong.[2]

His Highness Sultan Mohamed Shah, the third man to carry the title of Aga Khan, was a man of contrasts, complexities, and a few contradictions.[3] He was the spiritual leader of millions of Ismaili Muslims around the world who revered him as a descendant of the Prophet Muhammad's family. Beyond recognition from the faithful, though, there was also an unusual legal precedent recognizing his authority over the Ismailis.

In 1866 in the High Court of Bombay, Justice Sir Joseph Arnould was asked to rule on a religious dispute that had festered for decades. The Khojas were a group in India that did not adhere to a single religion. Instead, they followed a mix of Hindu and Muslim practices, and because of that dichotomy some of their members refused to pay the usual tithes to the first Aga Khan (the Aga Khan III's grandfather). The principal legal question for Justice Arnould involved the religious status of the Khojas and whether they were entitled to govern themselves without interference from the Aga Khan, who was named as a defendant in the case.

Although the lawsuit against the Aga Khan raised several related legal questions, attorneys for both sides agreed that the court's decision turned on the answer to only one question: whether the Khojas were Sunni Muslims or Shia Muslims. If the former, the Khojas owned no allegiance to the Aga Khan; if the latter, the Aga Khan gained legitimacy as their spiritual leader with a lineage stretching forty-eight generations back to Ali, cousin and son-in-law of the Prophet.[4]

Justice Arnould conducted a complicated and often convoluted examination of the centuries-old relationships between the Khojas, traditional Muslim and Hindu faiths, the Aga Khan, and important religious texts, among them the *Das Avtaar*. Justice Arnould then ruled that the Khojas at one point in their history had converted to the Ismaili faith—for legal purposes at least—and that the Aga Khan was thus the imam of the Khojas.[5] The decision marked the last serious legal challenge to the Aga Khan's leadership of the Ismailis.

The Aga Khan was recognized around the world as a tireless philanthropist who devoted his time, energy, and growing financial resources to the welfare of his Ismaili followers. He also was a gifted statesman—albeit one without an actual state—who served as the first president of the All-India Muslim League and as president of the League of Nations from 1937 to 1938.[6]

On the secular side, the Aga Khan enjoyed lavish celebrations held in his honor, the company of beautiful women, and his horses—some of the best runners in Europe from the early 1920s through the mid-1950s. He also was a connoisseur of good food and a lover of off-color stories that he told in as many languages as necessary—whether English, French, Italian, or Urdu—to get the punch lines across to his guests.[7]

The Aga Khan was revered by millions of Ismailis, who never seemed to begrudge him a lavish lifestyle that was worlds apart from anything they could imagine for themselves. The Aga Khan received his weight in gold for his Golden Jubilee, a celebration in Bombay (now Mumbai) that attracted more than thirty thousand people in 1936. Similar tributes, with appropriate gifts of precious gems and metals for his Diamond and Platinum Jubilees, followed.[8] Proceeds raised during the Aga Khan's various jubilee celebrations helped fund social welfare and development projects and institutions in Asia and Africa.[9]

The Aga Khan's goals as a young sportsman were simple: to win the Viceroy's Cup in India, to win the Epsom Derby in Great Britain, and to win a golf match over the Old Course in St. Andrews, Scotland.[10] Winning the Epsom Derby was the most important for both sentimental and economic reasons. Recalling the 1930s, when he was building the most dominant stable in England, the Aga Khan later told a friend that he needed to win the Derby at least every other year to avoid showing a loss.[11]

The Aga Khan's horses captured the Viceroy's Cup in 1928 and the

Epsom Derby three times during the 1930s and twice more in the post–World War II years. His record at St. Andrews remains unknown.

Ras Prince Monolulu, on the other hand, was a complete fraud. A self-proclaimed African prince with supposed roots in Abyssinia, he sported a tall headdress with ostrich feather plumes and colorful robes festooned with good-luck charms. For decades he made the rounds of British racecourses touting horses. He was an enthusiastic target for photographers, and coverage of major British races of the time more often than not included a still image or motion picture glimpse of the prince hawking his tip sheets and shouting, "I gotta horse!" or "Black man for luck!"[12]

He managed to pick the 1920 Epsom Derby winner, a rank outsider named Spion Kop, but his skill as a handicapper was neither obvious nor really important to the throngs of bettors that gathered around him. He was a character in the truest sense of the word, an outrageous figure who could make his good friend Groucho Marx appear relatively normal during an appearance with a woman who might or might not have been the prince's wife on *You Bet Your Life.*[13]

Win or lose, buying one of the sealed envelopes with a Prince Monolulu tip tucked inside was an experience to be savored.[14]

Prince Monolulu was friends with Jeffrey Bernard, a British journalist and raconteur whose drinking habits were legendary and whose beats included horse racing and daily life in the Soho district of London. In February 1965, Bernard's editor sent him to interview Prince Monolulu in a Middlesex hospital ward. Bernard appeared at the hospital with a box of Black Magic chocolates for his friend, a questionable choice considering Prince Monolulu's advanced age (eighty-two), and his ill health. Prince Monolulu lacked the strength to eat the chocolates on his own, so Bernard made an ill-conceived effort to help. He dug a strawberry cream from the box and pushed it into the old man's mouth. The prince tried to swallow the candy but could not; then he coughed and started to choke. Bernard summoned a nurse, but by the time she arrived, it was too late. Prince Monolulu had choked to death on the strawberry cream.

Bernard's biographer, Graham Lord, would characterize the unfortunate turn of events at the Middlesex hospital as just another in a series of many "odd things" that seemed to happen whenever Bernard was around. When things went wrong, Lord explained, Bernard generally was the "most unpredictable catalyst."[15]

But in 1930 Prince Monolulu was at the top of his game, although whether he managed to pick the winner of the Epsom Derby that year is unknown. There is a reasonable chance that he did, though. His tip sheets tended to favor long shots—anyone could pick a favorite, but to come up with the occasional surprising winner, when the odds were high and the payoffs large, was more impressive to the prince's patrons. And the winner of the Derby that year was indeed a long shot—dismissed by his owner, the stable jockey, and just about everyone else.

Homebred Rustom Pasha was a sentimental Derby choice for the Aga Khan because his dam, Cos, had been one of his first purchases in England. Cos also delivered the Aga Khan's first stakes win in England, in the 1922 Queen Mary Stakes. The Aga Khan liked Rustom Pasha's chances in the Derby, and so did the bettors, who made him the second choice. Favored was Diolite, the best juvenile of 1929 and winner of the Two Thousand Guineas a few weeks earlier.

Hardly anyone—including the Aga Khan—gave the stable's other runner, Blenheim, much of a chance in the Derby, and for good reason.[16] Blenheim was one of the top-rated juveniles in 1929, but each of his four wins that year came at five furlongs. The Epsom Derby is run over twelve furlongs, and Blenheim had done nothing as a three-year-old to suggest that he could live up to his stayer's pedigree.[17] Blenheim's potential as a stayer was tarnished even more when he failed to place in the one-mile Greenham Plate at Newbury and in Diolite's Two Thousand Guineas at the same distance.

Further complicating comparisons between the Aga Khan's runners was a stable practice of never training horses entered in the same race together.[18] The best evidence available to bettors was this: Paradine ran second in the Two Thousand Guineas, with Blenheim fourth, and

Rustom Pasha soundly trounced Paradine, giving up seven pounds, in the one-and-one-sixteenth-mile Nonsuch Stakes.

On paper, at least, Rustom Pasha looked to be around four lengths and seven pounds better than Blenheim, justifying the disparity in odds for the two horses. Blenheim had undeniable speed, but the colt had done little to prove that he could stay over a distance. Michael Beary, the Aga Khan's regular stable jockey, agreed with that assessment and chose Rustom Pasha; the mount on Blenheim went to Harry Wragg, a veteran rider who had won the 1928 Epsom Derby with Felstead.

Ultimately, Epsom bettors dismissed Blenheim at odds of 18-1. The Aga Khan reportedly did not even bother to place a bet on Rustom Pasha's stablemate.[19]

Drawn on the far outside in the seventeen-horse field, Blenheim broke poorly and lost three lengths, possibly more, when the starting tape went up. Wragg took his time with Blenheim, cantering along in last place during the early going. It was the same strategy he'd used with Felstead two years earlier, hanging back, staying on the outside through-out the race, and then making a run inside the final furlong.

As the horses rolled through Tattenham Corner and into the final run-up to the finish, charging past the huge crowds that lined the fences along both sides of the course, the Aga Khan was on his feet in the stands, cheering wildly. Seeing his colors in front, the Aga Khan shouted, "Rustom wins! Rustom wins!"—but he was wrong.

The Aga Khan was extremely nearsighted, had been all his life. He could make out the stable's green and chocolate silks in the lead, but he failed to see both Rustom Pasha and the favorite falter and drop back at the head of the stretch. Iliad, an unlikely contender at odds of 25-1, wound up in front with a furlong to go, but he had no chance. Blenheim had been picking up horses one by one under a patient ride by Wragg, and now the colt was moving fastest on the outside.

A man standing next to the Aga Khan gave him a quick elbow in the ribs as the winner crossed the finish line—it was a "hell of a dig," the sixth Earl of Carnarvon would recall years later—and shouted, "No! Blenheim wins!" Lord Carnarvon had license to gloat; he had bred Blenheim.[20]

"Well, it doesn't matter," the Aga Khan told Lord Carnarvon. "Rustom will win the Eclipse." Which the colt did a few weeks later.

As the Aga Khan pushed his way through the crowd and onto the racecourse to meet his first Derby winner, cheers from a raucous throng, which might have numbered half a million, swelled and rolled across the Epsom grounds. The Aga Khan swiveled his head left and right, doffing a gray top hat in acknowledgment.

Cheering crowds were nothing new to the Aga Khan. Expressions of devotion were an essential part of his birthright, accorded him by his status as the forty-eighth hereditary imam of the Ismailis. The throngs cheering him on this day were a different lot, though. They were racing fans who owed him nothing and who expected nothing from him beyond a winner from time to time. They were racing fans more interested in wagers than in spiritual guidance and the Aga Khan had come through for them, albeit in a way that he did not expect.

Below his thick, round-framed spectacles, a broad smile lit the Aga Khan's face. It was the sort of smile that well suited a man who had just won his first Epsom Derby, but there was also a touch of mischief in his expression. It was the grin of a schoolboy who had just managed to put something over on his friends and was thoroughly enjoying the moment.[21] One of those friends was Lord Carnarvon, who had bred Blenheim at Highclere, the family estate in the Berkshire hills, and who sold the Derby winner to the Aga Khan as a yearling at the second July sale in Newmarket.[22]

Various accounts of the sale have circulated over the years. The most interesting story, which is unfortunately untrue, is that a group of consignors reached the conclusion that the Aga Khan had more money than he needed and that with some collusion he could be relieved of some of it. When the conspirators noticed that the Aga Khan's agent, George Lambton, was interested in Blenheim, they joined the bidding, pushing the selling price up to 4,100 guineas, about twice what they thought the colt was probably worth.[23]

There actually was a bit of skullduggery at Newmarket surrounding the sale of Blenheim that fall, but it was unintentionally initiated by

Blenheim winning the 1930 Epsom Derby, giving His Highness the Aga Khan his first victory in the classic. (Keeneland Library/Cook)

the colt's breeder. The Earl of Carnarvon expected Lambton to bid on Blenheim for the Aga Khan's account and he instructed a friend, Jock Broughton, to stay in the bidding up to 4,000 guineas. There was nothing unethical about a seller bidding on his own horse, so long as there was an announced reserve price, but the Earl of Carnarvon failed to state a reserve for Blenheim. Broughton kept the bids moving up to the anticipated 4,000 guineas, and there he stopped; Lambton got the colt for a hundred guineas more.[24]

Although it took two more years, the Aga Khan finally got the last word. As he was leading Blenheim to the winner's circle at Epsom, Lord Carnarvon fell in beside him and suggested that he should get free seasons to Blenheim because he had bred the Derby winner.

"No," the Aga Khan replied. "You'll pay the full fee, same as everyone else."[25]

Lost in the pack that day was The Scout II, which finished fifteenth in the colors of William Woodward Sr., who owned Belair Stud near

Bowie, Maryland. Pierre Lorillard IV's Iroquois was the first American-owned and American-bred runner to win the Epsom Derby, in 1881. The Scout II had an opportunity to become the second and a victory in the race would have been a singular accomplishment for Woodward, but the colt failed. Jockey Joe Childs had no excuse for The Scout II's lackluster performance beyond the obvious, that the colt simply was not good enough that day to be competitive.

Earlier in 1930, back in the United States, Woodward's homebred Gallant Fox already had won the Preakness Stakes and the Kentucky Derby (run a week *after* the Preakness in 1930 but before the race at Epsom), and a win by The Scout II would have made Woodward the first owner to win both the Kentucky Derby and the Epsom Derby. On June 7, three days after The Scout II was outrun by most of the field in the Epsom Derby and with a sweep of American classic races on the line, Gallant Fox went to the post as the second choice in the Belmont Stakes.

Jockey Earl Sande, who came out of retirement to ride Gallant Fox, had his face swathed in bandages due to an automobile accident the veteran rider had suffered two days before the Belmont. Unfazed by his injuries, Sande hustled the Belair colt to the front at the start and never relinquished the lead. Gallant Fox finished three lengths ahead of favored Whichone, the champion two-year-old the previous year.[26]

Gallant Fox was the second Thoroughbred to win the Kentucky Derby, the Preakness Stakes, and the Belmont Stakes, following Sir Barton in 1919, but was the first to be widely recognized as the winner of a "Triple Crown."[27]

Winning the Epsom Derby was a decades-long pursuit for Woodward, but it was a goal he never achieved. The closest he came was in 1950, when homebred Prince Simon lost the lead in the stretch and finished a head behind Galcador.[28]

It was not until 1954 that an American owner and breeder duplicated Pierre Lorillard's Epsom Derby win with Iroquois. That year Robert Sterling Clark won the Epsom Derby with Kentucky-bred Never Say

Die, a 33-1 long shot ridden by Lester Piggott, a teenage jockey destined to become a legend in his own right.[29]

Blenheim never raced again after winning the Epsom Derby, and the question of how to measure his true ability became moot upon his retirement. The colt suffered a career-ending injury while training for the Eclipse Stakes and in August 1930 he was transferred to his owner's Marly la Ville for stud duty in France. Blenheim was an immediate success as a stallion. His first crop included Pampeiro, the top-rated juvenile in France in 1934; among his second crop was Mahmoud, winner of the Epsom Derby in the Aga Khan's colors, and Mumtaz Begum, the dam of Nasrullah.[30]

Interest in Blenheim as a sire peaked with Mahmoud's win in the 1936 Epsom Derby. The stallion was bred to a full book of mares that year, he had a full book scheduled for 1937, and subscriptions were already being taken for the 1938 breeding season.[31] It was a surprise, then, when the Aga Khan announced with little warning in July that Blenheim was being sold to an American syndicate for a price reported to be around $250,000, depending on the exchange rate. News of the sale came as a shock to just about everyone, but to none more so than breeders holding what they thought were confirmed bookings to the popular stallion in 1937 and 1938.

Buying Blenheim and bringing the horse to the United States was the idea of Mrs. Marion du Pont Scott, although no one knew her by that name at the time. Earlier that year, in March 1936, Marion was secretly married to actor Randolph Scott in Chester, a small town in rural South Carolina. The wedding was kept out of the press, which somehow was possible in pre–World War II America despite Scott's fame, and reports of the negotiations for Blenheim identify Marion as Mrs. Thomas H. Somerville.[32]

Other investors assembled for the Blenheim syndicate were William du Pont Jr., Warren Wright, John Hay Whitney, John D. Hertz, Robert Fairbairn, and Arthur B. Hancock Jr. Wright owned a one-quarter interest; the other syndicate members each owned a one-eighth interest in the horse.[33]

Although Blenheim stood at Hancock's Claiborne Farm near Paris, Kentucky, Wright was the immediate beneficiary of his ownership interest in the stallion. Blenheim's first crop of foals sired in the United States included 1941 Triple Crown winner and two-time Horse of the Year Whirlaway, which raced in the colors of Wright's Calumet Farm.[34] Blenheim's sixty-four stakes winners also included Jet Pilot, winner of the 1947 Kentucky Derby.[35]

News of Blenheim's sale ignited a flurry of criticism and ill will directed toward the Aga Khan. The transaction also generated at least one lawsuit, from a pair of bloodstock agents who claimed that they were cheated out of a commission. Raymond Dale and William Daiziell argued that they introduced the Aga Khan to the American syndicate that wound up buying Blenheim and that they were entitled to a £4,500 commission from the sale. The Aga Khan first argued that Mahmoud's win in the Epsom Derby increased Blenheim's value as a stallion so much that he was free to renegotiate a new sales contract for the horse, then settled the lawsuit for £1,500 plus costs.[36]

The Aga Khan attempted to silence his critics by reminding them of a provision in the breeding contracts for each of his stallions making the agreements valid only so long as he owned the horse, but hard feelings remained.[37] Gerald H. Deane, racing manager for Lord Astor, summed up the feelings of many breeders when he wrote: "If the Aga Khan advertises his stallions to cover for future years and invites breeders to book to them, are these breeders suddenly to be informed that the stallion has been sold? It is not easy to book nominations to Derby winners, and if these nominations are suddenly cancelled owing to the sale of the stallion, other Derby winners may already be booked full for 1937 and possibly for 1938."[38]

The Aga Khan justified the sale by explaining that he was keeping Blenheim's son, Epsom Derby winner Mahmoud, and that he already had a number of yearlings, weanlings, and coming foals sired by Blenheim.[39] He also had Bahram, who retired undefeated after winning the English Triple Crown in 1935 and who probably was the best racehorse among the Aga Khan's 1930s-era Epsom Derby winners.[40]

If the explanation quelled the discontent over the sale of Blenheim, the respite was short-lived. Four years after Blenheim made the Atlantic crossing from Southampton in England to New York on the White Star Line steamship *Berengaria,* the Aga Khan sold two more Epsom Derby winners for export to the States. When Bahram and Mahmoud were sold, the grumbling from breeders in England and France began again, albeit more subdued this time because of a major extenuating circumstance— the start of World War II and the Nazi campaign in western Europe.[41]

The Aga Khan was living in Switzerland at the time, forced there by the war and concerns for his family's safety. Cut off from many of his resources, the Aga Khan was in serious financial trouble. Selling Bahram and Mahmoud allowed him to maintain some semblance of the lifestyle he had enjoyed before the war.[42] Mahmoud was the more successful of the two in North America, where he was the leading sire in 1946 and the leading broodmare sire in 1957.

The Aga Khan raced two more Epsom Derby winners in the post–World War II years, My Love in 1948 and Tulyar in 1952. In February 1953, the Aga Khan sold Tulyar to the Irish National Stud for £250,000. He said at the time that he was offered nearly $1 million from an American syndicate for the horse but that he turned it down. Perhaps remembering the uproar when Blenheim, Mahmoud, and Bahram were exported, the Aga Khan said that he would never sell Tulyar outside of England or Ireland.[43]

Three years later an American syndicate purchased Tulyar from the Irish National Stud for $672,000 and shipped the stallion to Claiborne Farm. The reaction of Irish breeders when the sale was announced was predictable to anyone who remembered Blenheim. "This has been our greatest Thoroughbred loss in many years," said Frank Tuthill, a leading Irish breeder and steward of the Jockey Club.[44]

For the loss of Tulyar to America, at least, no one could blame the Aga Khan.

Despite the uproar that accompanied the export to America of four of the Aga Khan's Epsom Derby winners, the post–World War II sale of

Nasrullah proved to be far more significant on both sides of the Atlantic. As would be the case with Tulyar a few years later, losing Nasrullah to an American syndicate was not the fault of the Aga Khan.[45]

A son of Nearco and the Blenheim mare Mumtaz Begum, a daughter from one of the Aga Khan's most successful female lines, Nasrullah was an exceptional runner cursed with a miserable temperament. Sir Gordon Richards, champion rider in England twenty-six times from 1925 to 1953, called Nasrullah "the greatest mover I ever rode and a brilliant racehorse. It was his temperament which beat him, but if [trainer Frank Butters] could have raced him anywhere away from Newmarket, I am sure he would have proved himself one of the greatest horses ever."[46]

Nasrullah stood at Barton Grange Stud near Newmarket until 1944, when he was sold by the Aga Khan to Joseph McGrath and exported to Ireland. Five years later, the stallion was resold to a syndicate of American breeders led by A. B. Hancock Jr. for stud duty at Claiborne Farm. Nasrullah was the leading sire in England in 1951 and the leading sire in the United States five times, in 1955, 1956, 1959, 1960, and 1962. His son Bold Ruler was the leading sire in the United States eight times.[47]

The Aga Khan was a dominant force on the English turf for three decades. From 1922 through 1957—thirty-five years—he ranked among the top ten owners thirty-one times. He invested more money than just about anyone else, an estimated £100,000 during his first years as an owner, and he won the Epsom Derby five times, took the Triple Crown with unbeaten Bahram, and led the owners' list on thirteen occasions. He also was England's leading breeder ten times, in 1932, 1934, 1935, 1937, 1941, 1942, 1947, 1948, 1949, and 1952.[48] The Aga Khan's dominance in England was well established by 1949, when a bizarre accident forced the retirement of Frank Butters, his remarkably successful trainer for almost two decades.

Butters was one of the best Thoroughbred trainers working in the first half of the twentieth century. He trained first for the 17th Earl of Derby, working under a four-year exclusive contract, then opened a public training yard in Newmarket. His clients during the subsequent years included the Aga Khan, who had horses in training with him from 1931 through 1949. Butters was the leading trainer eight times between 1927, his first year at Newmarket for Lord Derby, and 1949, when he retired. For the Aga Khan, Butters sent out nine classic winners in England, three Irish Derby winners, and Prix de l'Arc de Triomphe winner Migoli.[49]

The Aga Khan had nothing but praise for Butters: "From 1931 I had the good fortune of having my very dear friend, Mr. Frank Butters, for whom my family have the greatest affection, train for me. . . . When he left Lord Derby and came to me, the tables were quickly turned and I took the front again as leading owner and breeder."[50] It was a special relationship between the two men, one that came to an unexpected and premature end late in the evening of October 17, 1949. Butters, who was in his early seventies at the time, was riding his bicycle on High Street in Newmarket when he was run down by a truck. His injuries were serious—severe shock, a concussion, and other head trauma—and they ended his career as a trainer.[51]

The Aga Khan had continued success with Butters's replacement, Lambourne trainer Marcus Marsh, who sent out Tulyar to win the 1952 Epsom Derby, the King Edward VI and Queen Elizabeth II Stakes, and the St. Leger. The relationship between the two nevertheless was strained. Tulyar would have swept the English Triple Crown in 1952 had he won the first of the year's classics, the Two Thousand Guineas at Newmarket. He looked like a horse which could have won that race, but Marsh chose not to run him, a decision that rankled the Aga Khan and added to the growing friction between owner and trainer.

Marsh's decision to pass up the Two Thousand Guineas, which in hindsight probably cost the Aga Khan a second Triple Crown, after Bahram in 1935, added to the owner's disillusion with racing in England. He believed the purses were too low compared to racing prizes in France, that bookmakers were taking too large a cut of the betting handle, and that the Jockey Club lacked the expertise to adequately address his concerns.

Late in 1952, in an unexpected move again prefaced with little warning, the Aga Khan departed England, moving his entire stable to France. The Aga Khan's son, Prince Aly Khan, kept a few horses in Eng-

His Highness the Aga Khan III, Laurel Park president John Shapiro, and Prince Aly Khan (father of His Highness the Aga Khan IV), mid-1950s. (Keeneland Library)

land with trainer Sir Noel Murless, including the classic-winning filly Petite Etoile, and in 1959 was the leading owner in England, Ireland, and France. Following Prince Aly's untimely death in an automobile accident in 1960, another eighteen years would pass before horses carrying the Aga Khan's stable colors would return in force to England.[52]

## 2

# Families

His Highness the Aga Khan III died on July 11, 1957, four months before his eightieth birthday. He had been the imam of the Ismaili community for a remarkable seven decades, since the untimely death of his father from pneumonia in 1885. He was eight years old when he inherited the title of Aga Khan and its attendant responsibilities; his inheritance also included a stable of some ninety horses and his family's passion for horse racing.

The Aga Khan III was one of the preeminent Thoroughbred owners and breeders in Europe during the first half of the twentieth century. Upon his passing, *Sporting Life* called him "the last emperor of racing."[1] Although less well publicized, his work as the spiritual leader and shepherd of the Ismaili Muslims was by all accounts equally successful, featuring a network of social programs and development projects spanning Asia and Africa.

Following the Aga Khan's death, solicitor Otto Giesen from the London law firm of Slaughter and May retrieved the old man's will from Lloyds Bank and delivered it to the family's villa in Versoix, a suburb of Geneva. In accordance with Shia Muslim laws of inheritance, the will disposed of the Aga Khan's horses as expected: a two-fifths share went to his son Prince Aly Khan; a two-fifths share to Prince Aly's half-brother, Prince Sadruddin Aga Khan; and a one-fifth share to his wife, the Begum Sultan Mohamed Shah. Prince Aly, the only one of the three with any interest in horse racing, consolidated his stable by purchasing the interests of Prince Sadruddin and the Begum.[2]

Two years later, in what the British *Bloodstock Breeders Review* recognized as "the Aly Khan's Year," Prince Aly swept the leading owner titles in England, Ireland, and France, becoming the first owner in history whose English runners earned more than £100,000 in a single season.[3] His wins that year in France, where the stable was based, included Saint-Crispin's controversial victory in the Prix de l'Arc de Triomphe, a win courtesy of a newfangled gadget—the film patrol—that had been introduced at the racecourse earlier in the season. The placing judges could not separate Saint-Crispin and Midnight Sun and initially ruled the race a dead heat, but a review of footage from film patrol cameras showed that Midnight Sun had twice interfered with Saint-Crispin.[4]

While there were no surprises in the disposition of the Aga Khan III's Thoroughbreds after his death, the reading of the will had its share of drama. There was news important enough for the front page (albeit below the fold) of the *New York Times*.[5] In naming his successor as imam of the Ismailis, which was his right, the Aga Khan III upset the usual order of father to eldest son with his decision, passing over Prince Aly Khan in favor of Prince Aly's son, Prince Karim, who was studying Oriental history at Harvard:

> Ever since the time of my ancestor Ali, the first Imam, that is to say over a period of thirteen hundred years, it has always been the tradition of our family that each Imam chooses his successor at his absolute and unfettered discretion from amongst any of his descendants, whether they be sons or remote male issue and in these circumstances and in view of the fundamentally altered conditions in the world in very recent years due to the great changes which have taken place including the discoveries of atomic science, I am convinced that it is in the best interest of the Shia Muslim Ismailia Community that I should be succeeded by a young man who has been brought up and developed during recent years and in the midst of the new age and who brings a new outlook on life to his office as Imam.
>
> For these reasons, I appoint my grandson Karim, the son

of my own son Aly Salomone Khan to succeed to the title of Aga Khan and to the Imam and Pir of all Shia Ismailian followers.[6]

The Aga Khan offered no further justification in his will for the decision to upset the expected order of succession. There was no requirement that he do so and he may have had reasons for skipping a generation that he chose not to share in his will.

After the unusual succession was announced, Prince Aly Khan faced reporters who raised the obvious questions, but he refused to offer any opinion about why he thought his father chose Prince Karim over him. Quintin Gilbey, a sportswriter who covered racing and who became friends with both the Aga Khan and Prince Aly during the 1930s, had his own theory about the matter. Years later he suggested in a memoir that the Aga Khan found his son's extravagant lifestyle excessive and inappropriate for a spiritual leader of the Ismailis.[7]

Prince Karim, on the other hand, was more forthcoming when a reporter asked if he intended to keep up the Thoroughbred empire founded by his grandfather and carried on by Prince Aly. "I'm not much

His Highness the Aga Khan IV. (John Crofts)

for sport," the new Aga Khan replied. "I don't know what I will do with the horses."[8]

The initial announcement of the will's succession provision did not include information about disposition of the Aga Khan III's vast estate, and newsmen apparently were unaware that the horses already had been divided among a group of relatives that did not include Prince Karim. The future of his grandfather's Thoroughbred empire was not the new Aga Khan's to worry about, not then at least.

In an ironic twist of fate, however, the Aga Khan Studs soon would become Prince Karim's concern after all.

Prince Karim's unexpected ascension to the role of Aga Khan IV—as the forty-ninth hereditary imam of the Ismailis—required a sudden and total reordering of his life. Returning to Harvard, where the twenty-year-old played a good game of soccer and had ambitions to pursue a doctorate in history, now was out of the question as he assumed both spiritual and temporal leadership of millions of Ismailis. In the process, he also became an immensely wealthy young man, with access to a yacht, his choice of fast cars, and residences in the Alps, on the Riviera, and in Paris.

His life was upended a second time when his father died in an automobile accident in 1960, just three years after the death of the Aga Khan III. Prince Aly Khan had consolidated the family's stables under his ownership, but now his will decreed that the horses would be divided again, this time with two-fifths going to the Aga Khan IV, two-fifths to Prince Karim's brother, Prince Amyn, and one-fifth to their half-sister, Princess Yasmin. Princess Yasmin was the daughter of actress Rita Hayworth, Prince Aly's former wife.

The sad but necessary ritual of selling horses to pay estate taxes, which occurred following the death of the Aga Khan III, was repeated after the death of Prince Aly. Prince Karim found himself in a position like that of his father three years earlier, having to decide whether it made sense to buy out the interests of his siblings and run the Aga Khan Studs himself. It had been an easy decision for Prince Aly. He was already a successful owner and breeder and he had been increasing his involvement in the running of the Aga Khan III's stable. For Prince Karim, on the other hand, charting a course forward was more difficult. His time was already filled with responsibilities as imam, plus he had little interest in—or knowledge about—horse racing. "I knew nothing about horse racing or breeding," Prince Karim told a reporter in 1964. "I asked myself seriously whether I could or should attempt to run the establishment. I also was not sure I would have time to spend on the stable, since I already was working six to 10 hours a day on Ismaili community affairs. And I certainly did not wish to operate a third-rate stable after the glory it had known under my grandfather and father."[9]

Years earlier, the Aga Khan III had reached a similar conclusion, embracing a "perfect or not at all" philosophy. He delayed buying his first Thoroughbred yearlings in England for nearly two decades, until 1921, because he was occupied with political work and sorting out the impact of World War I on his millions of followers and on the world. At least as important at the time, though, was the lack of funds sufficient to buy the high-quality bloodstock needed to operate a stable that could compete with Europe's top owners. Like his grandson, the Aga Khan III was not interested in a stable of second-string horses.[10]

The untimely death of Prince Aly Khan so soon after the passing of the Aga Khan III and the subsequent sales of horses to satisfy two rounds of estate taxes had reduced the stable from three hundred head to around one hundred. Many of the horses sold were some of the stud's best broodmares, tracing many generations back to Mumtaz Mahal, one of the Aga Khan III's early purchases. A gray daughter of The Tetrarch, Mumtaz Mahal possessed blazing speed. She won five stakes at ages two and three, and Dick Dawson judged her the best horse he ever trained. One of the foundation mares for the Aga Khan III, Mumtaz Mahal also was the seventh dam of Shergar, the first Epsom Derby winner for the Aga Khan IV.

There were dire predictions that such a decimated stable would have no success for years to come, but they did not materialize. Stakes

winners in the months after Prince Aly's death included Charlottesville (winner of the Prix du Jockey Club and the Grand Prix de Paris),
Sheshoon (the Ascot Gold Cup and the Grand Prix de Saint-Cloud),
Petite Etoile (the Coronation Cup), and Venture II (the St. James's Palace
Stakes and Sussex Stakes). At the end of the year, the new Aga Khan—
a man who professed little interest in horse racing—found himself the
leading owner in France.[11]

When the Aga Khan IV finally decided to continue racing and
breeding Thoroughbreds, after half a year's deliberation following his
father's death, he did so under two self-imposed conditions: first, the
Aga Khan Studs had to pay its own way, without the infusion of outside
capital; second, the time commitment could not impose on his existing
obligations to the Ismaili community.[12]

The sweeping reorganization of the Aga Khan Studs took two
decades to complete. Some of the farms in Ireland and France were sold,
new trainers were brought in, staff was added to replace people lost to
death and retirement, and an entirely new system for matching mares
and stallions was instituted. With major purchases of horses from the
estate of Thoroughbred breeder François Dupré in 1977 and from bankrupt textile millionaire Marcel Boussac the following year, the Aga Khan
IV had what amounted to a nearly clean slate.

It was time to race again in England.

In 1952, not long after his Tulyar won the Epsom Derby, the Aga Khan
III gave up on British racing, convinced that the sport was in a serious
state of decline. Disillusioned by what he saw as a miserly purse structure, an unreasonable share of the betting handle going to bookmakers,
and the inability of the Jockey Club to make needed changes, the Aga
Khan III moved all of his horses to France.

The situation in England improved during the ensuing quarter-
century, to the point that in 1978 the Aga Khan IV decided to race in
Britain on a regular basis. "I believe English racing has made more progress in the last five years than any other country, though the bookmakers
still take too much out of the game," the Aga Khan IV explained to his

friend the author Richard Baerlein. "As I breed in America, France, Ireland, and England, it is important to the international reputation of my bloodlines that they should be seen on the track in every important race in the country. It benefits the sales and I shall try and have representatives of all my main families running in England and France at the same time. Winners anywhere and everywhere are most important."[13]

The Aga Khan III had a genuine knack for matching the best person with the right job—trainers George Lambton, Dick Dawson, and Frank Butters in England and Alec Head in France all come to mind—and then listening to the advice he got from them. The practice served him well. Prince Aly Khan also relied on the counsel of Alec Head after taking over his late father's stable. The new Aga Khan kept Head as the stable's trainer in France for a time before moving his horses to the care of champion conditioner François Mathet. He made the change not because he questioned Head's ability as a trainer—he was one of the best in France. Instead, he had come to see Head, who was actively promoting his own bloodstock while training for the Aga Khan, as a serious rival with a potential conflict of interest.

With the new Aga Khan preparing to race in England on a regular basis after a twenty-five-year hiatus, the question was who would train the stable's horses. The Aga Khan IV settled on two young trainers, Richard Fulke Johnson Houghton and Michael Stoute. Houghton was the more experienced of the two as a trainer when he was tapped by his new client; six years younger, Stoute was something of a gamble, but it was one that quickly paid dividends. "I chose them very carefully," the Aga Khan IV told Baerlein. "I wanted men with good judgment who would prepare my horses with a stud career in the background. Therefore it was imperative to choose those who do not overrate their charges. Neither of my English trainers does this."[14]

Houghton took out a trainer's license in 1961 when he was twenty years old, becoming one of the youngest trainers ever to be licensed in England. His trainer's license was a matter of necessity because of an archaic Jockey Club rule. His mother, Helen Johnson Houghton, had tried to take over training the stable's horses after her husband was killed

Trainer Sir Michael Stoute.
(John Crofts)

in a fox hunting accident in 1952, but she was denied a license: at the time, the Jockey Club would not license a female trainer.[15]

Houghton brought with him an impressive résumé. For Charles W. Engelhard Jr. he trained Habitat, the best miler in Europe in 1969, and full brothers Ribocco and Ribero (both winners of the Irish Sweeps Derby and the English St. Leger); for David McCall he sent out Ile de Bourbon, winner of the King George VI and Queen Elizabeth Diamond Stakes.

Stoute, on the other hand, had been training for only six years. His credentials were more modest than Houghton's, but he had a reputation as an up-and-comer among young Newmarket trainers. He was already having the best year of his brief career in 1978, winning the Oaks, the Irish Oaks, and the Yorkshire Oaks with Fair Salinia, before an unexpected telephone call changed his life.

Stoute grew up in Barbados, the son of a high-ranking official in the national police force. The family lived near the historic Garrison Savannah racetrack on the outskirts of the capital, Bridgeport, and Stoute began hanging around the backstretch about the time he started grade school. He left Barbados for Ireland at the age of nineteen in

1964 and wound up working as an assistant to trainer Pat Rohan when another promised job fell through.

After three years with Rohan, Stoute moved to Newmarket, working first for Douglas Smith and later for H. Thomson Jones before setting out on his own at the start of the 1972 racing season. He saddled his first winner, Sandal, early that year; on April 28, the horse won in a photo finish over a horse trained by Stoute's former employer, Pat Rohan.[16]

The fateful telephone call came in September 1978 from Ghislain Drion, a Frenchman who was the Aga Khan IV's stud manager in Ireland. The Aga Khan IV was planning to race again in England, Drion said. Would Stoute be interested in training some of those horses?

Yes, Stoute said, he would be very interested.

The first group of yearlings from the Aga Khan Studs arrived at Beech Hurst, Stoute's training yard on the Bury Road north of Newmarket, a few weeks later. Among them was Dalsaan, which placed in stakes at three and won a minor stakes race as a four-year-old—a solid performer, but nothing spectacular.

Waiting in the wings, though, was a flashy bay colt with white on all four legs, a prominent blaze, and a walleye. Foaled earlier in the year at Sheshoon, the Aga Khan IV's private stud near The Curragh Racecourse in Ireland, the colt was a son of Great Nephew, the French champion at a mile and sire of 1975 Epsom Derby winner Grundy. The colt's dam, the Val de Loir mare Sharmeen, traced back seven generations to Mumtaz Mahal, one of the Aga Khan III's foundation mares.

The Aga Khan IV would name the colt Shergar. The luck of the draw would send him to Beech Hurst.

Michael Stoute saw Shergar for the first time at the Aga Khan IV's Ballymany Stud during a trip to Ireland in the fall of 1979. He was there to look at the yearlings that would be coming his way in a few weeks and Drion was showing him around Ballymany. He was not there to select the yearlings he wanted to train—those decisions already had been made—but just to look. To Stoute's eye, Shergar was just one colt among a group of yearlings grazing in a field.

Recalling that day years later, Stoute paused and then extended his arm, peering at his raised thumb, like an artist assessing a subject. It was easy to imagine Shergar on the other end of that thoughtful gaze. It was more difficult to imagine that the future Epsom Derby winner was not a standout as a yearling. In fact, he was just ordinary, even a little immature. "There was nothing to make you pick him out and say: 'I want him for my yard,'" Stoute explained.[17]

Shergar arrived at Beech Hurst in November and passed an uneventful winter settled in the fourth stall from the end of the shedrow, close to the path leading out to the Lime Kiln gallop. Stoute still did not know what he had in Shergar and it was not until the colt began serious work in the summer that he began to impress the trainer.

Racing legend Lester Piggott started riding Shergar for morning workouts late in August 1980 and apparently got along well with him. The veteran jockey was in the saddle when Shergar made his debut on September 19, starting favorite among twenty-three juveniles that came out for the Kris Plate, run over the straight one-mile course at Newbury. Piggott gave Shergar a confident ride, keeping the colt off the early pace, then moving him to the front with little apparent effort. Shergar finished two and a half lengths ahead of Chief Speaker but almost certainly could have won by more if Piggott had given the colt his head.

Shergar started next on October 25, in the William Hill Futurity Stakes, an important Group 1 race run over a mile at Doncaster.[18] Sent away the third choice behind Robellino and Recitation, neither of which placed, Shergar closed to within a length of Beldale Flutter in the stretch but could get no closer. Beldale Flutter drew away to win by two and a half lengths, with Shergar two lengths ahead of Sheer Grit in third.[19]

The William Hill Futurity was Shergar's last race as a juvenile. He was retired for the year with one win and one second-place finish and modest earnings of $39,232. He finished the year sound, though, and despite his loss in the William Hill Futurity, the colt probably seemed like a good prospect for the Two Thousand Guineas the following spring. Stoute had other plans, however, and they did not include another race at a mile. "We went into the winter hopeful that we had a good middle-distance horse," Stoute said of Shergar.[20] Beyond that hope, however, there were questions to be resolved.

Passing up the Two Thousand Guineas at a mile left the Epsom Derby as a logical target for Shergar, but who would ride him? For a trainer with classic aspirations the obvious answer—in 1981 or in any other year during the previous twenty-five years—was Lester Piggott. He rode his first Derby winner, Never Say Die, in 1954, then added Crepello in 1957, St. Paddy in 1960, Sir Ivor in 1968, Nijinsky II in 1970, Roberto in 1972, Empery in 1976, and The Minstrel in 1977.[21] Piggott rode Shergar in both his races in 1980 and obviously got along well with the colt, another factor in his favor.

Stoute's dilemma had little to do with Piggott, whose prowess as a race rider was unquestioned, and everything to do with Walter Swinburn, a young jockey who was earning good reviews from owners, trainers, and bettors. Son of a champion jockey, Swinburn inherited the genes to be a champion himself. He picked up a nickname, "the Choirboy," that belied a rider with a wealth of natural talent and a burgeoning reputation as a smart and aggressive rider. He had "marvelous hands," Stoute once said, and the ability to bring out the best in a fractious horse.[22]

Jockey Walter Swinburn.
(John Crofts)

Shergar and Walter Swinburn at Sandown Park, April 25, 1981. (Miralgo Publications Photo Archives/John Crofts)

Improbable as it was, considering his age (he was still a teenager) and lack of experience when put up against a rider like Piggott, Swinburn became Stoute's stable jockey over the winter. He got the mount on Shergar as part of the deal.

Bettors with a good memory and faith in omens might have recalled that decades earlier trainer Joe Lawson decided that a change of riders would benefit Never Say Die, which was being pointed toward the Epsom Derby. Lawson passed on veterans of the day, in part because some of them turned down the mount. He chose instead an eighteen-year-old jockey who, like Swinburn, was just starting to make a name for himself. That rider was Lester Piggott and he won the 1954 Derby with Never Say Die.[23]

With the rider matter settled, there remained another question that was out of Stoute's control: what about Storm Bird, the season's champion two-year-old and the consensus favorite for the next year's Epsom Derby?

# 3

# Black Swans

Until the end of the seventeenth century, Europeans held a simple and distinctly monochromatic view of swans: all swans are white. There was no reason to think otherwise. No one ever had seen swans of any other hue, so the conclusion was based on the available historical evidence. The logical conclusion was wrong, of course, as Dutch explorer Willem de Vlamingh discovered when he encountered black swans in Australia around 1697.[1]

Centuries later, philosopher and author Nassim Nicholas Taleb popularized the nonavian idea of a "Black Swan" as any event that could not be predicted based on contemporaneous empirical evidence but in hindsight was both "explainable and predictable" and had serious consequences.[2] The theft of Epson Derby winner Shergar by a gang of armed men in 1983 was just such an event.

The theft was unpredictable for a simple reason—although a few other prominent Thoroughbreds had been stolen in the past, no one had ever taken a horse of Shergar's immense value and popularity, not in Ireland or anywhere else. Theft of a Thoroughbred breeding stallion was so unlikely, in fact, that security at Ballymany Stud in the early 1980s—as at most other Thoroughbred breeding farms around the world at the time—was almost nonexistent.[3]

In hindsight, though, a connection between the theft of Shergar in 1983 and events set in motion in Northern Ireland and in the Republic of Ireland more than a decade earlier is inescapable. It is impossible to make sense of Shergar's theft as an overtly political act—which it surely was—without an understanding of what was happening in Ireland.

One of those watershed events was largely political, the other purely economic. They seemed unrelated at the time, but in retrospect the theft of Shergar, or of a horse like him, was inevitable. The first of the two events turned a long-simmering dispute between Protestants and Catholics over civil rights and rampant discrimination into the "Troubles," three decades of violence, death, and destruction in Northern Ireland.[4] The second changed the face of the horse industry in the south and in the process transformed the Republic of Ireland from something of a backwater for high-class stallions into an international leader in Thoroughbred breeding.

While the armed struggle approached civil war proportions in parts of Northern Ireland throughout the 1970s (and for two decades more after that), the Irish Thoroughbred industry thrived in the south, largely untouched by the violence. In lieu of a clear victory, the Irish Republican Army adopted a "long war" philosophy to wear down the British and eventually force them out of the country.[5] On a more peaceful note, Thoroughbred breeding became a bright spot in the Republic of Ireland's dismal economy and foreshadowed the emergence of the "Celtic Tiger."[6]

Hardly anyone expected the status quo to change. Northern Ireland and the Republic were, after all, two different countries and there was no reason to expect that the troubles in the north would spill south across the border.[7]

The situation changed dramatically, in a way no one could have predicted, on February 8, 1983, on a picturesque stud farm in County Kildare, some thirty miles southwest of Dublin.

Trouble was inevitable when partition in the early 1920s gerrymandered the six counties of Northern Ireland to carve out a new country with a Protestant majority in a traditionally Catholic land. Northern Ireland remained a part of the United Kingdom after partition, and for half a century the Unionist Party, loyal to Great Britain and mostly Protestant, ruled Northern Ireland with almost no effort made to include members of the Catholic community. Discrimination spread through every

Map of Ireland showing the location of events central to the Shergar story.

level of society in Northern Ireland, and the growing activism on both sides closely mirrored the struggle for civil rights in the United States.[8] Clashes between civil rights protesters on one side and loyalists on the other became more frequent and grew progressively more violent.[9]

Things came to a head in 1969 when partisan demonstrations and rioting spread from Derry to the streets of Belfast. It was obvious by mid-August that the Royal Ulster Constabulary (RUC), the predominately Protestant national police force in Northern Ireland, had lost control of the situation. Parts of Belfast became, for all practical purposes, a war zone off limits to the RUC. Admitting defeat, the government finally requested military assistance from Great Britain to maintain order. On August 14, the first British troops were sent to Derry; they moved on to Belfast shortly thereafter.[10]

It was not the first time that British soldiers had been deployed to the northern counties of Ireland to oppose the Irish Republican Army. In 1920, at the height of the Irish War of Independence, thousands of British troops were sent to prop up the Royal Irish Constabulary, which was losing the IRA's guerrilla war. The soldiers, who quickly became known as the Black and Tans because of the colors of their uniforms, later got paramilitary support from a group of ex-army officers from England who were looking for a place to fight after the end of World War I.

A truce finally was negotiated in July 1921, leading to Irish independence from the United Kingdom as the Irish Free State and separation of six counties in the northeast to form Northern Ireland, which is still a part of the United Kingdom.[11]

The reappearance half a century later of British troops for day-to-day security and law enforcement in Catholic areas of the cities in Northern Ireland generated an almost immediate reaction from a group of militant republican sympathizers.[12] Dissatisfied with what they saw as an inadequate response to the overt British military presence, the "Provisional" Irish Republican Army—the "Provos," as the splinter group came to be known—in late 1969 broke away from the so-called official Irish Republican Army that had fought the British during the War of Independence.[13]

The principal philosophical difference between the two factions of the Irish Republican Army was a fundamental question about the use of force: could a campaign of violence be an effective means to drive the British out of Northern Ireland? The official IRA took a more moderate stand than the radical Provos, who were armed and ready to fight.[14]

The Provisional IRA initiated a long-term guerrilla action to oust what its members saw as a British occupation force. Fueled primarily with weapons and money from the United States and from Libya, the campaign lasted three decades and cost the lives of more than thirty-five hundred people.[15] Ten years after the split from the official IRA, when the usually reliable sources of money and arms were disrupted, the Provisional IRA turned to kidnappings for ransom, often operating inside the Republic of Ireland.[16]

Somewhere along the way the IRA decided to steal a horse. On *I Was There,* a news program about the theft of Shergar broadcast by BBC 5 Live on February 12, 2016, Sean O'Callaghan said that the plot was conceived by IRA man Kevin Mallon during a stay at Portlaoise Prison. A reformed Provo who switched sides to become an informer for the police, O'Callaghan said that the scheme had appeal as an IRA fundraiser for three reasons: Shergar would be a valuable hostage; the timing of the theft, just before the start of the breeding season, would put pressure on the horse's owners; and the erroneous belief that stealing a horse would generate less public outrage than kidnapping a person.

It would have been a laughable idea when the Provos began their campaign against the Northern Ireland government and the British—there were few, if any, horses in the Republic valuable enough to command a decent ransom in 1969. By the early 1980s, though, things had changed.

The Irish love horses—always have, probably always will. The love affair ranges from pagan times, when belief in an afterlife promised an eternity of nonstop horse racing, to illustrations of riders in the ancient Book of Kells to racing at The Curragh starting as early as the third century and continuing today.[17] Thoroughbred farms in Ireland always produced some good runners, mainly because the farms had quality broodmares. Irish stallions, on the other hand, traditionally were best known as sires of steeplechasers and sport horses, not classic winners.

For the owners of high-end stallions—these were the well-bred horses that could be syndicated for seven and eight figures and could be expected to sire a succession of major winners—there was little incentive to abandon England and France and come to Ireland. Little incentive, that is, until Charles J. Haughey almost single-handedly created one.

Haughey was the quintessential politician. He served three terms as Irish prime minister and held several other important government posts in the Republic of Ireland. Depending on who was offering an opinion, Haughey was either an extremely cunning tactician who helped engineer Ireland's economic resurgence in the 1990s or a self-serving schemer who parlayed his political influence to accumulate a vast personal fortune. The truth is probably somewhere between the two.[18]

Haughey had family ties to the republican movement, at least for a time. His father was an active member of the official Irish Republican Army when the family lived in County Derry around the time of partition. That association ended, however, when the family moved from Northern Ireland to County Mayo in the Republic. Later, when Charles was finance minister in the south, he was implicated, but later acquitted, in an alleged plot to purchase weapons abroad and smuggle them into Northern Ireland.[19]

Haughey was friends with former British spy and novelist Frederick Forsyth, who lived with his family in Dublin from 1974 until 1979, about the time the IRA began planning its campaign to kidnap business executives. Concerned about an IRA kidnap attempt on his wife and children, Forsyth decided that it was best for his family to abandon Ireland for a home in England. Haughey wanted his friend to stay. He promised in no uncertain terms that the IRA posed no threat to the author or his family. "The only way he could have known that," Forsyth recalled in a memoir, "was if he had given a flat order to the Army Council of the IRA. Not many men could do that."[20]

The Taoiseach had friends in horse racing and a passion for the sport himself.[21] In 1969, during his term as finance minister in Jack Lynch's cabinet, Haughey pushed through the Dáil (the powerful lower house of the Irish Parliament) a tax reform measure that made stud fees earned in Ireland exempt from income tax.[22] The legislation helped Haughey's friends in the business, which may have been its purpose, but overnight the legislation also created in Ireland a powerful incentive for serious investments in Thoroughbred stallions.[23]

A few years later, in what may or may not have been merely a timely coincidence, Robert Sangster, Vincent O'Brien, and John Magnier hit upon a scheme to try to corner the market on potential classic winners and champions that could be syndicated for millions. A trio that became known as the "Brethren," Sangster, O'Brien, and Magnier for years were the preeminent force in the international Thoroughbred world. Sangster was a wealthy businessman whose father founded the lucrative Vernons betting pools business in England during the 1920s; O'Brien was one of the leading Thoroughbred trainers of the twentieth century; and Magnier owned Coolmoor Stud in County Tipperary.

In the mid-1970s, the Brethren's blueprint meant combing auction catalogues around the world for sons of Northern Dancer and then buying as many of them as possible when they came up for sale as yearlings. Sangster would supply the money, O'Brien would train the horses, and the best of the colts would stand at Coolmore until they could be syndicated for a profit.[24] It was a numbers game that led to a decade of spirited bidding wars and record prices for nicely bred Thoroughbred yearlings.

One of the first success stories for Sangster and crew was The Minstrel, a son of Northern Dancer purchased for $200,000 at the 1975 Keeneland select yearling sale. The Minstrel won the Larkspur and Dewhurst Stakes as a two-year-old and the Epsom Derby, the Irish Derby, and the King George VI and Queen Elizabeth Diamond Stakes against older horses at three.[25] (Shergar would sweep the same three races in 1981 on the way to his Horse of the Year crown.)

The plan came to fruition when Sangster and his partners sold a half interest in The Minstrel back to the horse's breeder, Canadian E. P. Taylor, for $4.5 million. The Minstrel still was in training when the deal was done and the plan at the time was to send the colt to France for the Prix de l'Arc de Triomphe and then retire him to stud at Taylor's Windfields Farm in Canada.[26]

The Minstrel never made it to the Arc, however. Instead, he was retired earlier than planned when word reached Taylor, Sangster, and the other owners that the US Department of Agriculture was about to impose an embargo on the shipment of horses to America from England, Ireland, and France. The purpose of the sudden embargo was to prevent the spread to the United States of contagious equine metritis (CEM), a highly infectious equine venereal disease that first was diagnosed in England in 1977. The effort came too late, however. Two stallions imported from France prior to the import ban carried the disease to Kentucky, where an outbreak of CEM closed breeding sheds early in the 1978 breeding season. A conservative estimate of the economic loss to the Thoroughbred industry was more than $13.5 million.[27]

The Minstrel was hustled onto a plane and was settling in at the USDA quarantine station in Clifton, New Jersey, when the travel ban went into effect. The Minstrel stood his first seasons at Windfields Farm before being moved to Overbrook Farm in Kentucky.

A few years later, similar travel restrictions imposed on horses moving from Europe to the United States because of CEM would become a factor in the Aga Khan IV's decision to syndicate Shergar for stud in Ireland.

Investing in untested yearlings like The Minstrel was a risky gamble, and an expensive one, but it worked. The partners' Coolmore Stud in County Tipperary soon became one of the world's leading stallion operations, generating millions of dollars in tax-free stud fees each year.[28]

The members of the Coolmore triumvirate were not the only horsemen who recognized the value of Haughey's tax legislation. The Maktoums, from the ruling family of Dubai, invested heavily in Ireland, as did the Aga Khan IV, who already had a base there, established by his grandfather decades earlier.

Perhaps the biggest surprise in the early years of rapid growth for Ireland's Thoroughbred industry was the Aga Khan IV's decision to pass up more lucrative offers from America to syndicate 1981 Epsom Derby winner Shergar to stand in Ireland. Winner of the Irish Derby at The Curragh, a sprawling racecourse adjacent to the Aga Khan's Ballymany Stud, where he would stand his first season in 1982, Shergar was a national hero in Ireland. The horse was also one of the most recognizable sports personalities—horse or human—in Ireland by the time he was paraded down the main street in Newbridge following his retirement from racing. "Today, the assembled dignitaries [which included the Aga Khan IV and his family] have come to pay tribute to a beautiful horse which has added so immeasurably to the fame of Irish bloodstock throughout the world," Newbridge town council spokesman Tom Corcoran said from the viewing stand at the parade. The "wonder horse," Corcoran added, "returns to the cradle."[29]

Whether the men who plotted the theft of Shergar were among the crowd that lined the streets of Newbridge that October day is not known. Even if they were not, though, news of Shergar's well-publicized successes at Epsom, The Curragh, and Ascot; the wealth of the Aga Khan IV; the horse's multimillion-dollar syndication; and his retirement to Ballymany Stud reached every corner of Northern Ireland and the Republic.

The general hoopla surrounding Shergar created only one conclusion—here was a very valuable horse that likely would command a handsome ransom. Here was a horse worth stealing.

# 4

# Assassination

The bomb exploded at 11:45 in the morning on August 27, 1979. The force of the blast rattled windows in the village store and in the old post office, startled guests in the Pier Head and Beach Hotels, and raised a general alarm among the residents of Mullaghmore, a popular holiday destination in County Sligo. A few hundred yards away, flaming debris from the explosion rained down around the wreckage of the *Saturn V,* a fishing boat now adrift on Donegal Bay. A witness to the explosion would later say, "The boat was there one minute and the next minute it was like a lot of matchsticks floating on the water."[1]

The night before, on the eve of what promised to be a beautifully clear bank holiday perfect for boating, Lord Louis Mountbatten dined with his family at Classiebawn Castle. An early Victorian mansion perched high on a hill overlooking the village and the bay, Classiebawn was the centerpiece of a fifteen-hundred-acre estate acquired by Lord Mountbatten through a complicated chain of inheritance. He had scheduled annual vacations there for years and continued to do so, despite growing concerns from his security detail about threats from the IRA in Northern Ireland.

Lord Mountbatten had been working out the details of an elaborate state funeral—his own—for some time. This was no real surprise for a war hero who had celebrated his seventy-ninth birthday two months earlier, and sometime during the family gathering the subject came up again. "I can't think of a more wonderful thanksgiving for the life I have had than that everyone should be jolly at my funeral," Lord Mountbatten said.[2]

Now the man was dead, the victim of a gelignite bomb hidden under the deck planking of the *Saturn V,* a converted launch he used for fishing and to check his lobster pots in the bay.[3] The bomb had exploded almost directly under Lord Mountbatten's feet, breaking both his legs. The pathologist's report said that he had been rendered unconscious by the explosion and had drowned. When his body was pulled from the water, rescuers noted with some irony that the jersey he was wearing bore the emblem of the HMS *Kelly,* a British destroyer that had been sunk by an enemy bomb while under his command during World War II.

Also killed in the blast were Nicholas Brabourne, one of Lord Mountbatten's grandsons; the Dowager Lady Brabourne (who survived the blast but died later in the hospital); and Paul Maxwell, a boy from the village who was aboard the *Saturn V* only because the family's regular boatman had been unable to make the trip to Mullaghmore that summer. Lord Mountbatten's daughter, Lady Patricia; her husband, Lord Brabourne; and another grandson, Timothy Brabourne, survived their injuries.[4]

Suspicion immediately fell upon the Provisional Irish Republican Army. Three days later, the Provos accepted blame for the bomb in a public statement:

> In claiming responsibility for the execution of Lord Mountbatten the I.R.A. state that the bombing was a discriminate act to bring to the attention of the English people the continuing occupation of our country.
>
> The British Army acknowledge that after 10 years of war it cannot defeat us, but yet it continues with the oppression of our people and torture of our comrades in H Block.
>
> Well, for this we will tear out their sentimental imperialist hearts.
>
> The death of Lord Mountbatten and tributes paid to him will be seen in contrast to the apathy of the British Government and the English people to the deaths of over 300 British soldiers and the deaths of Irish men, women and children at the hands of their forces.[5]

Overshadowed in the extensive press coverage of Lord Mountbatten's death was a second deadly IRA attack on the same day, at Warrenpoint in County Down, Northern Ireland. Late in the afternoon, as a British military convoy drove past Narrow Water Castle, a massive seven-hundred-pound bomb hidden in a hay wagon by the side of the road was detonated by remote control. The bomb was surrounded by cans of gasoline, and the fireball from the explosion engulfed part of the convoy. Six members of the Parachute Regiment were killed by the bomb and two others were injured.

A short time later, another bomb exploded, this one more powerful than the first and timed to coincide with the arrival of reinforcements. The second explosion killed twelve soldiers from the Parachute Regiment and injured three others. With the death toll at eighteen, the attacks marked the British Army's greatest loss of life in a single incident during three decades of policing Northern Ireland.

Investigation of the bombing at Mullaghmore fell to Chief Superintendent John Courtney, who ran An Garda Síochána's "Murder Squad" during the 1970s and 1980s. Based in Dublin, the Murder Squad was the Irish version of a major crimes unit. It grew in numbers and importance following the outbreak of the Troubles in Northern Ireland in 1969 and an attendant rise in kidnappings and crime in the south.[6]

The problem Courtney faced in the investigation was a unique one. He already knew the source of the bomb that killed Lord Mountbatten; the statement from the IRA claiming responsibility for the attack answered that question. The predicament was that the two men Courtney suspected of planting the bomb had what appeared to be an unshakeable alibi: both men already were in Garda custody when the bomb exploded.

At 9:40 in the morning, some two hours before the blast that killed Lord Mountbatten, a Garda named J. Lohane stopped a car on the outskirts of Granard, a city in County Longford situated about seventy miles southeast of Mullaghmore. Although the stop was routine—the officer intended only to verify that required paperwork for the vehicle was in order—neither the driver nor the passenger had identification and both appeared quite nervous. Garda Lohane became suspicious and took both men into custody for questioning. Although there was no reason to suspect the two men of anything, let alone of planning a bombing that had not yet happened, Garda Lohane's intuition that something was amiss about the two earned him a promotion for his police work.

The men in the automobile were Thomas McMahon, an explosives expert and active member of the IRA, and Francis McGirl, an IRA sympathizer. They refused to make any statements at the time and both were arrested. During subsequent questions, without being asked, McGirl said: "I put no bomb in the boat." Asked: "What boat?" by the interrogator, McGirl responded: "No answer."

McGirl's spontaneous denial was a tenuous link at best to the assassination of Lord Mountbatten, but neither that statement nor McMahon's reputation as an IRA bomb maker was proof of anything directly related to the bomb attack. Instead, Courtney and the prosecutors relied on strong forensic evidence to link the two men to the crime.

Flakes of green and white paint and sea sand recovered from the men's vehicle matched samples taken from the wreck of the *Saturn V* and the beach at Mullaghmore. Dr. Jim Donovan, head of the Garda's Forensic Section, also found traces of both nitroglycerine and ammonium nitrate, the principal components of the gelignite explosive used in the bomb, on both men's clothes.

Although the evidence was purely circumstantial, the combination of bomb-making chemicals and paint flakes from both the interior and exterior of the *Saturn V* on McMahon's clothing was crucial to Courtney's investigation. While neither man could actually have detonated the bomb, the evidence convinced an Irish court that it was McMahon who had placed the bomb on the boat with the intention of killing the people on board. He received a life sentence. McGirl was acquitted due to a lack of evidence.

There were reports that an IRA man in a yellow Ford Cortina actually detonated the bomb by remote control, but a search of the area by the Garda proved fruitless.

Over the years, the Murder Squad compiled a nearly perfect record of successful investigations, and the conviction of Thomas McMahon was one of the unit's most visible triumphs. Things did not go so well, however, when Courtney began investigating the theft of Shergar, an assignment he took on a few days after the horse went missing on February 8, 1983.[7]

For the head of the Murder Squad to be assigned to the trail of horse thieves might have seemed like a demotion at the time, but years later Courtney said that was not the situation. Shergar was a "special horse that most people would recognize on sight," he explained. "It was big news. Everyone was talking about it." The people who took Shergar—Courtney remains convinced it was the IRA—committed a "serious crime," he added. "And that was my job, investigating everything big that happened."[8]

A grandson of Queen Victoria and a cousin and confidant of Queen Elizabeth II, Lord Mountbatten was among the best-loved members of the British royal family. He was a national hero in the truest sense of the word—admiral of the fleet, allied commander in chief in Southeast Asia, the last viceroy of India—a nobleman with an affinity for the common man. He also was an obvious target for the IRA, a member of the monarchy whose disdain for adequate security measures had been well known since his days of active military service.[9]

Mullaghmore was just a few miles south of the border with Northern Ireland. Neither the proximity of the Troubles nor the threat of an IRA attack were enough to convince Lord Mountbatten to utilize the security measures his advisors thought necessary. He chafed at the attention paid him by the Garda and refused to allow his security detail onto the *Saturn V* while it was moored or to accompany him on his excursions out into Donegal Bay. The officers instead were relegated to a watch point on a clifftop road when the *Saturn V* exploded.

The attacks at Mullaghmore and Warrenpoint infuriated Margaret Thatcher, who was facing one of her first major challenges since becoming Britain's prime minister. Her Conservative Party had won a resounding election victory a few months earlier, with campaign promises to rein in powerful trade unions, cut personal income taxes, and strengthen the military. Dealing with the Troubles was not a high priority for Mrs. Thatcher during the campaign, but the events of August 27 brought the situation in Northern Ireland to the forefront.[10] When Mrs. Thatcher died in April 2013 at the age of eighty-seven, a lengthy obituary in the *New York Times* dismissed her interest in the Troubles in a couple of sentences: "Despite the sectarian violence, Northern Ireland was not high on her agenda. Mrs. Thatcher saw the troubles there as intractable and her policies as simply preserving the status quo."[11]

That characterization was unfair. While resolving the stalemate in Northern Ireland may not have been at the top of Mrs. Thatcher's agenda when she took office or during her tenure as prime minister, the Iron Lady was a steadfast opponent of the republican movement. More important, she recognized that the Troubles were exacerbated by a steady stream of money and shipments of arms to the IRA from the United States.[12]

Mrs. Thatcher also recognized that curbing transfers of funds and arms from a foreign country could not be accomplished unilaterally by the British; international cooperation was an absolute necessity. With the election of President Ronald Reagan in 1980, Mrs. Thatcher had a friend in Washington who was willing to listen to her worries about American money and weapons propping up the republican movement in Northern Ireland.[13]

After years maintaining a general hands-off attitude toward IRA fund-raising and weapons procurement in the United States, the Federal Bureau of Investigation finally began to rethink that approach following the assassination of Lord Mountbatten and the deadly attack at Warrenpoint. A special FBI unit was established in 1980 under the leadership of veteran agent Lou Stephens to investigate domestic IRA activities.[14]

Even enhanced investigations could not bring a total halt to Irish American support for the IRA, but the special unit did seriously disrupt the money and weapons pipelines with high-profile court victories. In 1981, a federal district court in New York ruled that the Irish Northern Aid Committee (NORAID), ostensibly a fund-raiser for charitable work in Northern Ireland, really was acting as an "agent" of the Irish Republican Army.[15] Although the court ruled that the "uncontroverted evidence is that the defendant [NORAID] is an agent of the IRA, providing money and services for other than relief purposes," the decision did not directly address what those other purposes were.[16] In a subsequent federal trial, however, four men were convicted on charges of gunrunning for the IRA. Testimony at that trial from Michael Hanratty, an informer involved in an FBI sting, indicated that at least some NORAID funds were diverted to buy weapons in America.[17]

Not every special unit investigation resulted in a successful prosecution, however. A few months earlier, in a seven-week federal trial, a New York jury acquitted longtime IRA weapons supplier George Harrison and four other defendants charged with conspiracy to smuggle weapons to the IRA. The men never denied that they purchased weapons from a convicted arms dealer or that the weapons were destined for the IRA. Harrison even acknowledged that he had been sending arms to the Provos for twenty years (see chapter 7 for a fuller discussion).[18]

Disruption of the usually reliable sources for money and weapons in the United States could not have come at a worse time for the IRA, which was also experiencing cutbacks from another regular supplier of arms and money, Libya.

Colonel Muammar al-Qadhafi had seized control of Libya in a military coup during the summer of 1969.[19] Under Qadhafi's rule, Libya quickly became a "one-stop weapons depot for radical movements all over Europe and Africa."[20] Qadhafi took over Libya in the same year the Troubles erupted in Northern Ireland, and he sympathized with the IRA's violent opposition to British rule. For the next few years, until the relationship soured for a time in the late 1970s, Libya was a major supplier of weapons to the IRA. After a hunger strike begun in 1980 by IRA prisoners failed to sway the authorities, a second hunger strike the next year had more impact. The deaths of ten IRA and Irish National Liberation Army prisoners being held in the Maze Prison near Belfast rekindled Qadhafi's interest in, and support for, the republican campaign in Northern Ireland. Cash payments to the IRA, but no weapons shipments, resumed in 1981.

Large-scale movements of weapons and explosives from Libya did not start again until the mid-1980s, however, when IRA leaders were working out plans for a major action against the British, something along the lines of the Viet Cong's Tet Offensive in Vietnam.[21] Those plans would have to wait, however, because there was a more immediate problem.

With the United States largely out of the picture for weapons procurement, and facing limited support from Libya, the IRA was strapped for cash. The Provos were forced to shop for arms on the black market to keep their decade-old campaign against the British going—and they had few options. The Provos turned to kidnappings for ransom, targeting prominent businessmen in the Republic of Ireland.

On February 8, 1983, they stole a horse.

# 5

# Shergar Ascendant

Shergar at two was a minor star in a juvenile universe ruled by Robert E. Sangster's Storm Bird. Top weight on the Tote European Free Handicap for two-year-olds of 1980 at 133 pounds, 12 pounds more than Shergar, champion Storm Bird was a solid favorite in advance wagering for the Two Thousand Guineas and the Epsom Derby. The colt had everything in his favor. He finished the year sound, he had a flawless record against good company as a two-year-old, and in Vincent O'Brien he had a veteran trainer with as fine a record in the classics as anyone.

Sangster bought Storm Bird for $1 million at the 1979 Keeneland summer yearling sale as another installment in an ongoing attempt to corner the worldwide market for exceptional colts by Northern Dancer.[1] The ambitious plan had worked before for Sangster and his partners with The Minstrel, another Northern Dancer colt that far exceeded expectations.

The Minstrel was Europe's Horse of the Year in 1977. The consensus during the winter of 1980–1981 was that Storm Bird was at least as good as The Minstrel, and maybe even better.[2] The Guineas and the Derby seemed to be Storm Bird's for the taking in 1981—until suddenly and inexplicably they were not.

A few minutes past midnight on the morning of Wednesday, January 21, a twenty-year-old laborer named Donal O'Sullivan slipped into Storm Bird's stall at Vincent O'Brien's Ballydoyle training yard near Cashel in County Tipperary. He found a halter with the Derby favorite's name, buckled it on the colt, and clipped Storm Bird to a tie chain in the rear of the stall. Wielding a pair of yellow scissors he'd lifted from a drawer in his mother's kitchen, O'Sullivan started hacking at Storm Bird's mane and tail. The bizarre attack was discovered when the staff at Ballydoyle showed up for work in the morning.

Fortunately, Storm Bird was unharmed—by intent, as it later would turn out—although he lost more than a foot of hair from his tail and a good bit of his mane. The incident received extensive media attention, the second time within a few days that Storm Bird was in the news. Earlier the same week, announcement was made that the colt had been insured through Lloyd's of London for $15 million, with a $500,000 premium. It was a lofty valuation for a colt whose classic season was not scheduled to start for another three months.

The Garda made quick work of the investigation, and O'Sullivan was standing before a district court judge in Clonmel, County Tipperary, a few days later. The young man entered guilty pleas for going into O'Brien's yard as a trespasser intending to commit a felony, for "stealing a quantity of horse hair valued at £50," and for "causing unlawful and malicious damage" to Storm Bird in an amount of less than £50. Just how a monetary value for a handful of hair from Storm Bird's tail was determined is unclear. A two-month jail sentence was meted out but was suspended upon O'Sullivan's promise of two years of good behavior. He paid a fine of £10 for each of the three charges.

O'Sullivan's motive for the attack had nothing to do with Storm Bird. He and his family harbored a grudge against O'Brien and Storm Bird was merely a surrogate. "My mother, brother, and myself were not satisfied with the way we had been treated by Mr. O'Brien," O'Sullivan told the district court judge. O'Sullivan's father had worked at Ballydoyle his entire life, until his death in September 1979. His father had not been treated fairly while working there, O'Sullivan said, and the family had received no consideration after his death. "And as a result of this a hatred built up inside me against Mr. O'Brien. . . . The hatred had built up so much against Mr. O'Brien I decided I would get at Storm Bird. . . . I did not intend to injure the horse in any way but it was my way of getting revenge on Mr. O'Brien. . . . I am sorry I did it."[3] Storm

Bird, it seemed, simply had been in the proverbial wrong place at the wrong time.

Under other circumstances, the incident would have been dismissed as a minor oddity, no obstacle on the road to a championship season for Storm Bird, the sort of story told over a round of drinks. As the season turned out, though, the attack on Storm Bird was a harbinger of misfortune to come.[4]

Storm Bird's first race as a three-year-old was supposed to come in the Gladness Stakes, a Group 3 event run at The Curragh on April 4. A spate of coughing was running through Ballydoyle by the end of March, but Storm Bird was in isolation. The colt apparently was in good health in the days leading up to a race that was supposed to validate his status as favorite for the Epsom Derby. Such a triumph had happened before. Vincent O'Brien had sent out Charles W. Engelhard Jr.'s Nijinsky II to win the Gladness in 1970 as a prelude to that horse's impressive sweep of the Two Thousand Guineas, the Epsom Derby, and the St. Leger, but hopes for a repeat with Storm Bird vanished when the colt turned up lame in his right hind leg. The injury did not appear to be serious, but the colt was scratched from the Gladness on the advice of his veterinarian.

The next available prep for the Two Thousand Guineas was the Minstrel Stakes at Leopardstown a week after the Gladness, but Storm Bird missed that race as well. The colt's early-season absences were troublesome, but they had not become a pattern for the Derby favorite, not yet.

By mid-April, though, it was clear that the isolation measures at Ballydoyle had failed. Storm Bird was coughing and would miss the Two Thousand Guineas on May 2.[5] To-Agori-Mou, judged the second-best juvenile in 1980 in the Tote European Free Handicap, closed in the final furlongs to take the first English classic in Storm Bird's absence. O'Brien announced in early May that Storm Bird had recovered from the virus that kept him away from Newmarket and that the colt would run in the Irish Two Thousand Guineas. He told reporters that the race would have to serve as a trial for the Epsom Derby.[6]

But Storm Bird never made it to The Curragh for the Irish Two Thousand Guineas, no surprise to anyone paying attention to the growing list of his missed engagements. Kings Lake edged To-Agori-Mou in the Irish classic and ante-post bettors who made Storm Bird the solid early favorite for the Epsom Derby based on his form the previous year finally must have been questioning their optimism about the colt.

When eighteen horses went to the post for the Epsom Derby on June 3, Storm Bird was not among them. He had not been seen on a racecourse in almost eight months, not since he edged To-Agori-Mou by a half length in the Dewhurst Stakes, and there was no indication that the onetime pretender to the English Triple Crown would ever race again.

Amazingly, and despite a series of disheartening no-shows that sometimes defied explanation, Storm Bird's worth actually doubled during the first half of 1981, to twice his insured valuation. In July, around the time he bid $3.5 million for Storm Bird's full brother at the Keeneland summer sale, Robert Sangster announced that he had sold a three-quarter interest in Storm Bird to Dr. William Lockridge and Robert Hefner.[7] Total value for the forty shares, including the ten shares kept by Sangster, was variously reported as $28 million and $30 million.[8] Whichever figure was accurate, either topped the record $22 million syndication of three-time Eclipse Award winner Spectacular Bid a year earlier.[9]

Storm Bird entered stud in 1982 at Lockridge and Hefner's Ashford Stud near Versailles, Kentucky.[10] He sired more than sixty stakes winners, none more influential than leading sire Storm Cat, a son of the Secretariat mare Terlingua from Storm Bird's first crop. During twenty years at stud, Storm Cat sired eight champions, 108 graded stakes winners, and horses with total earnings of more than $127 million. He twice led the general sire list and for a time his stud fee was $500,000, the highest on record.[11]

The magnitude of the deal left many people shaking their heads in wonderment. If a horse that had not even made it to the races as a three-year-old could command a $28-million price tag (or was it $30 million?), how much would a record-setting Epsom Derby winner be worth? The sky should be the limit.

The answer was a surprise, as unlikely in its own right as the Storm Bird syndication.

Dismissed in advance wagering for the Epsom Derby at odds of 33-1, Shergar cruised along under the handicappers' radar until it became apparent that Storm Bird would not run in the classic, and might not race again at all. For every misfortune suffered by the previous year's juvenile champion, it seemed that something went right for Shergar.[12]

Shergar with jockey Walter Swinburn and lad Dickie McCabe before his ten-length victory in the Guardian Newspaper Classic Trial at Sandown Park on April 25, 1981. (Miralgo Publications Photo Archives/John Crofts)

While Storm Bird was sidelined in April, Shergar made his three-year-old debut in the Guardian Newspaper Classic Trial, a Group 3 event run over one and one-quarter miles at Sandown. He looked good before the race and better at the finish. Favored at even money, Shergar won by ten lengths over Kirtling, a decent son of Grundy that had already won a stakes race earlier in the season. It was the first time Walter Swinburn was on Shergar in competition, and the performances of both horse and rider were flawless.

In May, while Storm Bird was still recovering from a cough that compromised his training, Shergar won again, in the Group 3 Chester Vase by twelve lengths over a mediocre field. Neither the Classic Trial nor the Chester Vase—the latter run over an uncomfortably tight, nearly circular course at the odd distance of one mile, four furlongs, and sixty-five yards—had the prominence or crowd appeal of the first classics of the year at Newmarket and The Curragh. Even so, both trials had proved at times to be reliable predictors of future success in the Epsom Derby.

Shirley Heights, Troy, and Henbit, winners of the Derby in 1978, 1979, and 1980, respectively, each had their three-year-old debuts in the Classic Trial. Troy and Henbit won, and Shirley Heights was narrowly beaten by Whitstead. Henbit also won the Chester Vase and then won the Epsom Derby as the second choice.

Impressive wins in the Classic Trial and the Chester Vase catapulted Shergar from a 33-1 long shot in advance Derby wagering to the pre-race favorite. By June 3, Shergar's odds had dropped even more and he started as the shortest priced choice for the race since Sir Ivor in 1968.

There was no guarantee that Shergar would live up to the promise he showed in his trials. Racecourses are littered with beaten favorites. If he did, however, the Epsom Derby figured to be a windfall for those prescient bettors who backed the colt over the winter at long odds. Cliff Lines was one of those bettors. Lines was head lad at Freemason Lodge, Stoute's training yard across the Bury Road from Beech Hurst, where Shergar was stabled. Lines rode Shergar most mornings, and he enjoyed the benefit of some insider information when it came to laying a bet.

Stoute and Swinburn were the media stars in the Shergar camp in

Shergar winning the Chester Vase by twelve lengths on May 5, 1981. (George Selwyn)

1981, but Cliff Lines, David Goodwin, and Dickie McCabe—the trio of lads who worked with the colt on a regular basis for two years—probably knew him best.[13] The English system is different from that in the United States, Goodwin explained. "Here the lads usually have three horses to care for and they really get to know them. Even if you don't ride the horses every day, you do everything else with them, start to finish."[14]

Years later, Lines still could point to one particular early morning workout that left him convinced that Shergar was a lock for the Epsom Derby. "I remember doing a piece of work with Shergar in the spring of the year, in 1981," Lines recalled. "We were working a mile with two other horses, one of them the winner of the Northumberland Plate. The other horses jumped off and went a racing pace, at least I think they did. They were running flat out. When I moved this horse out from behind the two of them, without my moving a muscle on him, he took off and finished ten or twelve lengths in front of them. Inside that last furlong, that's when I knew Shergar was something special And that's when I went and backed him at 33-1 for the Derby."[15]

Cliff Lines is in his eighties now, still active as his own head lad for the horses he trains out of the shedrow in his back yard. He lives in Exning, a village a short drive northwest of Newmarket, in an attractive house that doubles as a popular bed and breakfast. His home is a testament to a life well lived, a rich life filled with horses. The walls are covered with images of the Thoroughbreds he rode on too many early mornings to count—among them, of course, Shergar—and his two winners as an apprentice rider, one of them for Queen Elizabeth II. He treasures a bust of Shergar, a personal gift to him from the Aga Khan, and a bright yellow saddle cloth worn by J. O. Tobin in the 1977 Swaps Stakes at Hollywood Park. Both are mementos of the best horses Lines rode during a decades-long career.

J. O. Tobin was the top-weighted juvenile in Britain in 1976, when he won the Richmond and Champagne Stakes. After J. O. Tobin's trainer, Noel Murless, retired at the end of the season, the colt's owner, George A. Pope Jr., returned him to the United States. Pope put J. O.

Tobin in training with former jockey John H. Adams, but he wanted an exercise rider who was familiar with the colt. Lines had been riding J. O. Tobin for Murless, but he found himself looking for another position when his boss retired. He had an offer to move to Michael Stoute's yard and was prepared to take the job when Pope asked him to go to the United States. Stoute heard about the offer and told Lines to go.

Lines knows his way around a good horse, and he remembers J. O. Tobin as one of the best he ever rode. When he won the Swaps Stakes at Hollywood Park in the summer of 1977 with Bill Shoemaker in the saddle, J. O. Tobin handed American Triple Crown winner Seattle Slew his first defeat. He led from the start in the Swaps and finished eight and three-quarters lengths in front of Affiliate and sixteen lengths ahead of Seattle Slew in fourth place. J. O. Tobin's time for one and a quarter miles was spectacular, 1:58 $^3$/$_5$, just two-fifths of a second off the world record.

After nine months in the United States, Lines returned to Newmarket and took the job that Michael Stoute had been holding open for him at Freemason Lodge. Early in 1980 he started riding a flashy colt with a lot of white. Shergar also had a walleye, which some people believe indicates a horse that is skittish, maybe a little crazy.[16] "A lot of people don't like a horse with a walleye, but that's rubbish," Lines said. "It's like four white socks. Some people don't like horses with four white socks. But Shergar had four white socks, The Minstrel had four white socks. People believe strange things when it comes to horses."

There were no temperament issues with Shergar, Lines added. "He was an easy horse to handle. He never gave you any trouble."

Although Lines was on Shergar for many morning workouts, he was not the first person to put weight on the horse's back. That honor goes to David Goodwin, a crack bicycle racer and horseman from Largs on the Firth of Clyde in Scotland. Goodwin signed on with Michael Stoute in 1978, around the time that the first consignment of yearlings from the Aga Khan arrived. When the next group of yearlings came late in 1979, Shergar among them, Goodwin was one of a half-dozen lads assigned to start their training. "Shergar was a big, walleyed bastard,"

Goodwin said, "but he had no vices at all. He was straightforward to work with, very easygoing, a good pupil."

Goodwin rode Shergar off and on well into the colt's two-year-old year, but in June 1980 he lost the opportunity to handle his first Epsom Derby winner. "A girl named Rose had been working with Shergar, but one day she just quit," Goodwin said. "Dickie McCabe was there when the head lad pointed at Shergar and a few of the other two-year-olds. He looked at Dickie and said, 'Girl just left, you take that one, that one, that one.' That's how Dickie got Shergar and how I let him slip away. He didn't look bad and I thought he might make a decent horse, but I wouldn't have passed him up if he'd looked a little better. But that's the way classic horses often develop. Shergar wintered well and then he just kept getting better and started winning by ten lengths, twelve lengths. I let one Derby winner slip through my hands, but I did two more."

Goodwin left Stoute in 1980 and moved to Henry Cecil's training yard at Warren Place, where he worked with Epsom Derby winners Slip Anchor (1985) and Commander in Chief (1993). Stoute and Cecil were the dominant forces among Newmarket trainers for years. Stoute still is; Cecil died in 2013. Goodwin had the good fortune to work with two of the best. "I surfed the wave of the good horses," he said.

Dickie McCabe made the most of his serendipitous association with Shergar. Anyone who watched Shergar's races in 1981, whether in person, on television, or in newsreel or print media, knew him—maybe not by name, but certainly by appearance. McCabe was the well-dressed young man with bushy hair and a neatly trimmed moustache leading Shergar in to the winner's enclosure after the Epsom Derby, or maybe on the colt's head at Chester or Doncaster, or perhaps somewhere in the background. Wherever Shergar traveled that year, McCabe was there, too. Shergar, he said, was like a "machine, lovely to work with, a saint."[17]

McCabe was less complimentary about Michael Stoute and the Aga Khan. He believes that they should have taken him to Ireland for Shergar's retirement parade down the streets of Newbridge, but did not. "I took care of the horse," he said, "but they didn't take care of me."

Shergar as a three-year-old, with trainer Sir Michael Stoute and lad Dickie McCabe. (Courtesy of Laurie Morton)

# 6

# "You need a telescope to see the rest"

Rounding Tattenham Corner with Shergar going easily, tucked in behind Riberetto and Silver Season, Walter Swinburn felt like he was riding the favorite through a tunnel of people, awash with waves of sound. All Swinburn could make out among the shouts was "Come on, Lester!" and for the first time in the race, he panicked. He thought Lester Piggott might be catching up to him with Shotgun and he rapped Shergar right-handed with his whip.

There was no need to worry.

Shotgun was running in fourth place and presented no threat at all to the favorite. Shergar moved to the outside in response to Swinburn's whip, sprinted past the two leaders, and drew away through the run to the finish. He won by ten lengths and would have won by more if Swinburn had not pulled him up in the last few strides. The performance might not have been the equal of Secretariat's remarkable run in the Belmont Stakes, but it came close.

Glint of Gold, at 13-1, closed with a rush to finish second, but still was so far behind Shergar that jockey John Matthias thought for a moment he had won the race. "I told myself that I'd achieved my life's ambition," Matthias said later. "Only then did I discover there was another horse on the horizon."[1] That horse was Shergar, so far ahead of the others as to be almost out of sight.

Years later, Swinburn still felt a need to apologize for hitting Shergar that day in June. "I gave Shergar one last slap and he took off," Swin-

Shergar cantering to the start for the Epsom Derby on June 3, 1981. (Miralgo Publications Photo Archives/John Crofts)

burn said. "I didn't need to. I always regretted it. I never had an easier winner."[2]

The winter had treated Shergar well. The colt put on some muscle and filled out nicely during the break, and with his three-year-old season under way, potential stumbling blocks on his road to the 1981 Epsom Derby were disappearing. Storm Bird, the champion two-year-old of 1980 and the presumptive Derby favorite at the start of 1981, was out of action, although for how long no one was exactly sure. Shergar faced no serious challengers in either of his first two Derby trials, which he won by a total of twenty-two lengths, and then a week before the Derby his chief rival, Beldale Flutter, was injured and later scratched.

The only horse to finish ahead of Shergar to that point, by two and a half lengths in the 1980 William Hill Futurity Stakes at Doncaster, Beldale Flutter was held at odds of 7-1 in pre-Derby betting on

Shergar winning the Epsom Derby by a record ten lengths on June 3, 1981. (Ed Byrne)

the strength of a win in the Mecca-Dante Stakes at York. The victory was such a surprise that the York stewards demanded an explanation for the extreme reversal of form the colt showed since the Two Thousand Guineas at Newmarket, where he finished in fifteenth place. The stewards accepted trainer Michael Jarvis's explanation that Beldale Flutter had bumped another horse in the Guineas and that he preferred the longer distance of the Mecca-Dante.[3]

The week before the Derby, during a workout over the Long Hill gallops at Newmarket, Beldale Flutter bolted, threw his rider, and collided with Moorestyle, the previous year's champion three-year-old. Moorestyle went down and was injured; the riderless Beldale Flutter escaped onto the road, where he also fell and hurt a knee. Returned to the races three months later, Beldale Flutter won the Benson and Hedges Gold Cup, but was a disappointment in the Prix de l'Arc de Triomphe at Chantilly and the Washington, DC, International in the United States.[4]

The Derby at Epsom could not have been an easier race for Shergar and for Swinburn. Before the race, trainer Michael Stoute tried to put the young rider at ease. It probably was not necessary—Swinburn reportedly napped in the car while his father drove him to Epsom for the race—but Stoute explained that Swinburn had years to win a Derby. It was the older riders, the trainer said, who were running out of time.[5]

"All I had to do was steer him," Swinburn said about Shergar in *I Was There*, a February 12, 2016, BBC 5 Live radio broadcast. It might have been hyperbole colored by a bit of nostalgia more than three decades after the Epsom Derby, but Swinburn's win on Shergar was one of the easiest in the history of the race.

Shergar broke well, which is more than can be said for Lydian. The French horse refused to load and was left standing behind the starting gate when the starter lost patience and sent the rest of the field away without him. "It's a disgrace," Lydian's rider, Freddie Head, said afterward. "The starter never told me it was my last chance and I couldn't believe it when he called me 'out of the race.' I tried to go in three times and then the hood was put on. Lydian was standing to one side while they got the other French horse, Al Nasr, into the stalls. I was not going to stand there with the hood on, so I took it off, and the next thing I knew they were off without me."[6]

Swinburn kept Shergar near the lead, in fourth, then up to third, "brilliantly placed" during the early going, according to BBC radio commentator Peter Bromley. Lester Piggott tried to make a run at the leaders with second-choice Shotgun at the top of the hill leading to Tattenham Corner, giving a moment's hope to the fans who shouted his name, but Shotgun swerved to the right and lost any chance.

At the finish, Swinburn was standing in the irons and Shergar was slowing to a near canter. The winning margin, ten lengths, was the longest in the history of the Derby; time for the race, 2:44.21, was less spectacular, the slowest running since the end of World War II.

It was a magnificent ride by Swinburn, although he took little credit for the victory. "I was lucky enough to be a passenger on a very good horse," he told reporters after the race.[7]

Years later, on the thirtieth anniversary of Shergar's record-setting victory, the Aga Khan shared his memories of the race with Mick Fitzgerald on a BBC radio special. "It's a memory that can never, never go away," His Highness said.

> I've seen that film, I don't know, tens or hundreds of times. I keep trying to analyze where his remarkable performance came from. Every time I see the film, I feel that I have learned something. If you're in racing, the Epsom Derby is one of the greats. It always has been, so to win a race of that quality in itself is an extraordinary privilege. To win it the way he won it was more than that.
>
> I had watched quite enough races to be able to determine what the jockey was feeling, how the horse was going at the time when he came around Tattenham Corner, I couldn't believe my eyes, frankly.
>
> His victory up to this point in time was unique. Two things I found stunning—one was the ease with which that horse moved and second was the fact that during the finishing straight he just kept going away, going away, going away. That was really remarkable.[8]

Shergar was the first horse to win the Derby as the odds-on choice since Sir Ivor in 1968, and bookmakers quickly made the colt the odds-on favorite to win the Irish Sweeps Derby three weeks later. The horses Shergar would face at The Curragh were new—not one of the seventeen three-year-olds he had toyed with at Epsom turned out for the Irish Sweeps Derby. New, too, would be the colt's rider, at least since the William Hill Futurity Stakes eight months earlier.

Michael Stoute and the Aga Khan resisted any temptation they might have had to put a more experienced rider on Shergar for the Epsom Derby. For the Irish Sweeps Derby, though, they had no choice. Following a rough ride in the King Edward VII Stakes at Royal Ascot, when his mount Centurius bothered winner Bustomi through the stretch, Walter

Substituting for Walter Swinburn, jockey Lester Piggott guides Shergar to a four-length win in the Irish Sweeps Derby at The Curragh Racecourse on June 27, 1981. (Ed Byrne)

Shergar draws away to win against older horses in the King George VI and Queen Elizabeth Diamond Stakes at Ascot on July 25, 1981. (Miralgo Publications Photo Archives/John Crofts)

Swinburn received a six-day suspension.[9] Those days included June 27, the day the Irish Sweeps Derby was run.

It must have seemed like an instance of irony for Lester Piggott, who picked up the mount on Shergar with Swinburn on the sidelines.

In 1954, days after he won his first Epsom Derby, Piggott and his Derby winner Never Say Die were involved in a chain-reaction bumping incident with three other horses. The Royal Ascot stewards initially thought jockey Gordon Richards initiated the bumping but later assigned the blame entirely to Piggott.

The stewards disqualified Never Say Die, suspended Piggott for the rest of the meeting, and reported him to the Jockey Club. Before the next day's racing, after a hearing that lasted only twenty minutes, the Jockey Club stewards pulled Piggott's license and suggested that he might apply for reinstatement in six months.[10] The race in which Piggott suffered the longest suspension of his career? The King Edward VII Stakes at Royal Ascot.

There was little suspense in Shergar's races in 1981. What drama there was occurred away from the racecourse.

On Monday, June 15—it was exactly twelve days after the Epsom Derby and exactly twelve days before the Irish Sweeps Derby—Shergar tossed his rider, Steve Walsh, during an early morning workout over the Lime Kiln gallop. The colt cantered down the hill past a stand of trees, slipped through a gap in the hedge by the Boy's Grave, and started along the highway toward the village of Moulton.[11]

Stories differ about what happened next. Most accounts have Shergar making his way to Moulton, then turning right onto the road to Newmarket. He was being tracked all this time by either an automobile, a van, or a postal truck, depending on who is telling the story, with the driver unaware that the loose horse he was following was an Epsom Derby winner. When Shergar got tired and stopped to nibble some grass along the side of the road, the driver, or maybe it was the postman, caught the colt and delivered him either to Henry Cecil's Warren Place or back home to Beech Hurst around the time when Michael Stoute was leaving to go look for the horse.

Probably the best story has Shergar stopping at Warren Place on his own and wandering into an empty stall. That outcome would make Shergar the first Derby winner in Cecil's training yard years before the four that he actually trained. In any case, remarkably, Shergar managed to avoid traffic and got home without a scratch.

Shergar was the last of twelve horses loaded into the starting gate at The Curragh and the first of twelve to cross the finish line, with no real suspense in between. The Irish form book summary of the race was succinct and to the point, although often devoid of vowels: "Close up on inside; 3rd ½ way; switched out to ld entr str; qcknd clr 2f out; eased final furlong."[12] Translation: Shergar broke well and then settled in along the rail behind pacesetter Cut Above, with Jolly Heir and Kirtling keeping up on his left. Still third on the inside with six furlongs left, Shergar was running easily with Piggott riding high, his hands buried in the horse's mane. He edged Shergar out from the rail approaching the stretch, and with little urging from his rider the colt took charge and went to the front.

Piggott glanced over his left shoulder twice in the stretch but never moved his whip, content to let Shergar make his own pace. There was no need for Piggott to do anything, never a moment when the outcome was in doubt. Eased near the finish line as he was at Epsom, Shergar finished four lengths in front of Cut Above, with Dance Bid third. Time for the one and a half miles was 2:32.07.

There were no surprises during the Irish Sweeps Derby and none afterward. Shergar had barely passed the finish when bookmakers made him the favorite for the King George VI and Queen Elizabeth Diamond Stakes at Royal Ascot a month later and the Aga Khan confirmed that Swinburn would be the rider again when he returned after serving his suspension. "Walter is the stable jockey and he will be back," the Aga Khan said. "But I'd like to thank Lester Piggott for a great job."[13]

The only questions that remained after Shergar's second classic was whether the colt would race at four and if not, where he would stand at stud. Although the Aga Khan told reporters that it was too early to know for certain whether Shergar would stay in training for another year, there was almost no chance that would happen. He was too valuable and the risk of injury was too great.

The Aga Khan was noncommittal about retirement plans for Shergar, even though negotiations to syndicate Shergar already were under way. Those plans would come to fruition during the race meeting at Royal Ascot, where Shergar would be tested against older horses for the first time.[14]

Walter Swinburn resumed riding on July 3 after his suspension ended, failing to place on his only mount at Haydock that day. On July 4, riding Hard Fought in the Coral Eclipse Stakes at Sandown, Swinburn tried to muscle through an opening and appeared to interfere with a filly named Vielle. He was called before the Jockey Club stewards again, and again was suspended, this time for nine days. The good news for Swinburn was that he would be back from the suspension in time for the King George VI and Queen Elizabeth Diamond Stakes.[15]

The King George looked like a replay of the Epsom and Irish Derbies until the final turn, with Shergar on the rail, rolling easily along in third, a length or two off the pace set by Light Cavalry. This time, though, Shergar was boxed in by the filly Madam Gay, the only other three-year-old in the race, which had moved up on his left. Racing luck had nothing to do with Shergar's wins at Epsom and The Curragh, but at Royal Ascot the colt needed some help.

Shergar got the break he needed when Light Cavalry drifted out on the right-hand turn into the stretch. The colt accelerated through the gap, caught Master Willie, which was running far enough off the rail to give Shergar room, and drew off in the stretch. Shergar won by four lengths over Madam Gay in 2:35.04 for the one and a half miles.

Shergar's goal for the fall was the Prix de l'Arc de Triomphe in October, but Michael Stoute and the Aga Khan thought he needed a prep race between the King George and the Arc. They decided on the St. Leger, despite the fact that it was run at Doncaster, site of Shergar's only defeat.

"Usually, three weeks is what we consider to be the ideal time for a prep race," the Aga Khan told the late Kent Hollingsworth, editor of *Blood-Horse* magazine. "A month is too long, two weeks too close. The St. Leger we thought provided just the right time before the Arc, so we selected that one, even though it was at Doncaster."[16]

Run at Doncaster Shergar did, but not very well.

Shergar was slow breaking from the gate and he raced far back early, lagging behind, next to last in the seven-horse field. Swinburn appeared to be in no hurry to challenge the leaders until the final turn, when he finally got Shergar moving up on the outside. Third with three furlongs to race, Shergar looked to be in perfect position for a run to the finish, but he had no closing kick at all. He lost touch with the leaders through the stretch and finished fourth, eleven and a half lengths behind winner Cut Above, a colt that Shergar had defeated by four lengths in the Irish Sweeps Derby. The winner's time was 3:11.60.

It was a dismal effort that quickly erased any thoughts of going on to the Arc.

"It is very difficult to know," the Aga Khan said when asked what went wrong in the St. Leger. "Since the race, we have had a whole lot of tests carried out, and they were all fine. He was well after the race, so well that Michael Stoute was tempted to run in the Arc after all, but we all thought that because he had run an abnormal race—not just bad form, but abnormal—the three weeks between the Leger and the Arc just did not give us the necessary time to (a) understand exactly what had gone wrong, and (b) put it right."[17]

Rumors circulated in the days leading up to the St. Leger that Shergar was not training well, that he had become "mulish" after a hard campaign, and that he had missed an important morning workout, but Michael Stoute denied that there were problems with his horse. The problem, he said years later, was the ground at Doncaster. It had rained hard the night before the race and the ground was terrible, Stoute said. "He never should have run that day. Running him was a big mistake on my part, but I didn't have the bottom to keep him out."[18]

"On the day of the St. Leger, the going was dead," the Aga Khan told Kent Hollingsworth a few weeks after the St. Leger.

> There is a big difference over here between what they call heavy going and dead going. Dead going is really holding, sticky going. That was the sort of going at Doncaster last year when he was beaten.

So, all right, the going may have had its effect, the course may have had its effect, but really, although Shergar had worked well before the race . . . he was not right. All of us were unhappy with him. He clearly was not what he should have been. He was tense, distraught, a different horse from what he usually was.

He was just an exceptional athlete. All through the spring and summer he completely dominated European racing in a very dramatic manner, and after he had run so uncharacteristically in the St. Leger, we knew something had gone wrong, but we didn't know what it was, so it was an easy decision to retire him before the Arc.[19]

With the Arc no longer an option after the St. Leger and the syndicate agreement already in place, Shergar was retired to the Aga Khan's Ballymany Stud near The Curragh. He entered stud with a record of six wins, including two classics, from eight starts and the top ranking on the Tote European Free Handicap. The Aga Khan finished the season as England's leading breeder and owner and Michael Stoute was the year's top trainer, both titles courtesy of Shergar.

As Shergar rolled through his prep races, the Epsom Derby, and the Irish Sweeps Derby, dominating the opposition by a total of thirty-six lengths, European breeders grudgingly resigned themselves to the fact that they would lose the horse to deep-pocket breeders in the United States. There was a confirmed offer of $28 million to syndicate Shergar in America and unconfirmed offers for much more. That was too much money to pass up, the thinking went, even for a man as wealthy as the Aga Khan, who was certainly not strapped for cash.[20]

So it surprised everyone when the Aga Khan announced on July 9 that Shergar would be syndicated to stand in Ireland. There would be forty shares, with the Aga Khan keeping six of them, priced at £250,000 each, or about $467,500 at the prevailing exchange rate. The total value of the syndicate, including the Aga Khan's shares, was £10 million.[21]

There were conditions, though. All of the shares on offer had to be sold before the King George VI and Queen Elizabeth Diamond Stakes was run two weeks later and Shergar had to win the race before the deal would be finalized.

The Newmarket law firm of Rustons and Lloyd, one of the first proponents of Thoroughbred stallion syndications in the 1930s, drafted the agreement for Shergar. It included a provision for a five-person committee with authority to represent the shareholders in all matters affecting the syndicate. The committee had an international flavor, representative of the diverse group of shareholders in the syndicate, with prominent owners and breeders from England, France, Switzerland, and America agreeing to serve.

The members of the committee—Sir John Jacob Astor, Walter Haefner, Paul Mellon, Paul de Moussac, and Ghislain Drion, the Aga Khan's Irish stud manager—had no idea that the workings of their group would assume an unexpected urgency months later when a gang of armed men snatched Shergar from the Aga Khan's stud.

Michael Drake, a partner at Rustons and Lloyd, was at Royal Ascot when Shergar won the King George VI and Queen Elizabeth Diamond Stakes. He said that selling shares in Shergar, even at a lofty £250,000 each, was easy. "The syndicate was oversubscribed," he said. "The list was a who's who of international racing."[22]

Drake said that he was a "very junior partner" at Rustons and Lloyd in 1983 and that he happened to be the only partner in the office on February 9 when the call came in reporting that Shergar had been stolen. "It was a complete surprise to everyone in the industry," Drake recalled. Hs speculated that the Irish Republican Army was behind the theft, although he acknowledged that he had no special insight. He theorized that the Provos never took credit because they feared another public relations disaster like the backlash the IRA suffered following a bombing that had killed a number of soldiers and horses in Hyde Park the year before.[23]

"I am making a considerable financial sacrifice," the Aga Khan said when he announced the syndication. In was an understatement, considering that he probably could have syndicated Shergar for at least twice as much if he had wanted to stand the horse in the United States instead of Ireland.

This economic disparity between the United States and Ireland became obvious days before the King George, when Robert Sangster made an announcement of his own. Sangster's Storm Bird, a champion at two in 1980 but unraced as a three-year-old, had been sold to an American syndicate for a reported price of around $30 million.[24] (The actual price turned out to be less, reported to be between $21 million and $22.5 million, because Sangster retained a one-quarter interest in the horse.)

If there was a knock against Shergar that could have limited his appeal to an American market, it was a pedigree that was almost exclusively European: sired by Great Nephew out of the Val de Loir mare Sharmeen.[25] Central Kentucky pedigree consultant Anne Peters suggested that Shergar nevertheless would have been a good fit in many American breeding programs. "Shergar was a 1978 foal, so he came along in that period where Kentuckians were breeding to a large extent to attract the European market," Peters explained. "Turf pedigrees were the rage and a lot of horses were coming over from Europe to stand, so in that regard, he would have had real appeal. Brereton Jones imported the year-older Nikoli, another son of Great Nephew and winner of the Irish Two Thousand Guineas, to stand at Airdrie Stud in 1981.

Shergar suffers his only defeat as a three-year-old, finishing an uncharacteristic fourth in the St. Leger Stakes at Doncaster on September 12, 1981. The colt was retired after the St. Leger. (Miralgo Publications Photo Archives/John Crofts)

I'm not sure how popular he was, but he didn't last long here and ultimately went to South America. But he wasn't Shergar. We were also familiar with American-bred Mrs. Penny, by Great Nephew, so the sire wouldn't have been completely unfamiliar.

Windfields imported Val de l'Orne by Val de Loir, and Green Dancer was out of a Val de Loir mare, so that name was also familiar to the American market and with more successful imported sires. I expect Shergar would have been solidly embraced, at least initially, at a farm like Gainesway until he was proven a success or a failure.

I am reminded of something John Sparkman pointed out, that the European horses who succeeded in Kentucky were the ones who liked hard turf courses. A horse who preferred a softer course just wouldn't do well as a sire of dirt horses, although he could still have appeal selling back to the European market.

I think Shergar had enough "hooks" into American pedigrees that he would have been less of an outcross than you might think. Great Nephew's pedigree is very similar to Nearctic's pedigree, with most of the same key ancestors just reconfigured: Pharos/Scapa Flow, Hyperion, Nearco, Sister Sarah. On the dam's side, you have more Blandford, Prince Rose, Nearco again, and of course, going back to a half-sister to Nasrullah. I think his pedigree parallels could have been a great selling point instead of his outcross potential. He probably would have done just fine in that era. But not today.[26]

The Aga Khan acknowledged negotiating with American breeders, but he eventually made the decision to stand Shergar in Ireland to keep the stallion easily accessible for his own broodmares. The emergence of CEM and numbers dictated the decision. "There is logic in the Thoroughbred industry," the Aga Khan told a *New York Times* reporter a few months after Shergar was stolen, "and the larger number of horses you have, the greater the probability of having a good horse." Considering the marked difference between a good horse and a moderate one, he added, "it is justified to increase numbers to come up with that one exceptional Thoroughbred."[27]

For the 1982 breeding season, Shergar's first, the Aga Khan had some thirty broodmares in the United States and nearly five times that many in Europe. Considering the six shares in Shergar retained by the Aga Khan in the syndication agreement, four additional breeding rights for standing the horse at Ballymany, and the possibility of adding another breeding right in a draw every few years, the Aga Khan expected to breed at least ten mares to Shergar each season. He had a larger, and better, pool of mares to breed to Shergar with the horse standing in Ireland.

Shipping mares from Europe to America was not a viable option at the time. CEM, which keeps mares from conceiving, was first diagnosed at Britain's National Stud in 1977. CEM spread to the United States the next year and closed breeding sheds in Kentucky for weeks, with losses in the millions. The US Department of Agriculture imposed strict import restrictions on horses coming from Europe.[28]

The government restrictions were modified in subsequent years, making it somewhat easier to ship maiden mares to America, but the Aga Khan was not interested in sending unproven broodmares to Shergar. He wanted only the best mares for Shergar's book and since those mares were in Europe, with little prospect of leaving, keeping Shergar in Ireland made perfect sense.[29]

But that decision, coming at the height of the Troubles in Northern Ireland, also made Shergar a target.

7

# Guns and Money

Bobby Sands died in the Maze Prison near Belfast on May 5, 1981, sixty-six days after beginning a hunger strike to protest the conditions of incarceration for Provisional Irish Republican Army and other paramilitary prisoners being held by the British. The protest began after the government dropped special-category status for those prisoners. In effect since 1972, special-category status meant that members of the IRA were treated as political prisoners, allowed to wear their own clothes rather than prison-issued uniforms and granted other privileges not accorded to other inmates. Rescinding that status allowed the authorities to treat IRA members as common criminals instead.[1]

Before the protests were called off later in the year, ten prisoners had starved themselves to death.

The hunger strike protest had no direct connection to Shergar, although by a trivial coincidence the day Bobby Sands died also happened to be the day that Shergar won the Chester Vase. The protests nevertheless worked to make kidnappings and the theft of a valuable Thoroughbred seem more important to the IRA, and more likely.

The deaths of the IRA prisoners galvanized the republican movement in Northern Ireland and gave the "Brits Out" campaign more urgency. The protests also drove home the realization that the IRA was in desperate need of more and better weapons.

The Provos relied heavily on republican supporters in the United States and on Colonel Muammar al-Qadhafi in Libya for weapons, ammunition, explosives, and cash. It was one of the worst kept secrets in the history of the Troubles, if it ever was a secret at all.

76

"Brits Out" was adopted as a slogan by the Provisional Irish Republican Army near the start of the Troubles. (Poster courtesy of Captain Sean Berry)

An exact accounting of the material smuggled in to prop up the IRA during the 1970s is impossible. A few shipments were blocked in transit by Irish authorities and some transfers of arms from the United States were stopped before they ever left port. In 1973, the SS *Claudia* was intercepted off the Irish coast carrying five tons of arms from Libya; in a separate seizure, the FBI reported domestic seizures of "a large quantity of automatic and semiautomatic weapons as well as explosive destructive devices destined for use in Northern Ireland."[2]

George Harrison—a longtime IRA arms supplier, not the Beatle— reactivated a dormant network in the United States at the start of the Troubles, and for a decade he remained the principal domestic broker for IRA-bound weapons. The arms network finally collapsed in the early 1980s, the victim of stepped-up FBI pressure and trials in two New York federal district courts.

Logistics and other difficulties aside, however, there is no doubt that arms networks linking the United States, Libya, and the IRA were operating with some regularity during the first decade of the Troubles.[3] When those networks were disrupted in the late 1970s and early 1980s, however—by the FBI after the assassination of Lord Mountbatten and by a growing lack of interest in supporting the IRA on the part of Colonel Qadhafi—the Provos found themselves in an untenable position.[4]

Cash was tight and usually reliable sources of weapons were being cut off. During an interview on BBC 5 Live's news program *I Was There*, broadcast on February 12, 2016, Provo turned Garda informer Sean O'Callaghan explained the extent of the IRA's financial woes. Around the time Shergar was stolen, O'Callaghan said, the IRA was raising about £2 million, spending it all, and always needing more.

Compounding the shortfalls, money was being diverted away from the IRA's paramilitary operations to fund political initiatives by Sinn Féin.[5] To make up the deficits, the IRA looked south to the Republic and began a campaign of robberies and high-profile kidnappings for ransom. They also stole a horse in a particularly ill-conceived scheme to raise needed money for weapons.

Gabriel Megahey was not the average New York shopper, far from it. A republican sympathizer from Belfast and a member of the Irish Republican Army, Megahey wasn't browsing the high-end stores on Fifth Avenue or bargaining for a counterfeit Rolex or a knockoff designer handbag. He was in the market for weapons, lots of them—the more lethal, the better.[6]

Arms dealers were not hawking their wares on street corners in New York during the early 1980s, of course, but they could be found without much difficulty by someone who knew where to look. Megahey could easily tap into a well-established IRA network of sympathetic arms suppliers and moneymen operating in the United States. Locating reliable suppliers of the standard fare—pistols and long guns, ammunition, body armor, explosives, detonators, and the other hardware necessary for bomb making—was relatively easy for Megahey and his associates. Although George Harrison's weapons network was under heavy scrutiny, dealers saw the IRA as a trusted buyer with money to spend and the republican cause had substantial support among Irish Americans up and down the East Coast.[7]

Megahey already had brothers Eamon and Colm Meehan assembling a weapons shipment with dozens of ArmaLite AR-15 assault rifles, other submachine guns, an array of pistols, and electronic safety devices used to prevent premature explosions of improvised bombs. The weapons shipment would be bound for Northern Ireland hidden in containers labeled as roller skates and comforters.

What Megahey really wanted, though, was a far bigger score: surface-to-air missiles (SAMs) that the Irish Republican Army could use to blast British helicopters out of the skies over Northern Ireland. Andrew Duggan, another of Megahey's associates, said he knew someone, who knew someone else, who might be able to supply the SAMs for the right price.

The potential middleman for the missile purchase was Michael Hanratty, a legitimate retailer of surveillance and counter-surveillance devices and other sophisticated electronic equipment. Hanratty could not supply the items Duggan most wanted at the time, high-end remote-controlled detonators, but the two remained in contact. When meeting with Hanratty over the next few months, Duggan and the others sometimes spoke of a mysterious "moneyman" who controlled the purse strings for the IRA in the United States.

The "moneyman," whom Hanratty finally met in January 1982, was Megahey. He introduced himself as the leader of IRA operations in the United States and said that none of the group's activities were conducted without his knowledge. Megahey confided that he wanted to make himself known because Hanratty had become an important asset to the republican network in America. Two months later, Hanratty managed to obtain the bomb detonators and delivered them to Duggan.

The availability of SAMs came up again around the same time. Hanratty explained that he could not supply the missiles himself but that he had a contact in Florida, an arms dealer named Luis, who might be able to help. On May 2, 1982, Hanratty introduced Duggan to a man named Enrique, who would stand in for Luis during the preliminary negotiations for the SAMs. The first meeting went well. Duggan described himself to Enrique as a "buffer" who procured weapons for others. He said that he was interested in hand grenades and automatic weapons, but added that his priority was identifying a supplier of surface-to-air missiles. Duggan reported to Hanratty afterward that he thought Enrique and Luis, whom Duggan still hadn't met, had access to the missiles. A second meeting with the arms dealers and IRA technical people to evaluate the weapons was already in the works.

The deal was done in a run-down dockside warehouse in New Orleans. The arms dealers would deliver five Redeye missiles to the IRA for $50,000. The first operational shoulder-fired antiaircraft weapon, the Redeyes would be a good fit for the IRA's purposes and the price was right.[8]

Two weeks later, during a meeting held at the St. Regis Hotel in New York to finalize the details of payment and delivery, a suddenly wary Megahey introduced a new complication. He proposed an exchange of hostages between the buyers and sellers to guarantee that the transaction would proceed as planned. Megahey was worried about a police sting operation, and he reasoned that the authorities would not put an officer's life in danger or risk losing the SAMs. The arms dealers balked and the missile deal was called off.

A few weeks later, Megahey, Duggan, and the Meehan brothers were arrested by the Federal Bureau of Investigation and charged with weapons and conspiracy offenses under a seven-count federal indictment. Most of the arms destined for Northern Ireland were confiscated, although a couple of the disguised crates of weapons were left in the pipeline to allow authorities in Ireland to track the recipients. All four men were convicted in federal district court and their convictions were affirmed by the Second Circuit Court of Appeals.

The fix was in from the start.

After the initial meetings with Duggan and his colleagues in the summer of 1981, Michael Hanratty contacted the FBI with his concerns about the worrisome IRA connection. Agents did not ask Hanratty to initiate further meetings with Duggan and his associates, probably to avoid an entrapment defense, and subsequent meetings came about on their own. Agents did suggest that Hanratty try to introduce an undercover FBI agent into any future weapons negotiations. The ploy was successful. "Enrique," the supposed arms dealer who agreed to supply the SAMs, in reality was Enrique Ghimenti, a special agent of the FBI.

In early 1982, the FBI obtained an electronic surveillance warrant from a secret US court authorized by the Foreign Intelligence Surveillance Act ("FISA Court"). Wiretaps were placed on Megahey's home telephone on February 10, 1982, and his communications were monitored until his arrest four months later. The FBI also recorded various meetings involving Megahey, Duggan, and their associates. At the subsequent trial, the evidence against the defendants consisted mainly of Hanratty's in-person testimony, videotapes of meetings between the IRA men and undercover FBI agents, and audio recordings of conversations from Megahey's home telephone.

The convictions marked the first major successes for the FBI after the bureau increased its efforts to disrupt what for years had been a relatively free-flowing supply of weapons and money from the United States to Northern Ireland.[9] Megahey and the other defendants argued that Hanratty's alleged claims of an association with the Central Intelligence Agency gave them a free pass to purchase and export weapons for the IRA.

The defense was based primarily on a white laminated card printed with the words "Central Intelligence Agency" allegedly presented to the defendants by Hanratty. The argument failed after CIA officials denied any association with Hanratty. Arguing CIA involvement was not a total loss, however. The same defense had been successful in a similar federal trial a few months earlier.[10] One of the defendants in that trial was George Harrison, the legendary arms supplier for the IRA in the United States for a quarter century before he was replaced by Megahey.

During his trial, the prosecutor made the claim that Harrison had been supplying arms to the IRA for "six months." Harrison instructed his attorney to correct the misstatement. "Mr. Harrison is insulted," the attorney told the court. "He wants the court to know that there has not been a weapon sent to Northern Ireland in the last 25 years without Mr. Harrison."[11]

The Irish Republic Army's campaign to drive the British out of Northern Ireland depended on steady infusions of cash and weapons, but both were in short supply during the early 1980s. The arms network in the United States was in disarray after the replacement of George Harrison and the arrest and conviction of Gabriel Megahey, while arms shipments from Libya had slowed to a trickle and would not pick up again until 1985. The shortage was further compounded by the diversion of funds from the IRA's military operations to Sinn Féin, the political wing of the IRA, which was gaining prominence in discussions seeking a political solution to the Troubles.[12]

The future of reliable financial support from the United States was no longer a certainty, either. On November 22, 1982, according to declassified FBI files, the bureau initiated a comprehensive investigation into activities of the Irish Northern Aid Committee. Established in 1969 at the start of the Troubles in Northern Ireland, NORAID was billed as a charitable organization raising funds in the United States to support the families of IRA prisoners. At Gabriel Megahey's federal trial, however, FBI informant Michael Hanratty testified that at least some of the NORAID funds were being diverted to the IRA for arms acquisition.[13] "During the past two years," a confidential FBI communication acknowledged, "the New York Office has developed significant information and evidence which indicates that NORAID has been acquiring funds which are being funneled to purchase and ship arms to the Provisional Irish Republican Army."[14] NORAID still exists; its mission statement proclaims that the organization "supports through peaceful means, the establishment of a democratic 32-county Ireland."[15]

Kidnappings for ransom were a possible source of badly needed funds for the Provos, but past attempts had returned mixed results. The 1975 abduction of Dr. Tiede Herrema, managing director of a steel cord factory in County Limerick, had not gone well. The Garda eventually tracked the kidnappers to a private home, and after a seventeen-day standoff, Dr. Herrema was released unharmed. There were no public ransom demands from the kidnappers. Instead, they asked for the release of three IRA prisoners: Dr. Rose Dugdale, Kevin Mallon, and Jim Hyland.[16]

Mallon was a legend in the IRA. He commanded paramilitary units along the border between Northern Ireland and the Republic and was involved in a pair of sensational prison escapes. In October 1973, a stolen Alouette II helicopter cruised over the wall at Mountjoy Prison and settled down in the exercise yard. While baffled guards looked on, Mallon and two other high-level IRA prisoners climbed aboard the helicopter and vanished.[17]

Mallon was captured a few weeks later and sent to Portlaoise Prison, a high-security facility. He escaped again eight months later, along with eighteen other prisoners, when explosives smuggled into the prison were used to blast open the gates. Mallon was apprehended after five months on the run and returned to Portlaoise.

Although Mallon was never arrested or charged after Shergar was stolen, his name cropped up frequently in press reports linking him to

the theft and to a series of botched IRA kidnappings. He was specifically identified as the man who came up with the idea to steal Shergar by
Sean O'Callaghan, who had reason to know. O'Callaghan swapped sides
to become an informer for Irish authorities after years as a senior member of the command hierarchy of the IRA and was privy to operational
details of numerous IRA actions.[18]

Weapons shipments from the United States and Libya were in disarray, and little money was coming in from the usual supporters to buy
arms on the black market. Nor were robberies of banks and post offices
in Northern Ireland and in the Republic to the south bringing in enough
money to sustain the campaign against the British. Despite the failure of
the Herrema affair, the Provos began planning more kidnappings.

Ben Dunne, a wealthy supermarket executive with stores on both
sides of the border, was the first target. The authorities took an official position opposing the payment of ransoms, and initial attempts by
Dunne's family to pay the kidnappers were blocked.[19] It is speculated
that a ransom of approximately $1 million was eventually paid to secure
Dunne's release.[20] Many of the targets—first Dunne and later Galen
Weston and Don Tidey—were executives of supermarket chains, possibly targeted in the belief that grocery stores would have easy access
to huge amounts of used small-denomination bills ideal for untraceable
payoffs.[21]

After Dunne's kidnapping probably earned the IRA a ransom,
the Provos bungled the Weston kidnapping, and Tidey was recovered
unharmed after a shootout between the IRA and the Garda.

Galen Weston seemed an ideal target for a kidnapping. He was
wealthy, the president of a successful supermarket chain based in Canada with stores on both sides of the Irish border, and vice president of
a high-end department store in London.[22] Surely his return would be
worth a tidy ransom. Based on a tip, the Garda suspected that Weston
might be at risk and suggested that he and his family leave their lake-
side mansion in County Wicklow, south of Dublin, for a few days while
police set a trap for the would-be kidnappers.

When seven gunmen approached the Weston home in early

August, the supermarket executive was playing polo at Windsor Castle with Prince Charles. The Garda trap worked. Five of the kidnappers were arrested but two escaped during the ensuing gun battle. One of the men who got away was reportedly Kevin Mallon.[23]

Nearly four months after the incident, one of Weston's employees, Don Tidey, was kidnapped. Men posing as Garda officers flagged down Tidey's automobile, threw him into their bogus police car, and drove away. A few days later, the kidnappers demanded £5 million for Tidey's release.

Chief Superintendent John Courtney, head of the Garda's Murder Squad, ran the investigation into Tidey's kidnapping. The search lasted twenty-two days and ended in a shootout in a wooden area two and a half miles north of Ballinamore in County Leitrim. Part of the "Border Region" located south of the demarcation between the Republic of Ireland and Northern Ireland, County Leitrim was often identified as a likely destination for the thieves who took Shergar. Tidey was found unharmed, but a Garda trainee and an army private were killed.[24]

The spectacular failures of the Galen Weston and Don Tidey kidnappings were no surprise. With the exception of the ransom reportedly paid for the release of Ben Dunne, a decade of attempted kidnappings, beginning in 1973, had been disastrous for the Irish Republican Army.[25]

The decision to steal a horse only made the situation worse.

# 8

# A "Rough Patch" for the Garda

Dispatched late in 1983, a confidential memorandum from the American embassy in Dublin to the secretary of state in Washington, DC, the American embassy in London, and the US consul general in Belfast summarized a miserable year for An Garda Síochána.[1] The memorandum painted a grim picture: a burgeoning crime wave, especially in Dublin, while resources for the police dropped; a rash of kidnappings, from supermarket executives to bank managers, jewelers, and bookies; a feud between the new head of the Garda and the Royal Ulster Constabulary in Northern Ireland; and potentially serious threats to cross-border security cooperation.

Pushing the Garda even further, the memorandum added, and consuming valuable resources and time, was a massive search for a missing horse: "The Shergar Affair: In a country where stud farms and horse racing are big business the disappearance of a horse valued at over 20 million dollars in early 1983 was not a laughing matter. Yet, the Garda's handling of this case and its still unsuccessful investigation has been the cause for much criticism. More to the point—and more to the chagrin of the Garda—it has become the butt of jokes that are still enjoying something of [a] fad both in Ireland and—more damaging—on the British TV shows that reach Ireland by cable."

No laughing matter indeed.

The story broke early Wednesday morning.[2]

Julian Lloyd, a livestock insurance underwriter for the John Marsh Syndicate at the time, was staying at the Keadeen Hotel in Newbridge.

He had an 8:00 a.m. appointment that day to meet a veterinary surgeon from Sycamore Lodge Equine Hospital, a clinic located at The Curragh. The two were supposed to visit the Aga Khan's Ballymany Stud, just a mile down the road and situated between the hotel and the racecourse, to talk about a possible increase in insurance premiums. The veterinarian arrived in a rush as Lloyd was walking out of the hotel.

"We're in good time, Joe," Lloyd told his friend. "There's no need to hurry."

"Oh, no," the vet said. "Shergar was taken in the night."

"What?"

"He was taken."

"You mean he's dead, Joe?"

"No, you eejit, taken. Someone stole Shergar!"

"Oh my God!"

Lloyd tried to piece together the story of what happened to Shergar, but information was scarce and nothing he heard made any sense. The first reports were brief and confusing. An armed gang? Shergar missing? The stud groom kidnapped? Ransom? The Irish Republican Army?[3]

He spoke with Terry Hall, the lead underwriter for livestock coverage at Lloyd's of London, and several other insurance underwriters who held policies for Shergar. Because Lloyd was already on site, they asked him to stay in Ireland for a while to monitor the situation as their quasi-official representative. It proved to be an uneventful stay. Lloyd attended Chief Superintendent James Murphy's daily press briefings, played pool in the basement of the Garda station in Naas, and went along on several unsuccessful search expeditions.

"I spent quite a lot of time with some of the police during the investigation," Lloyd recalled. "It was days and days of going around to all of the Thoroughbred studs in the area with a picture of Shergar, asking, 'Have you got one that looks like this?'" It is unlikely that the searchers needed the photograph, though. Shergar was a national hero and with his distinctive blaze and four white ankles he was recognizable on sight for much of Ireland's population.

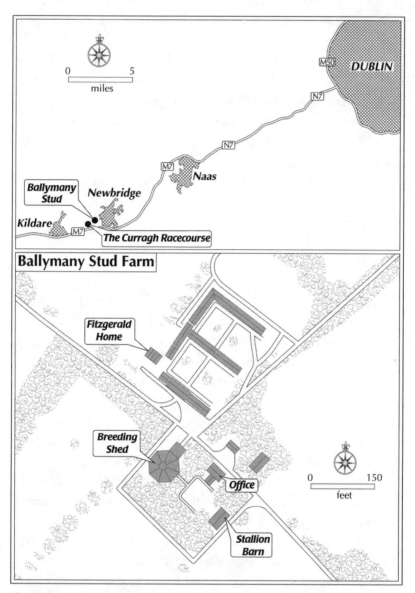

The Ballymany Stud Farm.

Over the next few days, a better picture of what happened began to emerge.

Tuesday, February 8, one of the coldest days in Ireland that year, started like any other for James Fitzgerald. A quiet man in his fifties, Fitzgerald had worked for the Aga Khan's family for his entire life, ever since 1945, when he was sixteen years old. Now he was the stud groom at Ballymany, a job his father had held before him, and one of the most valuable Thoroughbreds in the world was his responsibility. Fitzgerald took the job seriously, but never in his wildest dreams did he imagine being asked one day to put his life on the line for "his" horse.

Fitzgerald lived with his wife and children in a house a short walk from the four-stall stallion barn. The house was isolated, situated at the end of a narrow, tree-covered lane well off the road running between Newbridge and Kildare Town. Security at Ballymany consisted merely of a heavy wooden gate with a simple latch at the bottom of the lane. A sign for visitors read: "PLEASE CLOSE GATE."

Around 8:40 in the evening, a man wearing a long coat and peaked cap, the way a Garda officer might dress on such a bitterly cold and rainy night, walked up to James Fitzgerald's house and knocked on the front door. Fitzgerald, who had just returned from checking on Shergar one last time before turning in for the night, was upstairs and one of his sons, Bernard, went to the door. No one expected visitors at that time of night.

Hearing the knock at the door and then a commotion from the front of the house, Fitzgerald hurried downstairs. He found chaos, a scene that he could not immediately comprehend. Bernard lay pinned to the floor by a masked man and two other men in balaclavas were shouting, waving their hands, and pointing guns at his family.

"We've come for Shergar," one of the men said.

Other men wearing balaclavas and carrying guns rushed through the front door. They ordered the Fitzgerald children into one room and took Fitzgerald and his wife to the kitchen. The stud groom was terrified. He feared for himself and his family, and he feared for Shergar.

One of the men ordered Fitzgerald to accompany them to the stallion barn. Reports of the theft later suggested that the thieves needed his help to identify Shergar, but that is unlikely. Even if the men did not immediately recognize the horse with his distinctive white blaze, a large brass plate on the stall door—the stall at the northeast corner of the stallion barn—was engraved with Shergar's name. It would have been difficult to mistake him for another horse, even at night.

Fitzgerald was ordered at gunpoint to buckle a leather halter onto Shergar's head and then he was forced to help load the confused stallion into a two-horse trailer parked nearby. His help with this also may have been unnecessary. By all accounts, Shergar was gentle, well-mannered, and easy to handle for a stallion, and at least one of the thieves acted as if he had some experience with horses. More likely, however, the gang's purpose in coercing Fitzgerald's assistance and then kidnapping him was simply to intimidate the man into silence, at least for a while, and it worked. The Garda would not be notified for hours.

At 9:00 p.m., just twenty minutes after the bogus Garda officer first rapped on the Fitzgeralds' door, the trailer pulled away from the stallion barn with Shergar inside. At the end of the lane, a left turn onto the R445 highway would take the thieves into Newbridge and farther on, to the N7, at the time the busiest highway in Ireland, and Dublin. Turning right, the thieves would be heading toward The Curragh and into Kildare Town. The M7 motorway today intersects with R445 a few hundred yards south of the entrance to Ballymany. On current maps the M7 appears to be an excellent escape route, but the motorway was still in the planning stages in 1983.[4]

No one knows which direction the thieves turned when they left Ballymany that night. Even if there had been witnesses out and about in the bad weather, it is unlikely they would have noticed a horse trailer being pulled by a battered Hillman Hunter or Vauxhall automobile. Whether through careful planning or remarkable good fortune, the men who took Shergar selected the best night possible to steal the horse.

A single horse trailer on the road that night might have attracted attention, but one trailer among many would not stand out. Earlier in the day, in Kill, a few miles from Ballymany, Goffs sales conducted a large Thoroughbred auction. The sale ran late and a steady succession of vans and trainers was coming and going far into the evening. One more trailer on the road that night was unlikely to attract any undue attention. Who could know that this particular trailer happened to be carrying a stallion worth millions?

Whether the result of good planning, as Sean O'Callaghan suggested, or simply a stroke of good luck, targeting Shergar in early February, a few days before the start of the breeding season, was a fortuitous choice for the thieves. Some mares already would be shipping into Ballymany for breeding to Shergar and the other stallions standing at stud there, and this would make it more likely that an additional horse trailer would go unnoticed. The timing also allowed the thieves to avoid a general increase in activity at Ballymany once breeding season started, with added employees, mare owners, trainers, veterinarians, other service providers, and guests coming and going at all hours.

The situation might have been different if the Garda had been stopping vehicles searching for Shergar, but they were not. There was no reason for the authorities to be doing that, because no one had reported the theft. Other than the thieves who took Shergar, the only people who knew that the horse had been stolen were Fitzgerald and his family, and they still were under guard at Ballymany.

The gang took Fitzgerald back to the house after the trailer left with Shergar and kept him there for an hour. Around 10:00 p.m., with two armed men left in the house to watch the family, Fitzgerald was bundled into the back of a car and driven away. His three kidnappers wandered the back roads for two hours before they dropped Fitzgerald off near Kilcock, about thirty miles northeast of Ballymany, on the border between County Kildare and County Meath.

They left him by the side of the road with directions to the village and a message for Shergar's owners: if they wanted the horse back unharmed, it was going to cost them £2 million. They also gave Fitzgerald a code name to be used for ransom negotiations, King Neptune.

"Start walking," one of the men said. "Don't turn around and don't call the police." Fitzgerald did as he was told, relieved that he was being released but still worried about his family. He located a telephone in Kilcock and called his brother Des for a ride back to Ballymany. He asked his brother to let him out of the car a short distance from the gate, hoping a walk in the cold night air would clear his mind and help him decide what to do.

It was midnight and Shergar had been missing for more than four hours. The Garda still had not been notified.

It was after midnight, early on Wednesday, when Fitzgerald trudged up the lane at Ballymany. He found his family upset and frightened by their ordeal, but safe. At 1:15 a.m. he telephoned Ghislain Drion, manager of the Aga Khan's Irish studs. Drion lived a short distance away at Sheshoon, another of the Aga Khan's farms. When Drion arrived at Ballymany, Fitzgerald tried to convince him not to alert the authorities.

Reluctant to act on his own, Drion did not immediately report the theft of Shergar to the Garda. Instead, he tried to reach the Aga Khan for instructions. When his initial efforts to locate his boss were unsuccessful, Drion contacted Stan Cosgrove, the veterinarian who cared for Shergar and who also owned a share in the stallion. Drion collected Cosgrove and they drove back to Ballymany to see for themselves that Shergar really was gone. Satisfied on that point, they talked in person with Fitzgerald, who once again tried to convince them that they should not notify the authorities.

Cosgrove next telephoned his friend, retired army captain Sean Berry from the Irish Thoroughbred Breeders Association. Captain Berry drove to Cosgrove's house, arriving at 4:00 a.m. Drion had by then tracked the Aga Khan to Switzerland and asked whether the syndicate should pay the ransom without calling in the police as the thieves demanded. Drion was told that the police should be notified immediately.

The reasons were numerous: the syndicate committee was not in a position to deal unilaterally with such a criminal matter, the Garda and the press would learn about the theft anyway, and there was no guarantee that Shergar would be returned even if the ransom was paid. Perhaps most important, paying ransom for Shergar would put every other valuable horse in Ireland at risk. No ransom would be paid.

Drion had already called in a local Garda officer who was in touch with his superior, Chief Superintendent James Murphy. Captain Berry offered to call Alan Dukes, a personal friend who also happened to be the minister of finance. Dukes was scheduled to deliver his budget the following morning and he had neither the time nor the interest to talk about a missing horse in the middle of the night—even if the missing horse was Shergar. Dukes suggested that Captain Berry telephone Michael Noonan, the minister of justice.

Before ending the call, Dukes advised that the Garda should be contacted. Then he went back to bed.

Shergar had been missing for nearly eight hours.

The first telephone calls demanding a ransom for Shergar's return came around midnight, before Fitzgerald was back at Ballymany, made to the home of Northern Ireland trainer Jeremy Maxwell and his wife, Judy, and to the media. The caller, who did not identify himself, announced, "We have Shergar." The ransom demand was £40,000, he said, £1,000 for each of the forty shareholders, far less than the £2 million the men who held Fitzgerald had specified. (The ransom later would be raised to £52,000.)

The caller also made an odd demand that he would negotiate only with three British horse racing journalists, Derek Thompson, Lord John Oaksey, and Peter Campling. He said that he would use the code name Arkle in future calls.

The trio of journalists flew to Belfast, checking in at the "most bombed hotel in the world," the Europa.[5] They made it to the Maxwells' farm in Downpatrick by late afternoon.[6]

The ransom demand was repeated in a call to the Maxwells at 8:30 that evening, after the three journalists had arrived in Downpatrick, surrounded by large contingents of police and reporters. The original code word was changed by the caller first to Ekbalco and then in a later call to King Neptune—the code name given to Fitzgerald.

During calls at midnight and again at 1:30 in the morning on Friday, February 11, Thompson tried to keep the caller on the line so the calls could be traced. At the conclusion of the 1:30 call, which lasted more than ninety seconds, surely long enough to be traced by the authorities, Thompson asked if the police would now be able to work out where the call originated. One of the Garda officers who had accompanied the journalists said that was not possible. "I'm sorry to say the officer who traces calls went off shift at midnight."

There was one more call to the Maxwells at around 7:00 a.m. Things had gone dreadfully wrong, the caller said. There had been an accident and Shergar had been put down. When Judy Maxwell asked where the horse's body could be recovered, the line went dead.[7]

The Garda initially took the messages seriously but later the authorities were not so sure, and the syndicate committee dismissed the calls as hoaxes.[8] The timing of the calls to the Maxwell farm is important when judging whether those calls were genuine.

The first call to the Maxwells had come around midnight, less than four hours after Shergar was stolen and before the stud groom, James Fitzgerald, had made his way back to Ballymany Stud. When the first call was made, the only ones who knew that Shergar had been stolen were the people who took him, the stud groom, and members of the Fitzgerald family. It also is worth noting that the caller at one point adopted the name King Neptune, the code given to James Fitzgerald before the stud groom was released by his kidnappers. There is scant chance that the actual thieves and a pretender would independently come up with the same code.

A more likely scenario is that the Maxwell calls were from members of the gang that stole Shergar and were intended as a gambit designed to confuse the authorities and muddle the search. Not that the search needed further muddling. The eight-hour delay before bringing in the Garda accomplished that.

In one of his first press conferences, Chief Superintendent Murphy summed up the difficulties the Garda faced. "I'm slightly concerned about it," he said, "for the simple reason that a stallion cannot be kept by people who are not well up in the horsey field and do not know how to keep the animal." About the investigation, Murphy's assessment was simple: "I have no leads."[9]

That would become a familiar lament. The problem faced by the Garda, one that would prove insurmountable as the search moved forward, was the gap in time that gave the thieves ample time to escape.

Chief Superintendent John Courtney was involved in the investigation from the start. There was no murder, Courtney said, but it still was a "serious crime," the kidnapping of Fitzgerald especially, and that made it his job. The problem, he said, was the thieves' head start. "The affair was very badly handled by the people involved," Courtney said. "The Garda was not notified for hours. They told everybody that the horse had been stolen except the police. All James Fitzgerald had to do was call the police, but he didn't, because he was afraid for himself and for his family. But it was the most foolish thing that ever was done. We could have had the opportunity to set up roadblocks, but it was too late to check the horse boxes on the roads."[10]

The effect of the delay was compounded when James Fitzgerald was unable to provide information about the theft that could have helped the Garda. Explaining Fitzgerald's reluctance to talk, Murphy said, "The man is more than 50 years of age. He was forced to lie face down in the back of a van driven at high speed, probably over some rough roads, and his wife and seven children were in the house." Murphy went on, "He was afraid for his wife and family and did not want to do anything to risk the life or limb of his family," adding that Fitzgerald was suffering from "severe shock" and could provide no details about the incident.[11]

It would be days before Fitzgerald could provide anything useful to assist the investigation.

The only contact that the syndicate committee came to believe was legitimate began with telephone calls to Ballymany Stud late on Wednesday afternoon, February 9. This was the day after Shergar was taken, and more than fifteen hours after the first call to Jeremy and Judy Maxwell in Northern Ireland. Ghislain Drion spoke to the anonymous caller for the first time at 4:05 p.m.[12] The conversation was short and unproductive as the Frenchman, whose English was not fluent, struggled to understand the caller's words. Frustrated at the inability to communicate with

Drion, the man gave up. He called again at 5:45 p.m. "Speak slowly," Drion requested. The caller complied, asked for a contact number in France, and made a demand of £2 million for the return of Shergar. It was the same ransom demand communicated to James Fitzgerald the previous evening, along with the correct code word (and the third one used by the Maxwells' caller)—King Neptune. Drion provided a telephone number in Paris.

The game was on.

The next day, February 10, the *Irish Independent* confirmed reports that James Fitzgerald and his family remained reluctant to provide details to authorities about their ordeal. They were taking seriously the threats made by the thieves and feared reprisals if they cooperated with the Garda. "We do not want to press them too much for answers because of the threat they feel hangs over them," Murphy said.

Although Fitzgerald was reluctant to talk to the Garda, he had a poignant request for the men who held Shergar. He asked them to "give him some carrots. They are his favorite food and will cheer him up."[13]

The first call to the Paris telephone number came at 9:00 p.m. on Thursday. Drion was still in Ireland, and the Paris calls were handled by one of the Aga Khan's representatives who had a better command of English. The calls were monitored by the authorities, recorded, and reportedly traced to a public telephone.[14]

Whether the timing of that call was a coincidence is not known, but it was placed almost exactly forty-eight hours after thieves loaded Shergar into a horse trailer and vanished into the night. The caller repeated the £2 million ransom demand; the man negotiating on behalf of the syndicate tried to explain that coming up with the ransom would not be easy. Payment required the agreement of all the shareholders, he said.

It never was entirely clear whether the men who claimed to have Shergar really understood that the horse was owned by a syndicate with thirty-four members and that the Aga Khan was not the sole owner. Even if the syndicate members were prepared to pay a ransom—which a majority were not—the logistics of hammering out an agreement with people on both sides of the Atlantic would take more time than the Paris caller appeared willing to give.

The negotiator asked for proof that the caller had Shergar and that the horse still was alive and unharmed before committing to anything. The caller promised that the requested proof would be provided, but he gave no details about what that proof would be, or about how and when it would be delivered. That would come later.

Before breaking the connection, the caller threatened that Shergar would be killed if the ransom was not paid within three hours after the proof was delivered.

The next day, Captain Sean Berry announced to the press that the Irish Thoroughbred Breeders Association was offering a "substantial reward" for information about the theft, and offered to serve as a nego-tiator. The telephone calls started almost as soon as the newspaper hit the streets.[15] Two days later, Berry was quoted as saying that information from any calls would be kept confidential and that no information about callers would be passed on to the authorities.[16] That reluctance to share information would vanish a few weeks later when Berry found himself an active participant in negotiations for Shergar.

An anxious twenty-four hours passed in Paris with no contact from the man who called himself King Neptune. Finally, at 10:00 p.m. on Fri-day, February 11, the same caller as always rang the Paris number. He reported that the requested proof—he did not say what that proof might be—would be delivered the following morning, on Saturday, to the Crofton Airport Hotel outside Dublin. The contact should use the name Johnny Logan, the caller instructed. Logan was a popular young singer who looked less like veterinarian Stan Cosgrove, the man selected to col-lect the evidence, than just about anyone in Ireland.

Cosgrove was an odd choice for the job because the Paris caller clearly wanted a go-between who had no connection to Shergar or to the stud farm. Ballymany was one of the veterinarian's clients, however, and he owned a share in the syndicate. The caller also demanded that the police stay away from the Crofton Hotel while the exchange was made, but that condition was not met, either.[17]

Stan Cosgrove, aka "Johnny Logan," showed up at the Crofton Hotel early on Saturday morning at the time the Paris caller demanded, along with an ill-disguised contingent of Garda officers observing from the wings. No contact was made and the veterinarian came away empty-handed, probably because the thieves identified the Garda watchers, and maybe Stan Cosgrove as a man with connections to Ballymany, and fled.

At 11:15 a.m., the phone rang at the Paris number. The caller was angry and claimed that no one had been at the Crofton to collect the proof.

The caller telephoned again at 3:15 p.m. He said he knew that the negotiator was stalling and that he had an hour to obtain permission from the syndicate members to pay the £2 million ransom. The negotiator said that the shareholders now were afraid that Shergar was dead. The caller said that proof showing Shergar was alive had been delivered to the Rosnaree Hotel on the Dublin-Belfast road.[18] He demanded again that no police be involved.

The "proof" turned out to be Polaroid photographs of the horse's head. Some of the photos also included the front page of the *Irish News,* a Belfast newspaper, displaying a February 11 date.[19] To the syndicate committee, the photographs indicated that Shergar was alive on the 11th and that the horse was probably still in Ireland.[20]

Three days later, a Garda spokesman in Dublin denied any knowledge of the photographs, even though they reportedly were collected at the Rosnaree Hotel by a Garda officer.

"No such picture exists," a Garda spokesman said. "We don't have one and we have checked with the stud management, who said that they did not get a photograph of Shergar either."[21] Although members of the syndicate committee maintained that they cooperated fully with the Garda throughout the investigation, the official denial was not surprising, considering the level of secrecy maintained by the authorities.

"The police got a bad press because the media weren't getting any information," Garda Chief Superintendent Sean Feely explained later.

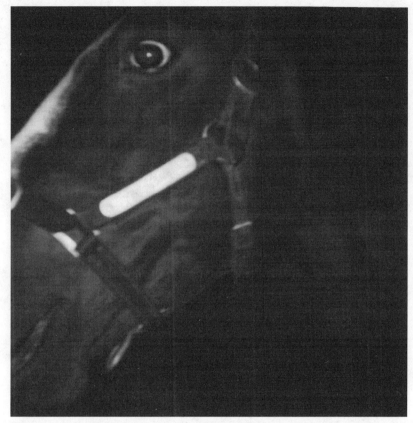

During ransom negotiations with the gang that claimed to have taken Shergar, the committee representing the syndicate that owned the stallion demanded proof that he was alive and unharmed. Polaroid photographs were then delivered to a hotel north of Dublin four days after Shergar was stolen. Although there is no definitive evidence that this photograph, never before published, was part of the proof offered, there is strong circumstantial evidence supporting that conclusion. (Photo from the stallion probe files of the Mobius Group)

"In those days, you didn't talk to the press. Murphy actually carried out a very detailed investigation but he didn't release any information. He kept it all to himself."[22]

There was another long call to Paris at 5:00 on Saturday afternoon, during which the caller demanded an immediate commitment to pay the £2 million ransom. Otherwise, he said, Shergar would be killed. "You may not pay for this horse," the caller threatened, "but you will definitely pay for the next one when you see what we do to this horse."

The syndicate representative tried once again to bargain for a delay in the negotiations. He explained the difficulty of convincing the thirty-four share shareholders to agree on anything, much less the payment of so large a ransom. It was obvious, though, that the caller was losing patience with negotiations that, from his perspective, were going nowhere.

The telephone in the Paris office rang again at 10:40 p.m. The conversation was brief and to the point. When the caller was told that the syndicate committee still was not satisfied despite the photographs of Shergar, he replied: "If you are not satisfied, that's it."

The line went dead.

Those words were the last heard from the man who claimed to have Shergar. The committee attempted to reestablish communications through articles in the Irish press, but without success.

The syndicate committee remained guardedly hopeful that Shergar eventually would be returned. At a meeting in October 1983, the committee reportedly agreed to increase the reward for the horse's safe return to a "six-figure amount." Lloyd's of London spokesman Stanley John told reporters that the underwriters agreed with the new offer, but cautioned that "any offer we're involved in is conditional on the horse being returned alive and the gang involved being convicted."[23]

Although the Aga Khan retained six of the forty shares composing the Shergar syndicate, he was not a part of the committee that represented the shareholders during the negotiations with the mystery caller. Interviewed months later in Newport, Rhode Island, where he was supporting Italy's first America's Cup challenger, the yacht *Azzurra,* the Aga Khan confirmed that there had been no further negotiations after contact with the supposed thieves stopped in mid-February. In light of the disappointing breakdown in communications, the Aga Khan admitted, "The presumption must be that the horse has been destroyed. He represented the best I had bred in 23 years. He was truly an exceptional Thoroughbred. One is obviously close to an individual like that."[24]

In hindsight, members of the syndicate committee found themselves questioning the motives of the thieves. In the comprehensive post-theft report to the shareholders, the committee listed a number of facts suggesting that creating confusion and publicity, rather than collecting a ransom, was the motive behind Shergar's theft:

- The ransom demand included £100 notes, which did not exist;
- Demands for delivery of the ransom were physically impossible to meet because of complicated travel schedules between France and Ireland;
- The committee representative in Paris was ordered to not call Ireland, where many of the shareholders whose permissions would be required before a ransom was paid had their homes;
- The demands "moved too fast for a proper response";
- The original demand, £2 million, never was negotiated downward.[25]

In a radio interview, Jonathan Irwin, managing director of Goffs sales, suggested that breeders who offered a reward for the return of Shergar and the Garda might be working at cross purposes. The authorities already had made it clear that they would block the payment of any ransom for Shergar, and the distinction between a "reward" and a "ransom" was not at all clear.[26] "It is not the job of the breeders to prosecute people," Irwin was quoted as saying. The thieves could not go to the police or to Ballymany for fear of being arrested, Irwin explained, while the breeders could act independently of the authorities. "We are not involved in the legalities. We can relieve them of the horse."[27]

Murphy, for the first time, speculated that Shergar might be dead. This was based not on evidence that the horse really was dead but on the lack of evidence that he was not. The Garda had "nothing to convince them he was still alive," Murphy said.[28]

Late in 1982, the Irish Republican Army kidnapped Patrick Gilmour from his home near Derry in Northern Ireland.[29] There was speculation at the time that Gilmour had been taken to pressure his son, an alleged IRA informer, to withhold information that would implicate more than two dozen Derry residents on terrorism charges. Gilmour's wife, Brigid, went public with her displeasure over the extensive press coverage of Shergar and the growing concern the public was showing for the horse. "Almost every national newspaper devoted space to express the shock and anger at the abduction of the animal," Mrs. Gilmour told the *Irish Press*. "Journalists, politicians, and the public all showed their concerns. Police are scouring the country from Mizen Head to Malin Head to try and find the animal." In contrast, "There was no such outcry when my husband was abducted. It is a sad day when the welfare of a human comes second to that of an animal."[30]

Ten months later, on September 26, 1983, Patrick Gilmour was released. His son never retracted his testimony.

Ghislain Drion reported that mares were arriving at Ballymany Stud, some of them among the fifty-five mares scheduled to be bred to Shergar in 1983. The only choice, Drion said, was to board the mares at the stud and wait for definitive news about Shergar's fate.

Jonathan Irwin speculated that the thieves' timing of the theft of Shergar was selected with the start of the breeding season in mind. "My own feeling is that it's not by coincidence he was seized on the eve of the breeding season," Irwin said. "I would say the gang are building up the pressure and are staying underground until well into the season. If Shergar does not appear by April the season will be in total disarray."[31]

The search for Shergar got a boost from John Brophy, chairman of the national horse committee of the Irish Farmers' Association. Brophy urged the organization's 150,000 members to search barns and fields all across Ireland for the missing stallion. "With the full cooperation of farmers and landowners," Brophy promised, "we can quickly eliminate the countryside from the search, and let gardai concentrate on the towns and cities."[32] The nationwide farmers' search would take place from February 28 to March 1, to no avail.

Chief Superintendent Murphy took a different approach to widening the search for Shergar. The Garda had received more than fifty tips from "clairvoyants, diviners, and psychic people," the lead investigator said. Just how useful those leads might be was difficult to judge. The "psychic people," Murphy said, placed Shergar in every county in the Republic of Ireland. Most of the tips, though, put the horse somewhere west of the Shannon River. Subsequent reports suggested that the Garda search in County Galway was based on tips from psychics rather than on intercepted ham radio transmissions.[33]

A week after the theft, the Garda released preliminary descriptions of three of the men who allegedly stole Shergar. One of the suspects, Murphy announced, was of the "jockey type," in his mid-twenties, about five foot three, with a dark complexion and hair combed down across his forehead. He had been wearing jeans and a denim jacket. The second man, in his early twenties, was about five foot seven and weighed between ten and eleven stone (140 and 154 pounds). He had dark hair parted on the left and wore a brown jacket. His most prominent feature was a very long nose. The third man, no estimate of age given, was about five foot eight, with a medium build. He was wearing a dark jacket and pants, along with a cap with a shiny peak. The outfit, Murphy said, resembled the uniform of a bus driver or a Garda officer.[34] It was likely that he was the first man who forced his way into the Fitzgeralds' home dressed as a Garda.

The press quickly dubbed the three suspects the "jockey," the "nose," and the "guard."

The Garda Technical Bureau later assembled "photofit" images of the suspects based on their descriptions, with copies intended only for the officers investigating Shergar's theft, at least initially. Two of the images were subsequently obtained by the press, however, and first published in the March 2 issue of the *Irish Independent*. The leak drew the ire of the Garda and a lawsuit against the newspaper for violation of Ireland's Official Secrets Act.[35]

Despite wide circulation of the images by the Garda and the *Independent,* the suspects were never identified.

At the same time that Murphy was sharing his descriptions of the suspects with the press, a contingent of Garda officers in uniform and plainclothes was searching the countryside looking for Shergar in County Galway, on the western coast of the Republic of Ireland. They were concentrating on that area because on Sunday, February 6, two days before Shergar was stolen, the Garda had intercepted a puzzling two-way radio conversation that, at the time, they did not understand.

The transmissions used what appeared to be a code of some sort, or maybe it was just gibberish, with phrases that made little sense: something about an "orange car" that was "a mile behind," "ahead of me," or "a mile behind"; a road that was "very bad for the box"; and someone or something named "Wendy" who was "here now." Reviewed in the context of Shergar's theft, however, the conversation sounded as if it could involve a plan to move a horse.

The *Irish Press* reported that an amateur radio operator in the Galway area had inadvertently tuned his radio to 147.990 MHz on the VHF band and picked up a conversation among four different stations. One of the speakers had what was described as a "cultured English voice." The others had Irish accents.[36]

The searchers checked isolated farms and fields, even a deserted mine near Tynagh. Like all the other leads, however, the search in County Galway turned up nothing. The trail leading to Shergar was still cold.

Murphy told the press that he believed that Shergar was still alive and that the search for the horse was spreading to all parts of the country. He also said that there was no indication suggesting that Shergar had been stolen by either the Provisional Irish Republican Army or the Irish National Liberation Army.

A week after Shergar was stolen, a Garda spokesman admitted that there had been no leads and no progress. "Realistically, we are still as much in the dark as when Shergar was taken out of his stable."[37] The investigation into the theft, which had little momentum from the start, had already stalled.

# 9

# The Man in the Trilby

Front and center in the search for Shergar, Chief Superintendent James Murphy had the look of a man plucked directly from central casting. He was tall and dour with a heavy Irish brogue, a decent nickname (Spud), and a quirky self-effacing sense of humor. He favored three-piece suits and wore a trademark felt trilby hat like Inspector Clouseau in the Pink Panther film *A Shot in the Dark*. He was the quintessential Irish cop, and the press loved him in the way a family loves a bumbling uncle who never seems to get anything right.

As the Shergar investigation dragged on with no discernible results, however, Murphy soon became the foil for reporters' more "serious" stories about the lack of progress in finding the horse and the men who took him. At one of the press conferences held almost daily on the steps of the Newbridge Garda station, a half-dozen reporters showed up sporting Murphy-style trilby hats. It was a heavy-handed way to poke fun at the chief superintendent and what was already beginning to look like a failed investigation on his watch.

One reporter called Murphy a "one-man media circus." Michael O'Mahoney, one of the attorneys representing the Shergar syndicate committee, said that he was "optimism personified. It was the biggest story around and he was at the center. He was like a character out of Mickey Spillane and the press ate it up. Even as the weeks went by with nothing, he kept looking for another angle."[1] Years later, an Irish film critic reviewing a Shergar documentary called Murphy "the most richly comic copper since Inspector Clouseau."[2]

Lost in the biting criticism was Murphy's record as a Garda—a good one—and his success in major cases.

Almost a decade earlier, Irish Republican Army sympathizer and former debutante Bridget Rose Dugdale led a raid on Rossborough House in County Wicklow. The thieves pistol-whipped Sir Alfred Beit and his wife, bound them, and made off with a batch of immensely valuable paintings, including Vermeer's *Lady Writing a Letter with Her Maid*. The paintings, worth an estimated $20 million, were recovered and Dugdale arrested a few months later. Murphy was among the officers involved in the recovery and arrest.[3] He also was part of the Garda team that located the kidnappers of Dr. Tiede Herrema and rescued the Dutch industrialist.[4]

The fundamental unfairness about much of the criticism leveled at Murphy had nothing to do with the press overlooking his record as a Garda or his investigative skills; both were excellent. Valuable Thoroughbreds had been stolen before, but never in Ireland. No one—not Murphy, not the authorities, not the shareholders, not the negotiators, not the press—ever had experienced a situation even remotely like the loss of Shergar. Pressure to solve the case was enormous from all sides, but with no past performances to guide them, the authorities were treading on unknown ground.

On June 25, 1977, Fanfreluche, a ten-year-old broodmare in foal to superhorse Secretariat, vanished from her paddock at Claiborne Farm near Paris, Kentucky. One minute she was there in the South Field adjacent to Barn No. 4; two and a half hours later she was gone. Fanfreluche was a champion racehorse in Canada and her first foal won the Queen's Plate. Her value was estimated at $500,000, but with Secretariat yearlings attracting top dollar at select auctions, Fanfreluche was easily a million-dollar horse.

Security at Claiborne was excellent, far better than at Ballymany Stud, with perimeter gates locked at night, a sentry manning the main entrance, and roaming guards in trucks with lights and radios. Daytime security, although less obvious, was there by virtue of some 140

employees on the grounds during working hours. The farm had a spot-
less record, with not a single horse stolen in more than seventy-five years.
Until, that is, Fanfreluche turned up missing in broad daylight on a
warm summer afternoon.

The Federal Bureau of Investigation speculated that the thieves had
pulled a horse trailer up a lane adjacent to Fanfreluche's paddock, lured
the mare over with feed, cut the sturdy wire fence, loaded her into the
trailer, and driven away without attracting any attention. The cut fence
was repaired with lengths of thin wire.

The lack of an obvious motive for the theft baffled the police. There
was no demand for ransom, no evidence of a political motive, and little chance of success if the thieves intended to switch the mare's foal for
another horse and run it as a ringer. After six months with no news of
Fanfreluche, Claiborne owner Seth Hancock assumed that the mare was
dead.

Nevertheless, the search went on, and on December 8, 1977, FBI
agents and Kentucky State Police officers tracked the mare to Larry
McPherson's small farm near Tompkinsville, Kentucky. A retired truck
driver, McPherson said he had found Fanfreluche wandering along the
highway near his house trailer in late June, shortly after she vanished
from Claiborne Farm. The McPherson family adopted the mare, named
her Brandy, and used her for a riding horse. They liked her so much,
McPherson said, that he refused a $200 offer to buy her. "I just didn't
feel right selling something that didn't belong to me," McPherson said,
"so I just kept her and waited for the day when somebody would come
claim her." It never occurred to him that Brandy might be the missing
horse he'd been reading about.

Fanfreluche still was in foal when she was recovered. Jean-Louis
Levesque, the mare's Canadian owner, named the foal Sain Et Sauf,
"safe and sound" in French. The authorities were led to Tompkinsville
through a tip from "unnamed individuals" who might have been trying
to collect a $25,000 reward posted by Levesque and Claiborne Farm.
The rest, according to FBI special agent Robert L. Pence, was "solid,
basic police work."[5]

Contacted by the *New York Times* a few days after Shergar was stolen, Kentucky State Police detective Robert Duffy said: "I wish I had some advice to give the Irish police, but about all I can tell them is look for the horse."[6]

Almost two years before Fanfreluche was stolen, another champion filly went missing, in Italy. Nelson Bunker Hunt's Carnauba was taken by thieves who demanded a $300,000 ransom. They had been hiding Carnauba in a girls' riding school. When Hunt refused to pay, they sold the filly for slaughter. Although Carnauba was recovered from a slaughter house, she was in such poor condition that she never raced again.[7]

The same year that Carnauba was stolen, 1975, two major thefts occurred in central Kentucky. A Thoroughbred broodmare named St. Elizabeth, worth an estimated $200,000, was stolen from Robert Alexander's Bosque Bonita Farm near Versailles, and two Thoroughbred yearling colts were taken from the grounds of the Keeneland sales facility near Lexington.[8]

Eight days after Shergar was stolen, Murphy stepped down as spokesman and Superintendent Noel Anderson, the senior press officer from Garda headquarters in Dublin, began conducting the press briefings in Newbridge.[9] Murphy remained in charge of the investigation, however, which plodded on, and he continued to deliver press briefings from time to time.

On February 16, the Garda released a detailed description of the horse trailer believed to have been used to transport Shergar from Ballymany. They were looking for a two-horse trailer, possibly manufactured by Rice, painted either light blue or light green, with a dual axle. The trailer had no license plate or working lights, and reportedly was "poorly kept." The trailer, being pulled by either a Hillman Hunter or Vauxhall automobile, brown in color, supposedly was seen pulling through the Ballymany gate around 8:30 p.m. on the night Shergar was stolen. The authorities were puzzled that a major lead in the case, identification of the horse trailer, had not produced any positive results. "It is rather strange that that the horsebox has not turned up since," Superintendent Noel Anderson said. "It must be very well hidden."[10]

The search for Shergar intensified on both sides of the border, with the Garda and the Royal Ulster Constabulary both taking part in an effort a Garda spokesman described as an endeavor "to flush out the gang and force them into flight."[11] The massive searches failed to turn up any sign of Shergar. What the searchers did find were caches of IRA weapons hidden all across the Republic of Ireland.

Irish bloodstock agent James Keogh said that many people in the south were sympathetic to the idea of unifying the country, even if they did not agree with the IRA's methods of achieving that goal. He estimated that the IRA lost half of its safe houses in the Republic "almost overnight" as a direct result of the search for Shergar. "They never found Shergar," Keogh said, "but the police started 'finding' lots of guns and explosives. There were weapons everywhere."[12]

Amid rumors that Shergar had been spirited out of Ireland, perhaps to the Middle East or to France, the Garda asked Interpol to assist in the search.[13]

Brid Wynbs, a spokeswoman for the Garda, told the Associated Press, "There is nothing concrete to report. We are still receiving several phone calls and are following up several new leads. But as yet that have all proved fruitless."[14]

Growing frustration was evident. "There must be someone, somewhere in the industry, who knows something," a Garda spokesman said.[15]

Three days later, puzzled that releasing a detailed description of the horse trailer believed to have been used in the theft had produced no useful information, Murphy announced a "reassessment" of the search for Shergar.[16] Days later, after two weeks of little progress, Murphy explained what he meant by a reassessment. He disclosed that the search for Shergar was being scaled down, but he did not elaborate on what he meant.[17]

As February wound down, and with nothing new to report, press coverage of the Shergar theft became sporadic. There also were communication concerns developing within the syndicate that owned Shergar.

Captain Tim Rogers, one of the shareholders in the syndicate, complained to the media about the lack of information the syndicate committee was sharing with shareholders. "I find it quite extraordinary that the members of the syndicate are being told nothing. I received a telegram informing me of the theft on the day after Shergar's disappearance, and since then there has been no further communication."[18]

A year later, the syndicate committee acknowledged the sparse communications between themselves and the rest of the shareholders: "During this time [since the theft of Shergar] it has been the firm policy of the committee to maintain strict confidentiality about all aspects of the case. This policy has been pursued on the firm advice of, among others, the Irish Police and the Irish Government. . . . Therefore, even in respect of you, the shareholders, the Committee have heretofore only made sporadic reports and requested absolute discretion toward the Press."[19]

On February 26, a spokesman for the Garda told the *Irish Independent* that detectives had interviewed more than one hundred jockeys in the Republic, Northern Ireland, and England. The purpose of the interviews, the Garda spokesman explained, was to gather information. "There are many more jockeys who travel between here and Britain and we will be trying to get talking to as many of them as possible." There was no indication that these interviews were related to the Garda's earlier description of one of the thieves as looking like a jockey.[20]

After no trace of Shergar was turned up during the first day of a two-day search of the Republic by members of the Irish Farmers' Association, a member of the Shergar syndicate speculated that the horse had been moved out of the country. Lord Derby told BBC radio that he was certain Shergar was no longer in Ireland. "It is inconceivable that somebody would not have recognized him by now. I believe the horse could have been flown out of Ireland immediately after he was stolen, but one has very little to go on."[21] There was no evidence to support Lord Derby's theory.

In early March the Garda positively identified the horse trailer linked to the theft of Shergar as one stolen in County Louth, near the border with Northern Ireland. The positive identification was based on modifications made to the trailer by owner Patrick Kelly and identified by Shergar's groom, James Fitzgerald.[22]

Meanwhile, rumors that members of the Shergar syndicate were negotiating on their own with the gang that stole Shergar were straining relations between the Garda and the syndicate committee. Captain Rogers denied reports published in a British newspaper, the *Daily Express,* that he had said such negotiations were under way.[23]

A little over a month after the theft, Chief Superintendent Murphy, while denying suggestions that the Irish Republican Army had stolen Shergar, acknowledged that no progress had been made in the investigation. "We've got nothing further than what we had on day one," he said, "and that is very disheartening for us. Someone, somewhere has vital information which they haven't given us. I cannot for one moment believe that no one saw the three vehicles leaving Ballymany Stud on the night of the kidnap."[24]

In late May the Associated Press reported that the Garda and the Royal Ulster Constabulary in Northern Ireland had abandoned the search for Shergar.[25] "It all eased off after about three months," Murphy later told a reporter for the *Washington Post.* "Now I work on many, many things. You have to take into account more serious things. A person's life is involved in a murder, not a horse's. But we keep looking. You can never feel dispirited, though; you have to take into account the lapse of time. We follow up on anything. You can't call the case closed until it is."[26]

As of this writing, the case remains open and the Garda files remain closed.

# 10

# "Rugby" and the Captain

The highway from Dublin runs through the center of Kildare Town, with Market Square, Saint Brigid's Cathedral, and the Round Tower on the north side of the road and the old, vaguely medieval-looking Garda station to the south. A few minutes before 9:00 on the evening of May 5, a man wearing tweed against the brisk night air hurried purposefully toward a pair of public telephone kiosks standing back to back outside the station house. He wore no uniform or insignia, but he carried himself with the confident bearing of a man who had spent a fair amount of time in the military.

There was no reason for anyone to pay attention to the man, none at all, and he was pleased with the anonymity he enjoyed. He was there to speak with someone he had never met and probably could not trust, to bargain for the return of the most famous horse in Ireland.

As the official investigation stalled in the days after Shergar went missing, a question often asked reflected a growing concern: What can we do? Captain Sean Berry suggested that the Irish Thoroughbred Breeders Association (ITBA) sponsor a reward for the safe return of the horse. The organization took him up on the suggestion, and a few days after Shergar went missing newspapers in Ireland announced that the ITBA was offering a "substantial reward" if Shergar was returned safe and sound. Berry volunteered to serve as negotiator; callers with information could contact him through his office in the Irish Equine Centre, at the number provided.[1] "Our association represents all horse breeders," Berry explained, "and we decided on this course of action as a gesture on behalf of the entire breeding industry. It is vital that Shergar be found safe and well."[2]

The language of the offer was more than just an exercise in semantics. Chief Superintendent Murphy advised members of the Shergar syndicate that a ransom should not be paid because of the reasonable fear that doing so would put other valuable horses at risk.[3] The syndicate members apparently agreed, although rumors of secret negotiations between the syndicate and the thieves persisted—and were denied.[4] Calling the proffered money a "reward," the thinking went, was something else entirely.

The Garda agreed to the reward-but-not-really-ransom plan, with one important condition: that they be allowed to tap the telephones in Berry's office and home. Concern for Shergar outweighing his misgivings about the intrusive wiretapping of his and his family's private conversations, with some reluctance Berry agreed. He hoped that thieves who might be unwilling to talk with the Garda directly would contact him instead.

The initial announcements did not explain what "substantial" meant in the context of the reward. The original figure proposed by the ITBA was £50,000, but Berry knew that he could go much higher if necessary. Calls started almost as soon as the papers hit the streets and continued for weeks, tying up one of his office lines during the day and monopolizing his home telephone in the evenings.[5]

There were calls from people who seemed to be sincere in their offers of help and pleas from animal lovers who were concerned about Shergar's welfare. Those people, Berry thought, were not really interested in a reward.

One individual asked if instructions on feeding and caring for Shergar could be printed in the newspapers. Berry went the caller one better and arranged a television appearance by a veterinarian who provided detailed instructions on how to care for Shergar. Another caller asked Berry to say a prayer with her and to place a relic from St. Martin de Porres in Shergar's empty stall at Ballymany. He did as she asked.[6]

Then there were other callers—the "cranks," as Berry referred to them. They called with far-fetched schemes for locating the missing horse and with suggestions that their neighbors or acquaintances were the thieves and should be arrested. A few of the callers made threats against Berry. The cranks usually telephoned late at night and quickly broke the connection when Berry explained that the Garda was tracing all of his calls and would investigate in the near future.

A few of the threats were taken more seriously, though, including one from a caller who told Berry that his home would be burned to the ground if he continued his involvement in the search for Shergar. Berry was a military man, confident of his ability to take care of himself, and he felt obligated to follow up on any lead that sounded even remotely legitimate. When those investigations took him away from home, however, he feared for the safety of his family.

Now, as he stood by the telephone kiosks in Kildare Town, he remembered those threats, the ones that he had taken seriously, and he hoped that his Garda minder was close by in case things took a bad turn.

One of the telephone kiosks was occupied so Captain Berry stepped quickly into the other. He lifted the receiver and placed it to his ear, but he made no call. Rather than dialing a number with his free hand, he broke the connection so that he appeared to be talking to someone when, in fact, he was waiting for the telephone to ring.

He carried with him that evening a piece of paper on which he had written two telephone numbers—21368 and 21625. These were not numbers he intended to call, however. The numbers were those assigned to the two public telephones, leaving no doubt that he was at the right place.

Berry expected a call from the stranger, the man he had spoken to in the past but had never met. He could identify the contact only by his voice, which he later recalled as "cultured" with an Irish accent, and through the code words Rugby and Fiat 127. For all he knew, "Rugby" might be watching from the shadows, biding his time, waiting to see if Berry could be trusted to come alone.

The minutes dragged on and Berry grew impatient. He still was confident that Rugby was legitimate and could provide information worth the £250,000 reward already negotiated, but he began to wonder if he had been lured into a trap that put his family, his home, and maybe himself in peril. No overt threats had been made by Rugby, but the identification codes insisted upon by the caller were troubling nonetheless.

Berry loved the game of rugby, a fact that he thought the caller must have known when he selected that particular word to identify himself. He also believed that "Fiat 127" was an obvious reference to the automobile owned by his daughter, Vivienne. Any doubt that Rugby knew Berry and that the captain had been under constant surveillance for some time was erased when the caller had addressed him by name during an earlier conversation.

A long hour passed before the telephone rang.

"Bloody time!" Berry snapped when the connection was made. "What nonsense are you up to now? Come on . . . let me have the proposition."

"Stop being so abusive and listen," Rugby said. "We want to know whether you are sure that you could positively identify Shergar."

"I'm 90 percent positive," Berry answered. "I would need to have a straight opportunity to examine him with no interference, no messing about, no threats. And no money until identification was positive and the horse was found to be fit and well."

"Will you agree to be picked up and taken to see the horse, without any money?" the caller asked. "If you do, you will have to remain where the horse is until the money is paid, a quarter of a million pounds. We are not going to let you go, we couldn't afford to do that, not once you have seen the stallion's hiding place. You realize that, don't you, Sean?"

There it is, my name again, Captain Berry thought, as his unease with the situation grew. Was Rugby a person he knew, maybe someone in the Thoroughbred business? More important, did Rugby really know the whereabouts of Shergar? Did he have the key that could solve a mystery that had baffled the authorities for nearly three months?

The two men never spoke again and the £250,000 reward Berry negotiated was never claimed. Berry is still uncertain whether Rugby, the caller with the "cultured" Irish voice, really was one of the men who took Shergar. He is confident, though, that the lead he followed that spring was as good as any.

Sean Berry now lives a quiet life on the outskirts of Kildare Town in a small, well-kept residence that has been his home for years. Mementos from tours of duty with the Third Battalion in Asia and in the Middle East give the house a curiously Oriental air. The man is gracious with visitors and generous with his time.[7]

Manager of the Irish Thoroughbred Breeders Association when Shergar was stolen, Berry was one of the first people notified of the theft, even before the police were called in. He knew his position at the ITBA would require him to deal with the aftermath of Shergar's theft, but never in his wildest dreams did he expect to be personally involved in negotiations for the horse's safe return.

Everything changed on March 17, 1983.

As time passed and the investigation stalled, Berry began to question his continued involvement in the search for Shergar. A couple of psychics from San Francisco had taken up residence in his home, to the consternation of everyone; his conversations were being recorded; officers were dogging his movements; he assumed the thieves also were watching his house; and a radio tracking device had been installed in his personal automobile. The Berry family no longer had any semblance of a private life, threats were being made, and there was no obvious end in sight.

Berry believed at the time that the theft of Shergar was a botched fund-raiser conducted by the Irish Republican Army, and he remains convinced of that today. He stayed the course partly out of his anger and disgust for the IRA and its violent methods and partly because he thought he could aid the investigation. Maybe most important, he was a soldier who felt a duty and obligation to Shergar and to an industry and a way of life that he loved.

Promising or not, every call had to be investigated by the Garda, in the process taking away valuable resources from the investigation. Com-

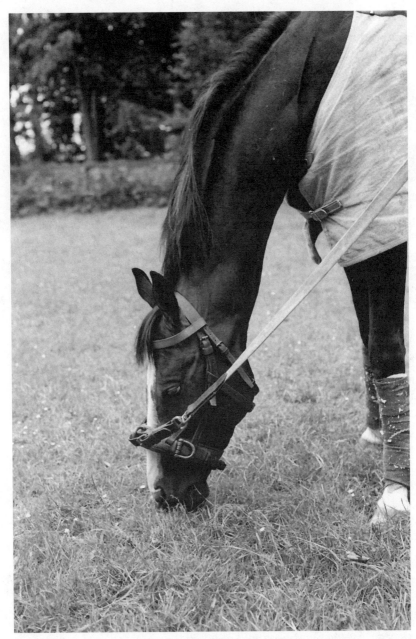

Shergar at three in 1981. (Courtesy of Laurie Morton)

bine the calls to Berry with the calls that were made to the authorities and to the media, and it seemed as if every person in Ireland who was capable of dialing a telephone had something to say about Shergar.

On the evening of St. Patrick's Day, Berry received a telephone call at home from someone asking about the reward. The amount of the ITBA reward had not been publicized beyond a suggestion that the reward was "substantial," and Berry told the caller that the reward was £100,000. The caller said £100,000 was "not enough." He passed the telephone to a second man, who proposed that the minimum sum for negotiations to begin was £250,000.

Berry said that he could raise that amount. He was not certain that he actually could come up with a quarter-million pounds, but he wanted to keep the man talking. In any case, he guessed that there was little chance the reward actually would be paid. Apparently satisfied, the caller gave Berry a code name to confirm his identity and promised that he would call back.

Code names had become popular shorthand for identification in the search for Shergar. The thieves who took the stallion gave James Fitzgerald the code words Neptune or King Neptune (there was some question about which was correct); a caller to a Northern Ireland horse trainer on the night Shergar was stolen used Arkle; and the names of celebrities like popular singer Johnny Logan cropped up from time to time.

In the future, the caller told Berry, Rugby was the code name he would use—confirmation for Berry that the caller was someone familiar with his likes and dislikes.

Rugby called four days later, again in the evening. Captain Berry told him that the reward now was £250,000. The call was short. Rugby said he would call again, and hung up. Garda men had by then joined the San Francisco psychics living with the Berry family and they cautioned their temporary landlord to be careful.

Berry took the offensive when Rugby called next, on March 24. The £250,000 reward could be available within twenty-four hours, he said, but only *after* receipt of conclusive proof that the caller really had Shergar and that the horse was alive and well. "Let me have the evidence or forget the whole deal. No more phone calls until then," Berry said. He was angry and almost shouting before he slammed down the receiver.

Well before Shergar's theft, Berry and his wife had scheduled a two-week vacation in the Canary Islands. He offered to cancel the trip after the March 24 call, when it looked as if the negotiations with Rugby might pay off, but the police told him to go ahead. Berry's close friend Jonathan Irwin volunteered to stand in for Berry and monitor the phones. There were no calls from Rugby while Berry was out of the country, which reinforced a worrisome concern that his home and his family were under continuous surveillance.

When Rugby next called the ITBA office on May 2, he said that the two of them should meet face-to-face. He instructed Berry to drive to the Keadeen Hotel in Newbridge near Ballymany Stud and wait there for a telephone call. He told Berry to use the name Mr. Davies and that their new code word would be Fiat 127, the obvious reference to his daughter's automobile worrisome to Berry.

The call for Mr. Davies came at 11:00 in the morning, precisely as scheduled. Berry would return to the Keadeen Hotel the following afternoon with £250,000, where he would be picked up and taken to see Shergar. He had already gotten identity and blood-typing kits from Weatherbys, and veterinarian Stan Cosgrove, who was as familiar with Shergar as anyone, would be recruited to go along to confirm the stallion's identity.

The next day, May 3, Berry returned to the Keadeen Hotel to await the next call from Rugby or Fiat 127 or whatever the mystery caller decided to call himself. When the phone rang a few minutes past 2:00 in the afternoon, Berry demanded that Rugby produce evidence that Shergar was alive and in good condition. Otherwise, he said, negotiations for the reward were over.

One of the policemen keeping watch, this one a plainclothes man from the Special Branch in Dublin, had been part of the backup on Captain Berry's trips to the Keadeen Hotel. He warned Berry that a man who had been watching him at the Keadeen the day before had been there again the next day. There was little doubt that the danger to Berry, and by extension to his family, was real. The Garda told Berry that he could quit the operation if he wanted, but he said no, he would keep talking to Rugby.

It was a difficult decision, putting his own welfare and that of his family at risk. Berry did not think of himself as a fearless crusader, but he was angry at what he called the "banditry and vandalism" that seemed to be taking over his country. He also loved horses, made his living from them. Besides, he thought, who else was going to step forward? He decided to stay in the game and do the best he could under the circumstances.

In the evening two days later, Berry got another call at his home from Rugby directing him to the telephone kiosks standing outside the Garda station in Kildare Town. During that call Berry explained that veterinarian Stan Cosgrove must accompany him to positively identify Shergar. Rugby said that he knew Cosgrove and that it probably was acceptable for the veterinarian to accompany Berry. He said he would call back with further instructions, but he never did.

Whether Rugby truly represented the thieves who took Shergar remains an unanswered question. Information not revealed until much later, however, suggests that Shergar had been dead for weeks before the St. Patrick's Day call to Berry.

Although communications with Rugby broke down before Stan Cosgrove could become involved, the veterinarian would play a different role in a subsequent attempt to recover Shergar.

In October 1983, around the time the shareholders in the Shergar syndicate were discussing whether to offer a "six-figure" reward for information, a combined Garda/military operation targeted a farmhouse in County Clare. They were searching for members of the Irish National Liberation Army. What they found was evidence of a previously unknown ransom scheme related to Shergar.

Although the raid had nothing to do with the theft of Shergar eight months earlier, letters seized from the farmhouse reportedly referred to a ransom that had already been paid to secure the return of the horse. The ransom plan, according to published reports, involved veterinarian Stan Cosgrove, Garda detective Martin Kenirons, and County Clare horse trainer Denis Minogue.[8]

Cosgrove reportedly had been contacted by a man he believed to be part of the gang that stole Shergar. The man demanded £90,000 for the return of the horse, the money to be delivered to Denis Minogue, with Detective Kenirons acting as a go-between for the two men. Minogue then was supposed to take the money Kenirons had received from Cosgrove, keep £10,000 pounds for himself, and turn the rest over to the men who claimed to have Shergar. Only then would the horse be returned safe and sound. It sounded too easy, too good to be true, and it was.

In a complicated scheme that involved an off-duty Garda officer, dead drops, telephone calls, and broken promises, Minogue was supposed to leave the £80,000 pounds he got from Cosgrove in the trunk of a car parked at a secret location near Ardnacrusha in County Clare. Only after confirmation that Shergar had been released was Minogue supposed to reveal the location of the automobile to the men who claimed to have Shergar. Minogue waited two days for a call that never came. When he eventually returned to the parked automobile, the money was gone.

Minogue later denied that he had done anything wrong. In a formal statement, he said that the Garda was aware of the negotiations and that "all monies given to me to negotiate have been handed back in full by me."[9] Minogue apparently was referring to the £10,000 he was supposed to keep as payment for his role in the scheme. That money was returned to Cosgrove. The other £80,000 was apparently never recovered.

In a cruel twist, Cosgrove was unable to shake off his involvement with Shergar. During the next decade, while he was waging a well-publicized battle against an insurance company that refused to pay on his mortality claim after Shergar was stolen, Cosgrove received several inquiries from individuals who wanted to lead him to the horse's remains—for a price, of course.[10]

*11*

# The Insurance Game

The underwriters at Lloyd's of London have a reputation for insuring anything, against any conceivable risk, but the Loch Ness monster? Who insures the Loch Ness monster?

The man who did that sort of thing, as it happened, was Terry Hall.

In 1971, as a publicity stunt, a whiskey distiller put up a £1 million prize for anyone who could produce the legendary creature supposedly lurking in a chilly Scottish lake. The offer seemed like a very safe bet, but the organizers of the promotion had second thoughts when it occurred to them that someone might actually try to claim the money. They came to Terry Hall's box at Lloyd's and he promptly wrote a £1 million cover with a £2,500 premium for twelve months of coverage.

"As far as this insurance is concerned," the underwriters' slip read, "the Loch Ness monster shall be deemed to be:

1) in excess of 20 feet in length
2) acceptable as the Loch Ness monster to the curator of the Natural History Museum, London."

Hall added the farcical provisions that the Loch Ness monster had to be caught through "fair angling," which to him meant rod and reel; that the creature had to be produced alive; and that it would become the property of the insurers in the unlikely event of a successful claim.[1]

Hall was not the cryptozoology expert at Lloyd's, even if there were such a thing, but he was the corporation's expert on insuring animals—

purebred cattle and dogs, flocks of chickens, pumas, guppies, ostriches, just about any other animal imaginable. The high-dollar premiums, though, came from insuring racehorses. In the mid-1970s, one of the most expensive Thoroughbreds on Hall's books was American Triple Crown winner Secretariat, insured for $6 million; by the early 1980s, one of the most expensive was Epsom Derby winner Shergar, with coverage totaling more than £10 million.[2]

Hall began work at Lloyd's at the age of nineteen, as the third man in underwriter George Butler's box. An underwriter's box on the floor at Lloyd's is an open-air office where the business of insurance is conducted. The boxes typically are oblong and sometimes very ornate—Hall's box was built of solid teak and had survived moves between three of Lloyd's buildings—with room for a half-dozen or more underwriters and their assistants to huddle around a center row of shelves piled high with books. Brokers sometimes approach the boxes with a level of trepidation, like mendicants, hoping to match their clients with underwriters willing to take up the risk.

Butler was a pioneer in the early days of livestock coverage, and working with him proved to be a good training ground for a man who would wind up underwriting multimillion-dollar polices on horses a few years later. Hall went out on his own in 1964 as an underwriter for his own syndicate, No. 627, where he stayed until his retirement in 1987.

From its beginnings as a tiny London coffeehouse in the mid-1700s to its incarnation as a state-of-the-art building occupying an entire city block with a prestigious Lime Street address in London's financial district, Lloyd's of London has been unique in the annals of the insurance industry. Lloyd's operates as a corporation, but not a corporation as most people understand the term. The underwriters who make up Lloyd's have some financial and ethical obligations to the corporation, but they are not employees. Instead, the underwriters are fully independent when it comes to insurance decisions; they work *at* Lloyd's, but they do not work *for* Lloyd's.[3]

The process at Lloyd's goes something like this: Agents solicit business from clients who need insurance, a horse owner, for example, or a member of a syndicate such as the group that owned shares in Shergar. The request for insurance then gets passed to a broker, who in turn takes the proposal to an underwriter at Lloyd's. In Shergar's case, the underwriter was Terry Hall. He does not remember the name of the broker now, but he remembers the amount, for a very good reason—it was around £10 million.[4]

Hall signed his name at the bottom of the slip for Shergar's cover and made a notation of the amount of the risk he was willing to assume, an underwriter's "line." Signing a slip and adding a line of coverage is a time-honored relic from the days when the business at Lloyd's was almost exclusively maritime; it is also the origin of the familiar term *underwriter.* By doing so, Hall was accepting a portion of the risk on behalf of his syndicate, a group of usually silent partners referred to at Lloyd's as "Names." Hall's personal line for underwriting was £1 million, which meant that other underwriters would have to take on the remainder of the risk.

Finding others to fill out the slip to cover the full amount was not a concern. The deal was done quickly. Hall had gained a reputation as the lead underwriter for livestock coverage at Lloyd's, and when he signed onto a slip, even for as much coverage as the amount sought for Shergar, other underwriters were quick to add their names below his.

Insurance for Shergar typically was all-risk mortality, which covered the death of the horse through accident, sickness, or disease, but not by natural causes, considered not an insurable "risk" but a certainty. Coverage for theft usually was included only if the broker requested it; many brokers made such a request, but some did not, even if the additional coverage cost nothing.

"The broker didn't ask for it," Hall recalled, "and I didn't write theft" for Shergar.

The bloodstock insurance business was very competitive at that time, Hall explained, and some underwriters offered theft coverage without charging an additional premium to get a leg up on their competition. But there was no history of risk and no reason to think that the failure to secure theft coverage for Shergar would matter. The lapse in coverage did not become an issue until an armed gang stole the horse, leaving those shareholders who had only mortality policies in a very precarious position.

Even if theft coverage had been included, Hall added, it might not have covered the loss of Shergar once the thieves asked for ransom. "The ransom demand made it extortion, not theft," he explained, which would not be a covered event under either mortality or theft policies.

The distinction between "theft," which seemed an obvious conclusion under the circumstances and would be covered by the appropriate policy conditions, and "extortion," which would not be covered, was a narrow legal question. One possible reason for making the distinction between the two, according to Julian Lloyd, was to prevent what he called "in-house scam operations" in which a bogus theft, an inside job, would be set up. "You'd set something up," Lloyd explained, "pay the ransom, and then the brother-in-law would wind up sitting on the money."[5]

In June 1983, Lloyd's agreed to pay some £7 million (approximately $10.6 million) to twenty shareholders of the thirty-four on their theft claims, despite what published reports called "areas of possible doubt" about the claims.[6] In doing so, the underwriters relied on advice from legal counsel that under the facts of the case, the theft of Shergar really was a theft that would be covered.[7]

Shareholders without theft coverage were left out in the cold. Among them was the Coolmore Stud triumvirate of Robert Sangster, Vincent O'Brien, and John Magnier, plus Shergar's veterinarian Stan Cosgrove. For Cosgrove, more than for any of the other shareholders, the loss of Shergar was financially devastating.

Shareholders in the Shergar syndicate were given two options to pay the Aga Khan. They could make either a onetime payment for the full cost of a share (£250,000) or a series of installment payments spread over four years. Shareholders opting for installment payments, nearly all of them, were obligated by the syndicate agreement to insure their outstanding

balances, with the Aga Khan as the beneficiary.[8] Shareholders also had
the option of insuring their own interests for the installment payments
already made, but were not required to do so by the syndicate agreement.
Shareholders who did not insure their interests did so at their own risk.

Sangster, O'Brien, and Magnier were among the shareholders who
chose installment payments for a final investment of £280,000 each: the
original share price of £250,000 plus an additional £30,000 paid to the
Aga Khan as interest. They obtained insurance for their interests in the
Epsom Derby winner through underwriters at Lloyd's of London, with
the British Bloodstock Agency (Ireland) acting as agent and Hughes-
Gibb & Company Ltd. serving as the broker. The term of the policy
started on October 15, 1982 and ran for a year.

The policies were for mortality only, with coverage for "all risks of
mortality and/or accidents necessitating slaughter," effective anywhere
"in UK/Eire/France, including transit therein," plus a "berserk extension
clause" that covered situations in which a horse became unmanageable
during shipment by air and was destroyed for the safety of the aircraft.
Although the policies did not specifically cover theft, they did not specifically exclude theft from the coverage.[9]

When the insurers refused to pay because there was no conclusive
evidence that Shergar had died during the term of the policies, Sangster, O'Brien, and Magnier filed lawsuits against the British Bloodstock
Agency (BBA) and Hughes-Gibb in the Chancery Court in London.
They had no claim against the insurers because of the policy limitations.
Instead, they claimed that the BBA and Hughes-Gibb had been negligent in failing to obtain theft coverage when it was available for the
asking.

This case was typical for the claims by shareholders who were covered for mortality but not for theft. Michael Payton, a solicitor for Clyde
& Co., a prominent London law firm, explained that there was no litigation brought against the underwriters. "We held the line on that," Payton said. Instead, lawsuits that were filed named agents and brokers and
alleged negligence for failing to secure theft coverage.[10]

The case finally made it to court in 1994, eleven years after Shergar was stolen. The question for Justice Rattee was whether the BBA and Hughes-Gibb had any obligation to ensure that theft coverage was included in the policies without specific instructions from the shareholders to do so. Attorneys for O'Brien and the other plaintiffs argued that they had little experience in equine insurance and that they had relied on the expertise of both the agent and the brokers to fully protect their investments. They said that the chain of instructions passed from the plaintiffs to the BBA, and then on to Hughes-Gibb, created a legal duty on the defendants to be certain that theft insurance was either included in the coverage or added to the policies if necessary. The plaintiffs also alleged that John Magnier had told the brokers from Hughes-Gibb that he always wanted the widest possible cover when insuring stallions, and that this language obviously included coverage for theft.

The defense to the claims was simple: if the plaintiffs wanted theft insurance, they could have—and should have—simply asked for it.

The theft of Shergar presented a unique case, Coolmore general manager Bob Lanigan testified during the trial. No one expected an attack on a stud farm, he said, because there would be no commercial use for a Thoroughbred stallion.[11] That testimony was accurate as far as it went: a stolen racehorse could not be substituted for another horse and entered as a ringer, nor could a stolen stallion be used for clandestine breeding because of sophisticated tests for parentage.

While it was true that no stallion had been stolen before, the argument ignored important facts about the Troubles in Northern Ireland, the growing financial problems faced by the Provisional Irish Republican Army, what appeared to be a campaign of IRA kidnappings, and the extreme vulnerability of a stallion like Shergar.

The value of a stolen horse, like that of a stolen Rembrandt or a stolen Vermeer, has nothing to do with possible commercial uses. After Shergar was taken, his value was whatever someone was willing to pay to get him back. His thieves must have expected, not unreasonably, that Shergar's owners would pay handsomely for his return. Although no one recognized it at the time, the theft of Shergar, or another valuable Thoroughbred like him, was inevitable under the circumstances.

After eight days of testimony and legal wrangling, Justice Rattee decided in favor of the BBA and Hughes-Gibb. "No one in Coolmore knew at that time of any previous theft of a race horse in Ireland," Justice Rattee wrote in his decision, "and in common with the vast majority in the bloodstock business, in particular Hughes-Gibb and BBA, thought that such a theft was exceedingly unlikely to happen." He went on, "Coolmore gave specific instructions as to the cover it wanted—mortality cover, or in other words, cover against the death of Shergar." The agents and brokers, Justice Rattee concluded, had fulfilled their duties by obtaining the coverage that Coolmore had instructed them to acquire.

Perhaps the most interesting part of the decision was Justice Rattee's comment that he was not even certain that the unlawful taking of Shergar by an armed gang, followed by ransom demands, constituted a "theft" under the criminal codes. This was the same concern Terry Hall recognized, that the legal issue was not really theft but extortion. It became a moot point, however, because both sides agreed that despite this bit of uncertainty, insurers would have paid those shareholders who had theft coverage on Shergar.

The plaintiffs in *O'Brien v. Hughes-Gibb* and Stan Cosgrove shared a similar problem, insurance policies with no theft coverage for Shergar and steadfast refusals by the insurers to pay out on a straight mortality claim. Cosgrove was in a more precarious position than the others, however, because he lacked the financial resources for a lengthy fight against the insurers in court. This does not suggest that the loss of Shergar had no impact on the finances of the other shareholders, far from it, but it is clear that they could absorb the monetary loss much more easily than Cosgrove.

He had already borrowed £155,000 to make the down payment on a share in the stallion and he was committed to pay an additional £125,000 under the terms of the syndicate agreement, even if Shergar was never recovered. Cosgrove, through his broker Chandler Hargreaves Ltd., insured his own interest for the £155,000 he had already paid with Norwich Union; coverage for the outstanding balance, £125,000, with the Aga Khan as beneficiary, was placed by brokers Hodgson, McCreery & Co. Ltd. with a variety of underwriters. In addition to being the sole insurer for Cosgrove's interest, Norwich Union also was a minor underwriter for the policy covering the outstanding balance.[12]

The coverage placed by Cosgrove's brokers for the benefit of the Aga Khan carried an annual premium of £4,343.75 (paid by Cosgrove) and ran through November 1, 1983. The policy included the following provision:

> *PROVEN THEFT*
> Notwithstanding anything contained herein to the contrary this insurance extends to include Loss by Proven Theft.

The Norwich Union policy, designated as "ALL RISKS OF MORTALITY INSURANCE," carried an annual premium of £5,936.50 (also paid by Cosgrove) and ran through November 10, 1983. The Norwich Union policy neither specifically included nor specifically excluded theft.[13]

Shergar was stolen on the evening of February 8, 1983. After the stallion went missing, Cosgrove pursued what he probably thought would be a straightforward claim under the Norwich Union policy. The insurer promptly denied the claim, however, triggering a dispute that thirty-five years later remains unresolved. Cosgrove still has not received any money from Norwich Union, which over the years has relied on a variety of justifications.[14]

On April 1, 1987, four years after Shergar was stolen and the claim for indemnification denied, Cosgrove's son James wrote to the claims superintendent at Norwich Union. He acknowledged the Norwich Union position that a successful claim required the elder Cosgrove to prove that Shergar was dead and that he died during the policy period, but disagreed that the conditions were reasonable. Cosgrove asserted that the proof of those conditions was more than mere speculation and that the insurer was "completely oblivious" to accepted theories about the disappearance and death of Shergar.

A response from Norwich Union came a few days later. Claims

superintendent T. Joyce said that a plausible alternate theory was that Shergar was "still alive and being used for breeding" and that evidence to refute that argument must be "conclusive and irrefutable." He also said that Stan Cosgrove could have protected himself if he had chosen to "pay the appropriate premium" for theft coverage.

The idea that Shergar was being kept at a secret location and used for breeding made no sense. Parentage testing available at the time was sufficiently reliable to have precluded that scheme. The suggestion that Cosgrove had failed to pay the "appropriate premium" was disingenuous and in fact wrong.

The premium for Cosgrove's insurance policy from Norwich Union was based on 3.83 percent of the insured value, £155,000. For the policy placed by Hodgson, McCreery for the benefit of the Aga Khan, however, the premium was calculated at a lower rate, 3.475 percent of the insured value, £125,000. Considering that theft coverage typically was provided for no additional premium, it was reasonable for Stan Cosgrove to expect full coverage for his premium. According to James Cosgrove, the claim for the Aga Khan's benefit was paid without dispute while the elder Cosgrove's claim was denied.

Cosgrove's dispute with Norwich Union languished until January 1993, when a newspaper published information provided by Sean O'Callaghan that seemed to offer the evidence that Norwich Union required, that Shergar was dead and that his death occurred shortly after he was stolen and while the policy was in force. O'Callaghan had been a highly placed member of the IRA before he switched sides to become an informer for the Garda and thus he should have been familiar with the facts of Shergar's death. He confirmed that the horse had been injured and shot to death within days after being stolen.

T. Joyce, now identified as "claims manager," dismissed O'Callaghan's account of Shergar's death: "I am sure you would not expect me to accept comments made by a known terrorist as being irrefutable evidence that Shergar was killed within the currency of the policy," Joyce wrote to James Cosgrove on January 18, 1993. "I certainly have no intention of making any payments under the terms of this contract." Joyce also noted that theft was specifically included in the policy related to the Aga Khan.

In a subsequent letter, dated February 26, 1993, Joyce also dismissed a signed statement obtained from O'Callaghan while he was incarcerated in Maghaberry Prison in Northern Ireland. The handwritten statement read as follows:

> *To Whom It May Concern*
>
> I was a senior I.R.A. volunteer from 1970 to 1985. Acting on Garda requests as well as my own initiative I investigated the Shergar kidnapping in 1983. The clear & consistent statements of those directly involved was that the horse was shot in February 1983. I informed the Garda accordingly at that time.
>
> Since the kidnappers were never convicted of the offence, they are unlikely to offer sworn evidence for a civil action.
>
> Signed this 18/2/1993.

The statement was signed by O'Callaghan and witnessed by David Horgan, a friend and associate of both Stan and James Cosgrove who for years worked tirelessly to resolve the dispute with Norwich Union.

In his letter rejecting this new evidence, the ubiquitous T. Joyce informed James Cosgrove that Norwich Union "regret to inform you that we are not prepared to reopen this claim at this late stage" on the strength of O'Callaghan's statement. Apparently for the first time, Norwich Union also declared that Cosgrove's claim was barred by a six-year statute of limitations.

In a separate letter two days later, February 28, Joyce reiterated Norwich Union's position. Stan Cosgrove's claim was time barred; the company had seen no evidence of Shergar's death that "would have brought the claim within the policy conditions had it been made in time"; and the refusal to pay the claim "was in line with the general approach where theft coverage was not provided by the policy."

Finally, Joyce added, there would be no more correspondence from Norwich Union about the claim. This was not quite true.

On January 14, 2002, David Horgan obtained a signed statement from Garda chief superintendent Sean Feely, who had been involved in the Shergar investigation nearly two decades earlier. Feely confirmed that statements made by O'Callaghan regarding the death of Shergar in his autobiography, *The Informer,* were consistent with Garda analysis and corroborated by other intelligence sources.[15]

Among other things, O'Callaghan wrote that Shergar had been destroyed by the IRA men who took him a few days after the theft.[16] Horgan sent the new information confirming that Shergar had died within the term of Cosgrove's mortality policy via facsimile to Norwich Union, where it came to the attention of Mike O'Sullivan, the manager of customer relations.

Feely's statement was "speculation," O'Sullivan said, and was not the "conclusive and irrefutable" evidence that Norwich Union required. O'Sullivan had closed the book on Stan Cosgrove once again.

With more than three decades of even modest interest added to the original amount insured with Norwich Union, Stan Cosgrove's unpaid claim now totals well over £1 million.

In addition to insurance for mortality and theft, the shareholders in Shergar's syndicate had another option to possibly recover their investments in the missing stallion and the lost income from stud fees. It was something of a long shot, but a few days after Shergar was stolen, attorneys for the syndicate filed a £20 million claim with the Kildare County Council.

The basis for the claim was the country's Malicious Injuries Act, which provides compensation for damage to property, including horses and other animals, under certain circumstances. As far as anyone could remember, the claim for Shergar was the largest ever made in the Republic of Ireland and if successful almost certainly would have been challenged in court.

The act was written to protect property owners from small claims, not in anticipation of a £20-million claim made by a group of wealthy owners for the loss of a valuable Thoroughbred stallion like Shergar. Emmet Stagg, chairman of the Kildare County Council, said that the entire county budget was only £18 million, which was not even enough to keep the roads in good repair.[17] An unidentified spokesman for the council put the annual budget higher, at £30 million, but whichever figure was correct, the claim was staggering. If successful, however, the claim would not bankrupt County Kildare because of a recoupment provision requiring the Department of the Environment to repay to the council annual damages over £120,000.[18]

Although the claim was filed within the fourteen-day requirement set out in the act, the syndicate made no effort to keep the process moving.[19]

## 12

# The Usual Suspects

Speculations about who took Shergar, and why, far outnumbered the bits of useful information that trickled in during the months after the horse was stolen. Suspicion almost immediately fell on the Provisional Irish Republican Army. There was no solid evidence to implicate the IRA, but the number of people and vehicles involved, the magnitude of the heist, and the obvious planning suggested a paramilitary operation. And at the height of the Troubles in Northern Ireland it was standard practice to blame the Provos for everything bad that happened.

The IRA never claimed responsibility for taking Shergar. This was out of character if the Provos really were behind the theft, and the omission led some people to discount the "IRA-did-it" argument. One explanation that makes sense is that the IRA did not claim the theft because they feared a backlash from the horse-loving Irish when what the Provos hoped would be a simple ransom scheme turned into a disaster.

The most credible theory, one that has persisted over the years, was that the theft was an IRA operation designed to raise badly needed money for arms purchases. Finances were tight for the IRA in the early 1980s, and the campaign to expel the British from Northern Ireland was an expensive undertaking.

Captain Sean Berry is convinced that the IRA was responsible for stealing Shergar, a belief shared by insurance man Julian Lloyd. The consensus—based largely on hearsay, Lloyd cautioned—was that the theft of Shergar was engineered by a few midlevel IRA men who were trying to improve their positions in the organization's hierarchy. The IRA never claimed responsibility for the theft because the operation was not approved at the highest levels.[1]

The first indication that Shergar's theft really was an IRA operation came a decade after the horse was stolen, although the information gathered then was not shared with the general public for several years.

On February 18, 1993, David Horgan met Sean O'Callaghan.

Today Horgan is a director of Botswana Diamonds with two decades' experience in mining and oil and gas exploration in Latin America, Africa, and the Middle East. In 1993 he was acting for a friend, Stan Cosgrove, who was mired in a bitter dispute with Norwich Union Insurance over the carrier's refusal to pay on a claim after Shergar was stolen (see chapter 11). Horgan hoped that O'Callaghan, with his obvious IRA connections, could shed some light on the details of Shergar's death.

O'Callaghan was a "supergrass," a senior member of the Provisional Irish Republican Army who had switched sides to work for the Garda as a confidential informer.[2] In 1988, concerned that other IRA members were becoming suspicious of him, O'Callaghan surrendered to the British police. He entered guilty pleas to two murders and forty other crimes related to his IRA activities and drew a sentence of 539 years. He was released in 1996.[3]

Their meeting took place at Maghaberry Prison near Lisburn in County Antrim, Northern Ireland, where O'Callaghan was a prisoner.[4] O'Callaghan told Horgan that he was not directly involved with the theft, but that within two weeks after the horse was stolen he spoke with one of the men who had taken part in the operation. He was told that Shergar went berserk and that the thieves could not control him. The horse was injured and had to be destroyed, O'Callaghan said, probably within twenty-four hours of being taken.

He identified Kevin Mallon as the IRA man who came up with the idea of stealing Shergar and said that Mallon knew that the horse was owned by a syndicate. That didn't matter, O'Callaghan said, because Mallon expected the major shareholders to pay the ransom anyway. He told Horgan to invite people from Norwich Union to visit him in prison if they had questions.

Following O'Callaghan's release from prison he chronicled his time in the IRA in a memoir titled *The Informer*. He devoted three of the book's nearly five hundred pages to the theft of Shergar and again named Mallon, along with Gerry Fitzgerald, Paul Stewart, Rab Butler, and Nicky Keogh, as members of the team that stole the horse. O'Callaghan said that he learned the "bare bones" of the story, which included details of Shergar's death, from Fitzgerald during a meeting in the Garden of Remembrance in Dublin.[5]

O'Callaghan also wrote about a prison visit from a solicitor who was acting for Stan Cosgrove. O'Callaghan wrote that he had cooperated as much as he could to help break up a logjam with Cosgrove's insurance company. O'Callaghan explained that he tried to help Cosgrove because, while he believed that the insurance was correct from a legal standpoint, he believed that the insurance company was being too strict with the veterinarian's claim.[6] Horgan is not named in the book, but the description and timing of the visit make it clear that the visitor was David Horgan.

Although the account of Shergar's theft and subsequent death in *The Informer* is consistent with Horgan's notes from his trip to Maghaberry Prison in 1993, neither the book nor O'Callaghan's signed statement from that visit are proof that he was telling the truth. He was, after all, a confessed informer whose life depending on his ability to weave a convincing web of lies. Without more evidence, O'Callaghan's story was just that, an interesting story.

Undeterred, Horgan continued his dogged search for evidence to salvage Stan Cosgrove's insurance claim. In January 2002, he contacted Garda chief superintendent Sean Feely, who had been involved in the Shergar investigation as a sergeant almost twenty years earlier. In a signed statement, Feely confirmed the accuracy of O'Callaghan's account: "I have studied the relevant sections of Sean O'Callaghan's book 'The Informer' and concur with his comments on the Shergar Case. This account accords in all material aspects with the Garda Siochana analysis both in 1983 and since, and is corroborated by other intelligence sources."[7] The statement also confirmed, by reference to "Intelligence Reports received through confidential sources," that Shergar was "injured and put down on the 11th or morning of the 12th February 1983."

Further evidence that the IRA took Shergar was the examination of a magazine containing twenty-seven rounds of ammunition found on the grounds of Ballymany Stud a few days after Shergar was stolen. Discovery of the magazine was not revealed by the Garda when it was found, or for some time thereafter. An officer in the ballistics section of the Garda Technical Bureau in Dublin determined that the magazine was manufactured for an Austrian-made "Stager-Damlier, Puch" submachine gun. This type of weapon had been used by the IRA in operations in South Armagh—"Bandit Country"—prior to 1983.

Chief Superintendent Feely's statement failed to sway Mike O'Sullivan, the manager of customer relations at Norwich Union, who called it "speculation" and not "conclusive and irrefutable" evidence.[8] As of this writing, however, and in the absence of access to Garda files, Feely's statement remains the closest thing to an official pronouncement by the authorities confirming IRA involvement in the theft of Shergar.

Among the arguments put forward in opposition to the conventional wisdom about Shergar's theft was that no Irishman would harm a horse. That argument fails to take into account the IRA's record of targeting military horses, both during the Troubles and as far back in history as the Irish War of Independence.

The sun was shining in London on Tuesday, July 20, 1982, as members of the Mounted Regiment of the Royal Household Cavalry, the Blues and Royals, made their way through Hyde Park to participate in the Changing of the Guard ceremony. At 10:40 a.m., a thunderous explosion rocked Hyde Park. An Irish Republican Army bomb, packed with four- and six-inch nails and at least twenty-five pounds of high explosive, had been hidden in the trunk of a blue Morris Marina automobile. The bomb was detonated by remote control as the soldiers and their horses walked past South Carriage Drive where the automobile was parked.

Three young soldiers were killed by the blast and a fourth, the company standard bearer, died four days later. Seven of the horses were either killed or so severely injured by the blast that they were euthanized. Another horse, a black gelding named Sefton, suffered serious injuries, including a severed jugular vein caused by a piece of shrapnel from the bodywork of the vehicle and more than thirty other wounds caused by flying nails or shrapnel.

Remarkably, Sefton pulled through and became a national hero, a living symbol of British opposition to the IRA. Major Noel Carding, the veterinary officer from the Knightsbridge Barracks who worked on Sefton, was, as far as anyone could tell, the first army veterinarian to treat war wounds on a cavalry horse since World War II.[9]

Two hours later, a second IRA bomb exploded under a bandstand in Regent's Park, killing seven musicians from the Royal Green Jackets.

After the bombings, Jonathan Irwin, along with the chairman and board of directors at Goffs sales, organized a private fund to raise money to help replace the lost horses. It would be, Irwin hoped, a way to show that not everyone in Ireland supported the IRA and its tactics, what he called a "quiet but symbolic, way of joining hands across the sea." The fund raised £47,000, all from private donations—enough to purchase six cavalry horses.[10]

Sadly, the tragedy at Hyde Park had consequences that lingered for years. Michael Pedersen, Sefton's regular rider, survived the bombing but afterward reportedly suffered from post-traumatic stress syndrome. On September 30, 2012, Pedersen killed his two young children and then committed suicide.[11]

Decades earlier, on June 22, 1921, when partition was a foregone conclusion, King George V traveled from England to Belfast to open the new Northern Ireland Parliament. The king was guarded by a contingent of the Tenth Royal Hussars. The next day, a troop train carrying several of the soldiers and more than one hundred of their horses to the Curragh Camp between Newbridge and Kildare was attacked.

A number of passenger carriages for soldiers and civilians, along with railway cars carrying the cavalry horses, were derailed and crashed in a ravine. Several soldiers and more than sixty horses were killed. Reports from the scene speculated that the derailment was caused by an explosion that tore up the tracks, but a later report from the Bureau of Military History covering military activities in County Armagh between 1918 and 1922 attributed the wreck to sabotage by IRA men who removed bolts that secured the rails to the rail bed.[12]

According to author Toby Harnden, soldiers forced local men to clear the wreckage and bury the horses, then returned a week later and made the men exhume the horse carcasses and bury them deeper. Like the Hyde Park bombing, Harnden said, "it was the dead animals rather than the dead soldiers who elicited most public sympathy."[13]

The Irish love their horses—the IRA, apparently, not so much.

# 13

# The French Connections

Garda press conferences in the days after Shergar went missing soon became a litany of "no's"—no clues, no arrests, no suspects, no horse . . . no news at all.

On one day, at around 5:00 in the morning, Chief Superintendent James Murphy sent out what sounded like an urgent call for reporters to come to the Garda station in Naas. Murphy must have been growing irritated by the constant attention, often critical, directed his way as the search for Shergar sputtered along. He announced to the reporters assembled on the steps of the station that he had called them in just to say that he had nothing to say.[1]

Journalists camped out in Newbridge, Kildare, and Naas, the small towns surrounding Ballymany Stud, soon found themselves with time on their hands, columns to fill, and little substantive information to report. Readers wanted news but there was nothing to report. Small wonder, then, that alternative theories about the crime began to appear, theories that bypassed the Irish Republican Army to focus on other, and far less likely, suspects, such as the Mafia, the Russians, and the Libyans.

One fanciful report had the police speculating that Shergar might have been stolen by a group of disgruntled Thoroughbred breeders who were not part of the syndicate that owned Shergar. Those breeders, whoever they might have been, did not want to pay the stallion's hefty stud fee for outside mares, so they stole him instead. "There is a possibility he was taken to service waiting mares in the hope the offspring will bring in the dividends," according to an unnamed Garda spokesman quoted in an Associated Press article that appeared two days after the theft.[2]

A few days later, another Associated Press story appeared under a headline that in other circumstances would have been funny: "Thieves May Have Shergar in 'Secret Love Nest.'" A Dublin veterinarian, who should have known better, speculated in the article that foals sired by Shergar "could make a fortune in races."[3]

Such a scheme might sound reasonable to people unfamiliar with procedures in place to verify the parentage of a Thoroughbred foal prior to registration. There is even a chance that it could have worked in 1967, when noted crime writer Dick Francis published *Blood Sport*. In an article appearing two days after Shergar was stolen, Francis reflected:

Fifteen years ago in *Blood Sport* I told the story of Classic winner Chrysalis who was hijacked not to be held for ransom like Shergar but to be used to cover mares at stud, to give greater value to the stallions who had supposedly fathered the race winning progeny which he then produced.

That does not seem to be the motive here, and perhaps with modern technology it would be possible to trace the paternity of foals fathered by Shergar while he is away from his rightful owners.[4]

By the early 1980s, blood-typing technology had far outpaced the plot in *Blood Sport,* making the clandestine breeding theory even less likely.[5] Altering Shergar's appearance and racing him under the name of another horse, such as the attempted "ringer" substitution thwarted by Sherlock Holmes in the short story "Silver Blaze," also held little promise. Although pre-race identification in England and Ireland was based on a horse's physical characteristics such as color and markings, rather than on more definitive lip tattoos, trying to disguise a horse as well known as Shergar would be a daunting task.[6]

Francis was working on his next book, *The Danger*, when Shergar was stolen. In that novel, Francis wrote about high-profile kidnappings among the racing community and Liberty Market Ltd., a company that specialized in risk analysis to help prevent kidnappings and ransom demands and supported recovery efforts for executives who have been taken. While Liberty Market was a fictional creation, such organizations do exist.[7] One of the best known is Control Risks Group Ltd., a private, and very secretive, crisis management company based in London with close ties to the kidnap and ransom division of insurance giant Lloyd's of London.

There were suggestions that Control Risks was involved in the efforts to locate and rescue Shergar on behalf of Lloyd's, whose underwriters carried much of the coverage on the stallion. While involving Control Risks in the search would have been a logical choice for the people at Lloyd's, rumors to that effect could not be verified. A spokesperson for Control Risks would neither confirm nor deny any involvement in the search for Shergar.[8]

Visiting Dublin to promote *The Danger* in October 1983, with the search for Shergar stalled, Francis said that he thought that the horse probably was dead. "I have been accused more than once of giving crooks ideas," he added. "I certainly hope I didn't give them the idea for what they have done with Shergar."[9]

According to Julian Lloyd, Shergar was stolen by mid-level IRA men who wanted to move up in the organization by raising a ransom for arms purchases from Libya.[10] The timing of arms shipments from Libya to the IRA, tapering off during the late 1970s and then increasing again by late 1984, also might suggest a connection between the Shergar theft and Libyan support for the IRA, but there is another explanation.

In April 1984, during a demonstration against Colonel Muammar al-Qadhafi outside the Libyan embassy in London, a police officer was killed by shots fired from inside the embassy. Police surrounded the building for almost two weeks before an agreement allowed Libyan diplomats to leave England. Following that incident, a subsequent attack against Qadhafi's military headquarters in Tripoli, and bombing raids by US planes based in England, the Libyan leader increased his support

for non-Western paramilitary groups around the world. One of the ben-
eficiaries of Qadhafi's renewed largesse was the IRA.[11]

Fanciful notions about the theft of Shergar aside, two of the theories
deserve a closer look because both involve revenge against the Aga Khan.
Both have roots in France.

Just before 3:00 p.m. on the afternoon of Monday, December 13,
1982, police and firefighters responded to reports of a burning automobile on Redd Road, a narrow, rural lane located less than two miles
from Keeneland Racecourse near Lexington, Kentucky. First respond-
ers found a badly burned vehicle, later determined to be a 1979 BMW
sedan, a one-gallon metal can typically used for transporting kerosene or
other flammable liquids, and a charred body.[12]

The body's torso was lying across the front seat on the driver's side;
the legs were outside the vehicle. On the ground near a rear tire, some
four feet from the body, police found a .38-caliber Smith & Wesson
revolver. All six cylinders were loaded, but only one shot had been fired.
Other cartridges had discharged due to the intense heat. The weapon's
wooden grips were destroyed by the fire, which also burned the body
beyond immediate recognition.

The vehicle, as it turned out after police traced the car's Kentucky
license number (EWC-664), was registered to Jean-Michel Gambet, a
Lexington bloodstock agent. Identification of the body was confirmed
the following day based on dental records. Dr. George Nichols, the
state medical examiner, performed the autopsy. He found a single bullet wound to the head, just above the right eye, and evidence of smoke
inhalation, indicating that Gambet had been alive when the fire started.

The death of Gambet and his connection with the Thoroughbred
industry in Kentucky generated intense scrutiny by local media and
national attention by horse racing's trade publications. The case moved
to the international stage two months later when Shergar was stolen and
reporters covering the theft learned that Gambet had been negotiating
with the Aga Khan IV for the purchase of a horse in the months leading
up to his death.

The new conspiracy theory went something like this: Needing cash to make a down payment on one of the Aga Khan's horses, Gambet negotiated a $500,000 under-the-table loan from the Mafia in New Orleans. The deal fell through, but Gambet could not repay the Mob loan because he had already spent the money on something else. The Mafia killed Gambet and stole Shergar because they thought the Aga Khan still owed them either their money or a horse.[13]

Although there were numerous loose ends to the theory, it gained some credibility when it turned out that Gambet actually was negotiating with the Aga Khan to buy a horse, Group 1 winner Vayrann, before the agent's death. According to one published report, Gambet had agreed to pay a nonrefundable deposit to purchase Vayrann in September and to pay the balance in October.

The story Gambet told his friends and potential investors was that he planned to syndicate Vayrann to stand at a farm he was buying in France. The deposit apparently was paid on schedule but the balance was not, and Vayrann remained the property of the Aga Khan.[14] The theory gained some credence when the deposit later was reported to be £350,000, which could have been covered by the loan.[15] A subsequent statement by Henry Carnegie, personal counsel to the Aga Khan in France, verified some details of the failed transaction.[16]

A major problem with the theory was the cause of Gambet's death. If the police investigation supported a finding of murder, the affair might really begin to sound like a Mob hit. If Gambet's death was a suicide, on the other hand, the supposed Mafia connection comes into serious question.

Almost from the start, the police investigated Gambet's death as a potential suicide. This was based on substantial circumstantial evidence, including massive debt, life insurance policies, the fact that the gun found at the scene was given to Gambet by a friend who was the registered owner, and Gambet's purchase of the kerosene can found in the car a few days before his death.

Gambet was heavily in debt when he died, and the police speculated that he attempted to manufacture a crime scene so his family could collect more on several current life insurance policies. The policies totaled at least $630,000. There were provisions to pay the full value in the event of a suicide, but additional provisions added payments totaling $200,000 if Gambet's death was the result of accident or murder.[17] Lieutenant Drexel Neal, now retired, led the investigation. Years later he said that there was enough insurance to get Gambet's family out of debt.

The investigation resolved the mystery of the supposed Mafia loan. Gambet did borrow $500,000, but from the American Bank and Trust Company in New Orleans. The loan was unsecured and co-signed by one of Gambet's friends, Echo Valley Farm owner Don Sucher. The loan, dated August 8, 1982, carried a hefty interest rate, 20 percent, which obligated Gambet to repay $523,013.70 when the note became due.

A statement from American Bank and Trust sent to Gambet, dated November 19, 1982, informed him that the loan would mature on December 1—twelve days before he died. Following Gambet's death, Sucher became solely liable for the debt.

The police concluded that Gambet committed suicide, which should have ended the matter, along with any speculation about a connection to Shergar. It did not, however, because of a coroner's inquest empaneled on March 2, 1983, at the request of Fayette County coroner Chester Hager to determine the cause of death. The inquest lasted two days and became a battle of experts over the caliber of handgun that caused the wound to Gambet's head.

Dr. Nichols, the state medical examiner who performed the autopsy, and Dr. David J. Wolfe, a state forensic anthropologist, both testified that a reconstruction of Gambet's skull showed that the wound was inconsistent with a .38-caliber handgun. Both experts testified that the entry wound was more consistent with a smaller weapon, either a .22- or a .28-caliber gun. Wolfe suggested that someone else had shot Gambet with a small-caliber handgun and then carried the weapon away after setting the vehicle on fire.

After six hours of deliberation, the six-person inquest jury determined that Gambet's death was a homicide, directly contradicting the conclusion of the police investigation.

Neal was incredulous. "I can't think of any death where a victim came to the scene with his own kerosene can and his own gun and had both of them used against him by someone else."[18]After the inquest, the police contacted Dr. Rudiger Breitenecker, a noted forensic pathologist and expert on gunshot wound investigation who had performed autopsies on Rev. Jim Jones and the victims of the Jonestown killings. The police asked him to review the entire record of the investigation and the inquest in the hope that he could "resolve conflicts in the evidence." Dr. Breitenecker discounted the testimony of Drs. Nichols and Wolfe and concluded that "the great preponderance of the evidence supports a suicidal manner of death."[19]

The authorities remained certain of their interpretation and in an internal police memorandum dated August 18, 1983—before Dr. Breitenecker's report was released—the department officially classified Gambet's death a suicide. On September 1, 1983, the police closed the case.[20]

At few weeks later, during a speech at the American Society for Medical Technology convention, Dr. Nichols defended his and Dr. Wolfe's conclusions about the cause of Gambet's death. When the local police refused to change their decision that the bloodstock agent committed suicide, Dr. Nichols said they had "sacrificed the truth."[21]

A few weeks after Shergar went missing, a reporter tracked down Lieutenant Neal and asked about a possible link between the death of Gambet and the theft. Neal was unequivocal: "There is absolutely nothing to connect Gambet with the kidnapping. We have never found any evidence that it was a homicide."[22] More than thirty years later, Neal's assessment has not changed. There is no reason to think Neal was wrong in 1983, or that he is wrong now.

Not everything about Gambet's death has been resolved, however. Tucked away in the police investigative file is a photocopy of check #945, drawn on Gambet's personal account at the Bank of Commerce and Trust Company in Lexington, Kentucky, rather than on a business account for his Euro-American Bloodstock Agency. The check is dated August 20, 1982, around the time that Gambet was said to be in Deauville negotiating with the Aga Khan for the purchase of Vayrann.

Check #945 is made out to S. A. Aga Khan in the amount of $166,000; the memo line reads "10% Vayrann," placing the value of the horse at $1,660,000. The check was never cashed, however. A box designated "Insf."—presumably meaning insufficient funds—was checked off. Why was Gambet unable to cover this check when, twelve days earlier, with the help of a friend, he had secured a $500,000 loan from a New Orleans bank?

After the inquest where it was determined that Gambet's death was a homicide, two of the jurors said the decision was, at best, a judgment call based on incomplete evidence. While questions about Gambet's death likely will remain unanswered, there is nothing in the evidence gathered by the police to suggest anything other than a coincidental link to Shergar.

In addition to Vayrann's peripheral connection to the Jean-Michel Gambet case in America, the Aga Khan's horse was also involved in a controversy in his own right in England. After winning the 1981 Champion Stakes at Newmarket, the Brigadier Gerard colt tested positive for anabolic steroids. That, at least, was the report from Horseracing Forensic Laboratories, the official testing laboratory for the British Jockey Club. The laboratory reported a positive result for estrane-3, 17-diol, a metabolite for the prohibited anabolic steroid 19 Nordstrom.

The Aga Khan questioned the validity of the test result and assembled an international panel of scientists who concluded that the steroid found in Vayrann's urine was a metabolite of a hormone found naturally in all uncastrated horses at the threshold level considered a "positive" by the testing laboratory. Proof that the prohibited drug had been administered to a horse in violation of the Jockey Club's Rules of Racing, the scientists argued, required a concentration much higher than the testing threshold in use at the time.

The Jockey Club accepted that argument and did not disqualify Vayrann from his Champion Stakes win, although the organization did not publicize the scientific basis for that decision.[23]

The matter did not end there, however. American Craig Singer, whose Cairn Rouge finished second, two lengths behind Vayrann, filed a lawsuit in the Chancery Court in London. Singer claimed that the Jockey Club had misinterpreted its own rules and thereby breached a contract with him. His lawsuit asked for damages amounting to the difference between the prize money for second place, which Cairn Rouge earned, and the first-place purse that Singer thought he deserved.

Singer argued that the Jockey Club had misinterpreted and misapplied its own rules by failing to disqualify Vayrann and that a contract existed between him and the Jockey Club that guaranteed the rules would be correctly applied in every case. Justice Scott acknowledged that there was merit to some of Singer's arguments but eventually ruled against the American.

Most interesting, perhaps, was Justice Scott's conclusion that even if a valid contract did exist between the Jockey Club and the owners, trainers, and jockeys, that relationship did not guarantee that every rule would be applied correctly in every situation. "No judge would ever guarantee that he had reached the right result," Justice Scott wrote, "and I do not see why it should be implied that the Jockey Club had contractually bound itself that its disciplinary committee would do so."[24]

The second semi-plausible attempt to link Shergar's theft to someone not connected to the Irish Republic Army was even less successful than the first. It involved Marcel Boussac, for decades one of France's leading owners and breeders, the Aga Khan IV, and a Kentucky bloodstock agent named Wayne Murty.[25]

When the Aga Khan IV decided in 1978 to begin racing in England after a quarter-century hiatus, one of the reasons he gave was that his French stables were overflowing. Money raised through the syndication of two-time champion Blushing Groom helped finance the purchase of eighty-three horses from the estate of François Dupré in 1977. The purchase of some two hundred horses from Boussac the following year stretched the capacity of the Aga Khan IV's French operation to the limit.[26]

Acquiring the Dupré and Boussac horses was an important part of the Aga Khan's long-term strategy for his breeding and racing interests, but the practice of making an offer for all of a breeder's horses in a single transaction was not original to him. Both his grandfather, the Aga Khan III, and his father, Prince Aly Khan, favored such package deals. They could select the horses they truly wanted from the consignment, and then sell the rest, perhaps making a profit in the process.[27]

It was a protracted legal battle in French courts over the Boussac transactions that led some reporters to cast Wayne Murty as a suspect in Shergar's theft.

Negotiating directly with the elderly and infirm Boussac on July 6, 1978, Murty purchased 57 horses—the best of the old man's stud—for $840,000. A few days later the Aga Khan bought 144 more of the Boussac horses, which he believed at the time to be all of the stud's horses, from the bankruptcy receivers for approximately $8.2 million. When the Aga Khan learned that he had acquired some, but not all, of the Boussac horses, he offered an additional $1.2 million for the 57 horses purchased by Murty.

Bad timing, at least for Murty, was the legal issue. When he made his purchase, only Boussac's corporate assets were part of the bankruptcy proceedings. His personal assets, including the horses, were not included. So far, so good, until the French bankruptcy court decided to include Boussac's horses and other personal assets in the bankruptcy proceedings. A week *after* the deal brokered by Murty, the court backdated the cutoff for all personal payments from Boussac to May 20, 1978. Transactions made after that date, including Murty's acquisitions, suddenly became subject to scrutiny by the bankruptcy receivers.

Based on an appraisal that put the approximate value of the horses purchased by Murty at slightly under $1 million, more than Murty paid but less that the amount offered by the Aga Khan, the receivers accepted the Aga Khan's offer for all the Boussac horses. An irate Murty argued against acceptance of the Aga Khan's offer, but the receivers stood firm. On January 4, 1979, the Commercial Court in Paris ruled that Murty had paid well below the fair market value for the Boussac horses, which was unfair to creditors and nullified the sale.

Murty appealed the decision but lost when an appellate court in Paris affirmed the lower court's nullification of the sale. The court did order the receivers to return some $400,000 that had been seized, however, along with an additional $40,000 for his expenses in keeping the horses during the litigation. Murty's initial payment, made directly to Boussac rather than the bankruptcy receivers, was not returned.

Murty's string of losses in the courts of France continued on November 19, 1979, when the Commercial Court ordered the Société d'encouragement, which governs racing in the country, to issue duplicate registration papers to replace those that Murty refused to return to the Aga Khan.[28] The papers were necessary for the Aga Khan to register foals produced by the Boussac mares.

Murty was incensed. He launched a flurry of lawsuits in France and England, and when those failed he tried to sue the Aga Khan in the United States. His process servers handed a summons to the Aga Khan as he was walking into the United Nations building in New York, but a federal district court judge dismissed Murty's civil lawsuit. The judge ignored Murty's argument that the Aga Khan wielded too much influence on the French courts for him to get a fair trial and ruled that the complaint should have been filed in France.[29]

Despite Murty's failures in court, rumors persisted that fear of his barrage of lawsuits forced the Aga Khan to alter plans for Shergar. Concerned that the horse might be seized by court order in the United States, the Aga Khan supposedly passed up the inaugural Arlington Million in Chicago, at the time the richest race in the world.[30] This was not true, according to Richard Baerlein, an author and friend of the Aga Khan IV, who said that the Arlington Million would not have fit into Shergar's training schedule in any event.[31]

Unsuccessful in court, Murty waged an intensive media campaign. He argued in the press that the Boussac horses belonged to him and that he should be allowed to export them from France to the United States; that the French courts were prejudiced against him in favor of the Aga Khan; and that a gift of three Boussac stallions to the French National Stud by the Aga Khan amounted to an unfair influence on the decision makers.

For good measure, Murty reportedly stormed into the office of a low-level official in the Ministry of Agriculture and slammed a bloody horse's leg down onto the man's desk.[32]

Losing a protracted legal battle over the horses acquired from Boussac certainly could have given Murty sufficient grounds to wage a feud with the Aga Khan, and his volatile behavior, if reports are true, raises questions about his judgment. Murty consistently denied any involvement in Shergar's theft. There never was any evidence linking him to the theft of Shergar that went beyond speculation and innuendo, and Murty gradually drifted off reporters' radars.

# 14

# The Pathologist and the Skull

A week after Shergar went missing, across the border in Northern Ireland, a gruesome discovery was made—a crudely severed hind leg of a horse turned up in County Tyrone. Paddy McCann, described as a "local horse enthusiast," said that it was the leg of a Thoroughbred. With concern growing about the fate of Shergar, the find drew the attention of the authorities in both Northern Ireland and the Republic.[1]

Initial reports suggested that the leg was from a recently dismembered horse that had been "professionally shod," bolstering speculation that the leg belonged to Shergar. A cursory examination proved that the leg did not belong to the missing Epsom Derby winner, however. The leg lacked Shergar's distinctive white ankle.[2]

The County Tyrone mystery leg, along with the body of a dead horse that washed ashore at the Dublin docks, were among the first pieces of physical evidence with possible links to Shergar. As time passed and decomposition took its toll, uncovered remains generally have been parts of a skeleton or smaller bits of bone. When suspected remains show up, as they still do from time to time, the final arbiter when it comes to a positive identification often is Des Leadon, a well-known veterinary surgeon and clinical pathologist at the Irish Equine Centre in County Kildare.

The identification process for suspected remains can be simple and straightforward. A cursory visual examination can be sufficient to discount many items. The County Tyrone leg was missing an easily identifiable characteristic, for example, and the horse's body discovered at the Dublin docks was that of a draft horse and obviously not Shergar. A closer call might require a more comprehensive physical examination of suspected remains.

One of the most promising pieces of evidence was discovered in spring 2000 when Tralee Urban District Council member Tommy Foley uncovered a horse's skull during an annual cleanup project in County Kerry. The skull was wrapped in a rotting coal sack and had what appeared to be a pair of bullet holes in the forehead. There was some speculation that the skull might be Shergar's because of a tenuous three-way connection between the town of Tralee, Garda informer Sean O'Callaghan, who was born in Tralee, and the Irish Republican Army.

"I found the head in a sack . . . when I was cleaning up," Foley said.

> There's a drop of 100 feet to the river bed, and the climb was so steep that we were on our hands and knees as we cleared the area of old bottles, washing machines, and other rubbish. It hadn't been cleared for 14 years, and I found a sack under a rock with briars and overgrowth covering it.
>
> The sack had obviously been there a considerable time because it disintegrated when I picked it up. In it was a horse's head, and there were two bullet holes through the forehead. It was obvious to me that the sack had been deliberately concealed under the rock. If it had been thrown there, it would have rolled down into the valley.[3]

Not surprisingly, Des Leadon was called in to evaluate the skull. A DNA test might be necessary to either confirm or rule out a positive identification, Leadon said, but that would be a last resort. "I have been dealing with Shergar episodes since the 1980s, and when we get a skull we have to begin with an evaluation of what we have got. We first have to confirm that it is fact equine material, and that is not easy when the skull is decomposed and fragmented." Severe decomposition did not seem to be a problem with the Tralee skull.

> Sometimes in the past, it has proved to be bovine material, and in other cases we have found it to belong to something that would have been more at home pulling a dairy cart than

appearing on a racecourse. If the answer is that this could be nothing to do with Shergar, we will be able to give it relatively quickly.

But if it's a case where absolute confirmation is going to be involved, it will take quite a long time. We would need to be scientifically certain and we would have to be right, because the police would want it for part of their forensic evidence.

A quick examination of the skull showed that it belonged to a horse substantially younger than Shergar would have been in 1983 when he was stolen. "This could not, therefore, be the skull of Shergar," Leadon said, "and we do not need to proceed any further or carry out any further laboratory tests. We know from the anatomical features of this individual that . . . he is definitely not Shergar."[4]

A DNA test was not needed for the Tralee skull, or for any of the other suspected remains that have come Leadon's way. Although a DNA profile has never been developed for Shergar, there is the potential to prepare one if necessary to augment a physical forensic examination, according to John Flynn, past head of Weatherbys Ireland blood-typing laboratory in County Kildare.

Discussing the identification of equine remains exhumed from a grave in Donegal in 1996, Flynn explained the complicated steps necessary to conduct a DNA test:

> The potential is there for a 100%, unequivocal identification that the carcass [discovered in Donegal] is that of Shergar— but there is a very long and difficult time ahead. There will have to be a complete and thorough testing procedure and we will be relying on how the owners of Shergar's offspring respond.
>
> A DNA profile has to be built from the carcass and then matched with the DNA profiles from other material, sources of hair which have come to light and Shergar's offspring. If all three were to match up, that would amount to overwhelming

evidence, but the material is between 12 and 13 years old and it is a very protracted and uncertain business.[5]

The results of any examination conducted on the remains from Donegal were not publicized.

When Flynn spoke of "sources of hair which have come to light," he likely was referring to a few hairs two veterinary students supposedly plucked from Shergar's tail as souvenirs during a visit to Ballymany when Shergar still was alive.[6] In an email message to the author on August 21, 2017, Flynn explained: "Lots of stories circulated regarding hair samples, but there was no DNA profile developed for Shergar."

Shergar vanished on Tuesday, February 8, 1983, snatched from his stall at Ballymany Stud and driven away into a cold and rainy night, never to be seen again. Since then, the horse's remains have become a holy grail of sorts, and the search for them a noble quest in Ireland. Although official efforts to locate the remains of the Epsom Derby winner ended decades ago, the search undoubtedly will continue. The lingering question, though, is where to look.

IRA man Sean O'Callaghan said that the thieves took Shergar north to County Leitrim, near the border with Northern Ireland. That would have been a logical escape route for the Provos. If O'Callaghan is correct that Shergar was killed shortly after he was stolen, it stands to reason that his remains were buried in County Leitrim or at least in that general area.[7] The police and thousands of farmers searched the whole of the Republic, including the border region, without success, however.

A large cadre of psychics divined after the theft that Shergar could be found in every county across Ireland. Chief Superintendent Murphy encouraged their unconventional assistance, a decision that he probably came to regret. When he mentioned at a press conference that more than fifty "clairvoyants, diviners, and psychic persons" had been in contact with his office offering to help recover Shergar, the reporters laughed at him.

Undeterred by the criticism, Murphy defended his unconventional approach. The Garda searched in County Galway, on the western coast of the Republic, Murphy told reporters, "because of information we have received from different clairvoyants, diviners, and psychic persons that the animal is there. We cannot ignore all of this, irrespective of what you might think of them. They could come up with the answer."[8]

None of those tips panned out, and most of the psychics' suggestions, even if they had turned out to be accurate, were too general to be helpful. There was some consensus among the psychics that Shergar was being hidden "west of the River Shannon."[9] Rising in Northern Ireland, the River Shannon flows southwest through eleven counties in the Republic, from County Cavan in the border region past the city of Limerick and on to the Atlantic Ocean. The River Shannon divides the western counties of Ireland from the eastern ones, but the predictions still were not specific enough to be useful to searchers.

As of this writing, every attempt to locate Shergar or the horse's remains has failed. But what if everyone so far has been looking in the wrong place?

# 15

# The Stallion Probes

The mystery of Shergar's disappearance was the last thing on Michael Payton's mind when the lawyer settled down on a late September evening to watch an episode of *Horizon,* a popular BBC series that was ushering in a new season that night. Almost eight months had passed since Shergar was stolen from Ballymany Stud, insurance carriers had paid out millions of pounds for theft claims a few months later, and public interest in the missing Epsom Derby winner had shifted to other things.[1]

Shergar was gone, end of story—time to move on.

*Horizon* is a quirky series with topics that run the gamut from science to philosophy and beyond. The September 26, 1983, program Payton was watching—*The Case of E.S.P.*—moved from controversial parapsychology experiments performed by Dr. B. J. Rhine at Duke University during the 1930s to possible applications for remote viewing, a form of long-distance clairvoyance. Remote viewing, many researchers believe, is a technique that allows individuals to "source non-local information," or, in plain English, to "see" or sense things that are physically located somewhere else.

The possible applications for remote viewing are endless. The "thing" being viewed might be anything and the "somewhere else" might be anywhere, from the body of a missing girl in Pennsylvania to the wreckage of an airplane lost in the mountains to a secret military facility hidden somewhere in Russia to a ship resting on the bottom of the ocean. Remote viewing is not always successful, but when it works, the results can boggle the mind.

One of the people interviewed for the *Horizon* program was

Stephan A. Schwartz, a young researcher who retired from a civilian post as special assistant for research and analysis to the chief of naval operations under Admirals Elmo Zumwalt and James Holloway to start the Mobius Group. During his tenure with Zumwalt and Holloway, Schwartz reviewed and analyzed data for his bosses and drafted speeches, articles, and congressional testimony. The navy at the time was involved in experimental testing to evaluate whether extrasensory perception could be a viable method of communication with submarines. Schwartz was privy to classified data about those experiments and to information about similar investigations being conducted by the Soviets. He organized Mobius as a private and independent research organization to investigate remote viewing and possible commercial uses for the process.

By late 1983, when the *Horizon* program was broadcast, Schwartz already had a record of successful archaeological searches utilizing remote viewing. Among them were an expedition to Alexandria, Egypt, which resulted in the first modern mapping of the ancient Eastern Harbor of Alexandria and numerous discoveries: centuries-old shipwrecks, Mark Antony's palace, Cleopatra's palace complex, and the remains of the lighthouse at Pharos, one of the seven wonders of the ancient world. Schwartz also was involved in the Deep Quest Project, an experiment off the coast of Santa Catalina Island utilizing remote viewing and a submarine to discover a previously unknown shipwreck.[2]

Payton knew nothing about remote viewing, but his interest was piqued when, toward the end of the *Horizon* broadcast, the program narrator suggested that "for $5,000 Mobius will help you solve a murder." He was sold on the idea of contacting Schwartz when he learned that Mobius remote viewers had successfully located the body of a missing girl—a murder victim, as the case turned out—for the Lancaster County Police Department in Pennsylvania. Local police were directed to the location of the girl's body by remote viewers working for Mobius at the group's offices across the country, in Los Angeles. The authorities had provided Mobius with a photograph of the girl, and two of the Mobius viewers had identified both the location of the girl's body and the cause of her death. Maybe Schwartz could work the same magic for locating Shergar, Payton thought to himself.

Remote viewing is not magic, of course, although at times it might seem that way.[3] There is evidence that remote viewing works and evidence that it does not. Nevertheless, governments in the United States and Russia have devoted substantial support to parapsychology research since the end of World War II.[4]

A psychic is a human "remote sensing device with a signal-to-noise problem," Schwartz explained on the *Horizon* program. "It is not a cure-all, not a magic bullet, not weird, but something to be studied"—and something to be used.[5]

Reaching out to Schwartz and his Mobius colleagues was a long shot, Payton knew, and people might think he was crazy for suggesting it. An Garda Síochána chief superintendent James Murphy had utilized "clairvoyants and other psychic persons" during the Shergar investigation to no avail, and he was ridiculed for it in the press.[6] Misgivings aside, the same question nagged Payton: what if the remote viewers really *could* find Shergar's remains? Associated with Clyde & Co., a prominent international law firm based in London, Payton was one of the lead counsels for underwriters at Lloyd's of London during the legal wrangling that arose after Shergar was stolen. He also had been serving as an unofficial "clearinghouse for all the ideas about where Shergar was, what happened to him, the nuts, the sightings. We had to follow up all the leads. It would be negligent to not do so." What was the worst that could happen if he made contact with Schwartz?

With some reluctance, Payton ran the idea by Terry Hall, the lead underwriter for livestock coverage at Lloyd's. "We have to try this," Payton urged. Hall was noncommittal and said that Payton "would have to take it to the market," to get approval from the underwriters who insured Shergar.[7] One of those underwriters told Payton it was the "stupidest idea you've ever had," but the eventual consensus was "We'll do it, but we won't pay much."

Payton also talked with the Aga Khan. The lawyer was "jittery" about the meeting, but he got the go-ahead from the Aga Khan, who was grateful for anything that could be done. There was only one condition —that one of the Aga Khan's men, a retired Special Air Service (SAS) officer named David J. Walker, had to be involved.[8]

The initial contact with Mobius came in a letter dated October 3, 1983, from Clyde & Co., the London law firm that employed Payton. Schwartz, Randall J. De Mattei, the executive director of Mobius, and Payton met in London three weeks later, and in a letter from Clyde & Co. dated November 4, 1983, the terms of the arrangement were set out.

The contract was for £5,000, £3,000 in advance, with the following conditions: the investigation would be undertaken based on assumptions that Shergar (or, presumably, his remains) was in Ireland and that the horse was not being moved, and an agreement that the results of the investigation would remain confidential. The final requirement was necessary, the letter from Clyde & Co. explained, because the firm's clients "believe that the whole affair, including your contribution to its solution, is dynamite, and they wish us to keep as tight a control" as possible.

A subsequent letter confirmed the reimbursement for "reasonable" expenses. Those expenses, Schwartz already knew, would include a trip to Ireland.

Physical objects and photographs often are used to facilitate remote viewing sessions, and Schwartz requested from Payton items with a connection to Shergar. Payton, through an intermediary named Jeff Oliver, sent a sheaf of photographs and newspaper clippings, one of the shin boots worn by Shergar when he was in training, and several small pieces of thick felt from a saddle pad worn by the horse.

The package also included a grainy and slightly out of focus Polaroid photograph that showed a frightened and wide-eyed horse with a wide blaze that, from the left side at least, matched Shergar's distinctive white face (see photo in chapter 8). No details about the Polaroid image were included, and contact information for the person who supplied the material to Mobius, Jeff Oliver, has been lost over the years. The image matches the description of photographs reportedly provided as "proof" that Shergar was alive during negotiations with the supposed thieves, however, and it is reasonable to believe that was the original source of the Polaroid photograph sent to Mobius.[9]

The requested items arrived at the Mobius office around December 1, 1983. The first remote viewing sessions began shortly thereafter in Los Angeles, winding up in January 1984.

There typically are two components to remote viewing: off-site "probes" and, when practical, on-site fieldwork. In the former, remote viewers try to describe a location or scene, sometimes with the aid of a photograph or physical object that has a connection to the target. In the latter, the remote viewers travel to a site, or sites, in an attempt to verify their impressions.

Remote viewing is not a group exercise. The best results are a consensus, derived from several individual sessions at different times involving different viewers. For the Shergar probes, the initial remote sessions were conducted with nine remote viewers. The Shergar sessions were generally conducted in one-on-one meetings with the remote viewer and an interviewer, usually Schwartz or De Mattei. Some sessions were conducted by telephone and on a few occasions remote viewers provided written comments after being provided materials by mail.

A basic outline for the sessions was provided by De Mattei, although expecting adherence to an outline was optimistic and ultimately impossible. The sessions tended to stray from the plans depending on the responses from the viewers. But based on De Mattei's proposed outline, the primary goal of the sessions was to "identify present location and condition of the Stallion" and provide other desirable information such as how Shergar was guarded, the description of vehicles at the location, and descriptions of the people involved.

The initial viewing sessions generally started with a brief introduction setting out the problem—a missing horse in Ireland. The remote viewers then were given a package containing a map of Ireland, items relating to Shergar (the shin boot and saddle pad felt), and the photographs. The maps were standard tourist maps, reproduced in black and white to guard against a viewer being influenced by colors in one area or another.

"This stallion is missing," the interviewer might begin, sliding the photographs across the table, "and we would like to learn its present location. Please spread the map out in front of you and mark an area where you feel that the stallion might be found." The maps from all of the remote viewers participating in the probes would be collected and the marked areas transferred to a single "composite map" that would help guide the on-site fieldwork.

Other questions that might be asked included the viewer's perceptions of the area marked on the map, such as the appearance of the location and any prominent or unique identifying features, including sensations of sound, smell, touch, and maybe even taste; the physical condition of the horse; descriptions of the people who had the horse; and details of the theft, the perpetrators, their vehicles.

The initial remote viewing sessions, completed in December 1983 and January 1984, produced results that sometimes seemed overly general, confusing, and contradictory. In the context of consensus, however, several themes emerged.

Seven of the nine remote viewers thought that Shergar was alive, although the responses regarding his physical condition varied. Two of the viewers thought the horse was dead.

One of the most difficult aspects of remote viewing, Schwartz explained, is attaching a specific time frame to images sensed by a viewer. Impressions that Shergar was alive when the initial sessions were conducted, for example, seem to be contradicted by subsequent evidence indicating that the horse was killed within a few days after he went missing.

That does not necessarily mean, however, that the information from the remote viewers that Shergar was still alive was incorrect, Schwartz said. Such a discrepancy might arise if a viewer had a strong impression of Shergar being alive, but in a different—in this case earlier—temporal context. Strong impressions, Schwartz is saying, might linger.

Six people thought that Shergar's appearance had been altered in some way to avoid detection. Other responses led to the conclusion that if Shergar still were alive, however, he most likely was being hidden inside a barn or other structure.

Seven viewers commented on how Shergar was being moved. Five favored ground transportation; two thought that Shergar had been moved by air. Schwartz, De Mattei, and project analyst Richard S. Thompson later discounted the air carrier scenario.

Four viewers thought that Shergar was being held somewhere "close" to Ballymany, although estimates of the actual distance varied widely.

Six viewers described an old and dark wooden structure, with natural and unpainted wood exposed, perhaps a collapsed roof, and possible evidence of intentional camouflage. The other three descriptions were of buildings similar to those at Ballymany Stud.

A majority of the viewers described the area surrounding the barn as "well kept" and believed that the general locale was the site of many horse farms.

Six people described a house, probably white with a roof and trim in a different color, near the disused barn.

Five people described fences, although none were the traditional white board fences often associated with horse farms.

The viewers described an old, small, and nondescript village in the vicinity of the target location, with an unusually ornate church and at least one pub where the individuals guarding Shergar spent time.

General impressions from the remote viewers, like those provided by Chief Superintendent Murphy's psychics, were seldom helpful. Every village of any size in Ireland has a church (in the Republic of Ireland, most likely a Catholic church) and a pub or two. Impressions that Shergar was near a village with a church and a pub would not eliminate many locations.

What Schwartz and De Mattei wanted were descriptions or impressions that would be specific to a particular area or location. Several of the remote viewers drew sketches of their impressions, which tended to be more useful than verbal descriptions. Most valuable of all were impressions of unique features likely to be found in only one location, ones that a remote viewer would have no reason to fabricate, either intentionally or inadvertently through a process Swartz called "analytical overlay." Unconsciously associating a "barn" with a probe involving a horse would be an example of analytical overlay.

One unique impression was that of Shergar being held in a barn on a well-defined estate, with a "stone bridge standing over nothing in the middle of a field." That image would drive the on-site fieldwork to come.

The "map exercise," in which the remote viewers indicated on a map of Ireland a general area of interest, also appeared inconclusive. At the end of the initial sessions, the maps were placed onto a large light table. The indicated areas on the individual maps then were traced onto a single composite map. The composite map, like the session results, showed little apparent consensus. Analysis of the results would take time, some two hundred hours to review the maps, the interview transcripts, notes, and drawings made by the viewers.

Inconsistent results produced by different remote viewers were neither discouraging nor even a surprise to Schwartz. While remote viewing can, at times, identify a specific location, he said, the process is equally valuable—often more valuable—in eliminating potential areas for search. Results from the remote viewing sessions and the map exercise identified several areas of interest, but equally important, they eliminated from the search area vast parts of Ireland.

Schwartz, De Mattei, and two remote viewers, Hella Hammid and Keith Harary, flew to London in late March 1984 to begin their fieldwork. Hammid had been involved in the Shergar probes since the start, while Harary was seeing the material for the first time. Before leaving London for Ireland, they visited first with Payton and later with the Aga Khan IV and David J. Walker, the SAS man who would monitor the investigation and provide assistance if necessary.

Hella Hammid, an artist, photographer, and gifted remote viewer, often worked with Schwartz at Mobius. She was featured on the *Horizon* program undergoing a remote viewing test in which she successfully performed an "outbounder-beacon" experiment. The outbounder-beacon protocol was developed by parapsychology researchers at the Stanford Research Institute (SRI) in an attempt to devise a reliable and repeatable procedure for testing remote viewing. In a typical experiment, a team of researchers would select a sealed envelope from among several at SRI. They would open the envelope after leaving the facility and drive to the location identified in the envelope, usually a nearby landmark. At a preset time, while the "outbounders" were at the randomly selected site, a remote viewer at SRI would attempt to describe or identify the target site.[10] In the *Horizon* test, the outbounder team drove to a randomly selected Los Angeles location unknown to Hammid. She then successfully described the location.

Payton was intrigued by Hammid's apparent remote viewing prowess, but skeptical. When the two met for the first time in London, the attorney asked Hammid to perform a test for him. "Where am I going to be tomorrow?" he asked.

Hammid, who never had been to England before and who knew nothing about Payton, indicated the city of Birmingham on a map. She said that she saw the attorney in a large, imposing building, situated on a grassy knoll.

Payton was supposed to attend a funeral the following day, at a place he never had been to before. He got lost driving to the funeral, but finally found his way to the service. It was being held in a large building, sitting at the top of a grassy knoll. Payton was stunned by the accuracy of Hammid's prediction. "When I walked into the funeral," Payton recalled, "people said that I looked like I'd just seen a ghost."

Payton might have thought that remote viewing was nothing more than a clever parlor trick before, but meeting Hammid in person changed his mind. He took a chance with Mobius as a last resort, Payton recalled, because "everything else had failed." In the end, though, working with Schwartz, Hammid, and the others from the Mobius Group turned out to be a "great privilege."

From London, the Mobius researchers and remote viewers flew to Dublin for on-site research, arriving on March 29. The two-car caravan—

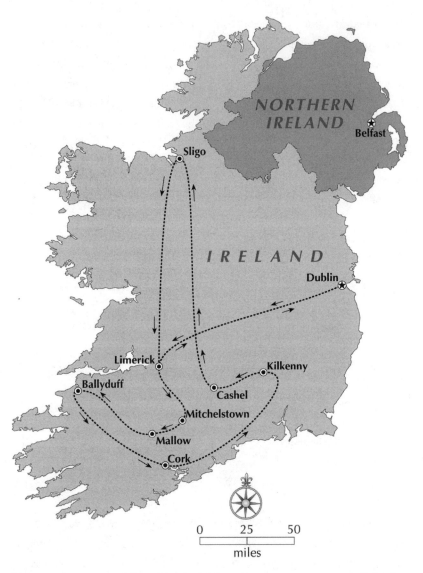

The meandering route followed by the Mobius Group remote viewers in Ireland in 1984.

Schwartz and Hammid in one rental car, De Mattei and Harary in a second—made its way southwest to Limerick, farther south to Mitchelstown and Mallow in the Blackwater area, then to Ballyduff on the southwestern coast. From Ballyduff, they drove to Cork in the south, then to Kilkenny and Cashel, both near Tipperary, where Coolmore Stud is located.

So far, the teams had stayed in the southern half of the Republic of Ireland, the general area indicated by a majority of the remote viewers during the advance map sessions conducted in California. From Cashel they drove north to Sligo, near the bay where Lord Mountbatten had been assassinated, then back south to Limerick and on to Dublin for the trip home.[11]

"There is a big jump from paperwork in the office to fieldwork," De Mattei said. "We set up parameters before we got there with a general idea of where we were going to search. We were trying to narrow down the search areas in advance. We'd go into one of the marked zones that we'd already identified and just drive around. We'd wait for the respondents in the car to give the driver directions. We also conducted probes while we were in Ireland, all four of us in the same car."

De Mattei explained, "Narrowing down the right zones might be the most important thing that we do" before staring the fieldwork. He compared the process to a blood type. "You can't use a basic blood type to identify an individual, but you can use a blood type to eliminate large segments of the population."

Some perceptions, such as a barn with a collapsed roof, turned out to be far too general to be useful. "When we got to Ireland," De Mattei said, "we found out that half the barns in the country were dilapidated."

It was outside Mallow, some twenty miles north of Cork on the southern coast of Ireland, that the Mobius team found what they were looking for, a guiding feature identified in the remote viewing sessions so unique that there could be only one: "a stone bridge standing over nothing in the middle of a field."

It was dark and rainy the first night in Mallow.

The Aga Khan's man, David Walker, took charge as the Mobius team staked out the stone bridge property. De Mattei recalled that Walker was "very professional, even if he didn't believe us."

Earlier in the day, when Schwartz and Hammid had stopped their car in front of the estate where the stone bridge was located, men came rushing out of a guardhouse near the entrance to the property and confronted them in the roadway. They were the sort of men, Schwartz recalled, who you knew on sight could be dangerous. Schwartz and Hammid pretended to be visiting university professors lost during an excursion and, with a map spread out on the hood of the car, they got directions from the men, who were helpful once they determined that the visitors posed no threat. Schwartz and Hammid drove away and did not stop there again that day.[12]

Schwartz, De Mattei, and Walker returned that night. As their car rolled slowly past the property, Walker told Schwartz, who was driving, not to stop. "They can see the headlights from the house," Schwartz recalled being instructed, "and headlights don't stop here."

Schwartz slowed the vehicle as Walker opened the door and rolled out onto the wet pavement. They picked him up a few hours later, soaking wet, with an expression on his face that De Mattei called "reality vertigo. A lot of what we'd told him in advance about the estate turned out to be true," De Mattei recalled. "He was struck by the accuracy."

Both De Mattei and Walker slipped onto the property the next night, which again was dark and raining, perfect for trespassing. They climbed a high fence by the road and were walking up a small knoll when Walker motioned for De Mattei to stop. The SAS man was a professional at this sort of thing, and he had spent the previous night memorizing the layout of the land, De Mattei realized.

The men moved past cattle, some sleeping, some snorting—a "looming presence," recalled De Mattei, who had little experience with livestock. He was close to panic when one of the cows bumped him in the dark. De Mattei flicked on the flashlight he was carrying, but he had it turned 180 degrees. The light hit his eyes and nearly blinded him. He looked for Walker, but the man had already made his way to the other side of the barn. The door was chained, but Walker could shine his light inside.

"The barn was empty," De Mattei said. "In the back of the barn there was a wall that didn't go all the way across the aisle. You couldn't see everything behind the wall, where there might have been a stall where a horse could have been hidden, but Walker was certain that there was not a horse there. We didn't find the horse, and we went home."

Schwartz was disappointed but not discouraged. More than three decades later, both he and De Mattei still have faith in the process. One of the dilemmas presented by remote viewing, as noted above, is that it often is impossible to match a viewer's perceptions and a particular time frame. The fact that Shergar was not present at the stone bridge farm when the searchers got there does not mean that he had not been kept there at some point in the past.

Walker had walked out of the first planning meeting between Schwartz and the Aga Khan and Schwartz still remembers the man's "hostile body posture" at the time.

Recalling conversations that he had with Walker about the Mobius Group, Michael Payton said that the SAS man told him that he "didn't believe in any of that nonsense" when he first met Schwartz. "I wouldn't be here if the Aga Khan had not said to help," he told Payton. Walker was totally skeptical at first, Payton recalled, until he spent time riding around with the group from Mobius.

Ireland is crisscrossed with narrow, winding roads. Sometimes when Walker was with Schwartz and Hammid, Payton recalled the man saying, Hammid would make spur-of-the-moment comments about what lay ahead. They were on the right road, Hammid might say, because there is a church around the next bend—and a mile or so later, around a corner, there would be the church. Payton said that Walker was especially impressed with Hammid's ability to know what was coming around the next corner, even though she never had been on the road before.[13]

A few days after Schwartz and the others returned to California, in a message to Schwartz dated April 17, 1984, David Walker laid out his objectives. The search for Shergar, which Schwartz might reasonably have assumed was over, had taken a new turn.

There were two prime objectives, Walker wrote. The first was to determine how, where, and at whose hands the horse had died—almost a year after Shergar was stolen, the assumption was that the horse was dead—and to put together a strong enough case to prove those things in court. The purpose was twofold, to allow the claim under the Malicious Injuries Act to proceed and also to "remove lingering doubts within and without the Bloodstock Industry (which I do not suffer from myself!) as to what happened to the horse and who was behind it. In order to produce such evidence in court, we almost certainly need the dead body of the horse." The second objective was to punish the people involved.

Walker explained that the identities of some of the men who stole Shergar were known, but that there was insufficient evidence to convict them. The police seemed uninterested in interrogating those individuals, he said, even though they had been identified to the authorities. Walker suggested three possible ways to proceed.

A "slow and painstaking" investigation might result in the "serendipitous discovery" of an important clue, but Walker thought that the cost and time would be prohibitive. He also thought that there was little chance of success.

The second option was through the resources of Mobius, but that approach had already proved unsuccessful.

The third option was similar to the first, although without help from the Garda. "I believe the best chance we have of discovering the truth is by getting ourselves into positions where we can listen to the intimate discussions of those who were involved, and hope that eventually they will let slip something that we need." (It was not clear from the correspondence whether this eavesdropping was to be conducted by conventional methods or through extrasensory perception.)

To help with the last option, Walker suggested some questions that the Mobius Group might want to consider:

• Information about the veterinary surgeon who was involved. Where does he come from? Is he married? Children? What age group is he? (Walker probably was referring to a veterinarian who was rumored to be part of the gang that stole Shergar but who backed out at the last minute, not Stan Cosgrove.)

- Information about an "insider" who provided information to the gang. (The possibility of an inside job had been considered but dismissed, according to Julian Lloyd.)
- Information about a possible "French connection" (see chapter 13).
- Information about the "operational organizer" of the theft.
- Information about the location of the horse trailer used to transport Shergar.

These requests were well beyond the scope of the original agreement Schwartz struck with Michael Payton, but he moved forward anyway. The final report from Mobius, "The Stallion Probe IV," eventually was completed, and the 256-page document was sent to Payton late in 1985.

The report first concluded that the scenario presented when Mobius was hired, that the theft of Shergar was "an IRA operation, although peculiar in some ways," was correct, but incomplete. Subsequent probes and research, including the trip to Ireland early in 1984, led Schwartz and his colleagues to expand their original reports to include discussions of possible motives and detailed information about some of the individuals involved.

An individual identified in the report as the "Mastermind" coordinated the theft of Shergar to "to fulfill a grudge" against the Aga Khan. The report suggested that while revenge was the overriding motive, the Mastermind also intended to use Shergar, or at least the horse's semen, for his own breeding programs, for both Thoroughbreds and non-Thoroughbreds.

The "Lieutenant" is identified as an IRA "officer" retained by the Mastermind to hire men from the lower ranks of the IRA who would carry out the theft. He would serve as the field commander of the operation.

The report speculates that Shergar's theft had been in the planning stages for six months to a year, initiated by a small group of Muslims who thought it necessary to try to limit the role of the Aga Khan in the power structure of Islam. The "Council," the name given to the group by Mobius, feared a direct attack on the Aga Khan would create sympathy for the Ismaili Muslim followers. The Council reasoned that an attack on Shergar, which they viewed as a "costly western toy," would not have such an effect.

The Mastermind was identified in the report as a "non-English-man, in the upper echelons of English society" who knew the Aga Khan and who was involved in Thoroughbred racing. The remote viewers provided a detailed physical description of the Mastermind along with information about his London office and a description of the Lieutenant. The ransom calls, the report concluded, were never about ransom, but were made to create confusion and to make it clear to the Aga Khan that he was the actual target.

"In conclusion," the "Executive Summary" to the report said, "we feel that this case can be taken further, mostly by careful traditional policework. Whether that is an appropriate commitment of energy and time is beyond the scope of this report."

In a letter to Stephan Schwartz dated December 5, 1985, Michael Payton reported that there would be no follow-up. The Aga Khan, Payton explained, "most definitely wishes not to be reminded about the affair, and the other Shareholders have no continuing interest. As for the Underwriters at Lloyd's, they remain fascinated, but have largely lost their passion, anyway to the extent of not wanting to spend their Members' money unless it could be shown to be justified."

More than three decades later, Payton confirmed that no further investigations were ever conducted based on information in "The Stallion Probe IV."

The last official search for Shergar was over.

"Just because we were unsuccessful," Schwartz said of the Mobius effort to locate Shergar, "doesn't mean that we were wrong."

# Epilogue

How good was Shergar?

A contemporaneous assessment of his racing prowess is straightforward. Finding Shergar's place in history, both as a runner and as a sire, is more complicated, and far more speculative.

There can be little doubt that Shergar was the best of his generation as a three-year-old. He won the Epsom Derby by ten lengths, a winning margin never equaled before or since. Despite a relatively slow time for the race and a disappointing fourth-place finish in his last start, in the St. Leger, Shergar was the consensus choice among a group of international handicappers as the best European runner in 1981. Their totals buoyed by Shergar's record as the season's leading earner that year, the Aga Khan was England's leading breeder and owner and Michael Stoute was the leading trainer.[1]

Michael Church, a prolific author and noted Epsom Derby historian, picked Shergar as the best Derby winner of the 1980s.[2] Shifting context to the twentieth century, and providing fodder for endless argument among his fans and detractors, John Randall and Tony Morris ranked Shergar eighteenth among the "World Top 200 Flat Champions" with a Timeform rating of 140.[3]

The century's "top twenty" in the estimation of Randall and Morris were:

1. Sea-Bird (winner of the Epsom Derby and the Prix de l'Arc de Triomphe, with a Timeform rating of 145)
2. Secretariat (Horse of the Year; winner of the US Triple Crown in 1973)
3. Ribot (undefeated in sixteen starts, two-time winner of the Prix de l'Arc de Triomphe, with a Timeform rating of 142)
4. Brigadier Gerard (a classic winner with seventeen victories

in eighteen races; Horse of the Year in Great Britain, with a Timeform rating of 144)

5. Citation (Horse of the Year; winner of the US Triple Crown in 1948)

6. Hyperion (winner of the Epsom Derby, the Prince of Wales Stakes, and the St. Leger)

7. Tudor Minstrel (top-ranked juvenile in England; classic winner as a three-year-old)

8. Mill Reef (won twelve of fourteen races, including the Epsom Derby, the King George VI and Queen Elizabeth Diamond Stakes, and the Prix de l'Arc de Triomphe)

9. Spectacular Bid (American champion at two, three, and four; winner of the Kentucky Derby and Preakness Stakes)

10. Bayardo (winner in twenty-two of twenty-five races during three seasons; leading earner in Britain in 1909)

11. Seattle Slew (Horse of the Year; winner of the US Triple Crown in 1977)

12. Pharis (major winner in France in 1939)

13. Native Dancer (winner in twenty-one of twenty-two races, including the Preakness and Belmont Stakes; champion at two, three, and four)

14. Affirmed (Horse of the Year; winner of the US Triple Crown in 1978)

15. Nijinsky II (English Triple Crown winner in 1970; Horse of the Year)

16. Dancing Brave (winner of the Prix de l'Arc de Triomphe in 1986)

17. Vaguely Noble (major winner in France, with a Timeform rating of 140)

18. Shergar

19. Windsor Lad (winner of the Epsom Derby and St. Leger in 1934)

20. Abernant (champion sprinter in 1949 and 1950)[4]

Sea-Bird's 145 was the highest rating handed out by Timeform since the organization began collecting and analyzing data and appraising the comparative merits of Thoroughbreds in the late 1940s—the highest, that is, until Frankel. Unbeaten in fourteen starts spread over three seasons (2010–2012), Frankel won eight Group 1 races for owner/breeder Prince Khalid Abdullah. The horse earned a Timeform rating of 147 after an impressive eleven-length victory in the Group 1 Queen Anne Stakes at Ascot, the same rating he was assigned upon his retirement at the end of his four-year-old season.[5]

Michael Church acknowledged the problem of trying to sort out the relative merits of horses from different eras:

> It is difficult to compare horses two hundred years apart, not by times but against the standard of their time. For me Ormonde, the 1886 [British] Triple Crown winner, is probably the best Derby winner and then Gladiateur [1865 Derby winner]. As a rough guide, Shergar beat a very moderate field, while two years earlier Troy beat a field of future Group 1 winners.
>
> Also it is doubtful if Shergar, by Great Nephew, would have been a success at stud—Grundy [winner of the 1975 Epsom Derby] by Great Nephew was a failure and sent to Japan.[6]

Jonathan Irwin, head of the Goffs sales company when Shergar was stolen, shares the view that Shergar's potential as a sire might have been overrated. "The ironic thing is," Irwin said, "and you mustn't take this the wrong way, but I think the IRA did us all a lot of good. He [Shergar] only had one crop and most of them couldn't run faster than a fat man. As a stallion, things were looking really, really grim."[7]

Shergar was stolen a few days before the start of the 1983 breeding season and the racing success, or perceived lack thereof, of his only crop of foals is at best a glimpse into how he might have fared over the years as a sire. It is safe to assume, though, that Shergar was given the best chance for success by shareholders who provided a book of high-quality mares for the stallion's first season at stud.

Bred to forty-four mares in 1982, Shergar was represented by thirty-six registered foals, thirty-five of which were named foals, from his only crop—seventeen colts and nineteen fillies. Three of Shergar's progeny (two fillies and a colt) won Group races, another two runners won lesser stakes, and two were stakes-placed in Group 1 events.[8]

The best of the crop was Authaal. Produced from the Nijinsky II mare Galletto, Authaal won the Irish St. Leger (Group 1) at The Curragh and the Queen Elizabeth Stakes (Group 1) and the Underwood Stakes (Group 1) in Australia.

Authaal was the first of Shergar's foals to be sold at auction, as a weanling at Goffs International Breeding Stock Sale on November 20, 1983. The colt would have attracted the attention of high-end buyers on the strength of his pedigree alone—sired by a record-setting Derby winner out of a stakes-winning mare sired by another Derby winner—but the notoriety of Shergar's theft nine months earlier added a circus-like dimension to an already electric atmosphere at the sale grounds at Kill, near Dublin. Security was high before the sale, when the colt's movements were shrouded in secrecy, and increased even more after he arrived at Goffs.

At least eight camera crews and dozens of reporters roamed the grounds and there were standing room–only crowds any time Hip No. 303 was taken out of his stall and later in the sales pavilion when the colt was led into the ring. Everyone, it seemed, wanted a look at the son of Shergar.

Jonathan Irwin, managing director of Goffs at the time, predicted lofty prices for Authaal and for his dam, Galletto, which was catalogued for sale earlier in the session in foal to Alydar. Second to Affirmed in each of his Triple Crown victories in 1978, Alydar already was the sire of stakes winners Althea and Miss Oceana from his first crop of foals. Valentine Lamb, who served as editor of the *Irish Field* for thirty-three years, said the Goffs sale included "the best collection of foals and mares ever to be offered in Ireland.[9]

Authaal, the first foal sired by Shergar to be sold at public auction, as a weanling at Goffs in November 1983. (Courtesy of Goffs)

Authaal in the Goffs sales ring in November 1983, where he was sold as a weanling for 325,000 guineas ($374,400). A record-priced auction yearling the next year, Authaal won the Irish St. Leger in 1986. (Courtesy of Goffs)

Irwin's and Lamb's optimism was well placed. Bred in Kentucky by Robert Sangster's Swettenham Stud and several partners and consigned by Tommy Stack's Thomastown Castle Stud, Authaal exceeded all expectations.

Bidding for the colt started at 100,000 Irish guineas ($115,200) and moved steadily upward for three minutes, passing the European auction record for a weanling set earlier in the sale by a colt from the same consignment (290,000 guineas, or $334,080). The successful bid, 325,000 guineas ($374,400) paid by the British Bloodstock Agency's Joss Collins on behalf of an American syndicate, was a new record. Collins said that he was not at liberty to identify the buyers, but he said that they were a syndicate of owners from America and Europe.[10]

Galletto, the colt's dam, sold for 500,000 guineas ($576,000).

Authaal proved to be a remarkably good investment despite his record price as a weanling. Half a year later he went through the Goffs sales ring again, this time in the yearling consignment of Timmy Hyde's Camas Park Stud. Bloodstock agent Tote Cherry-Downes won a spirited bidding duel against Vincent O'Brien, who had trained Galletto, to get the colt for Sheikh Mohammed bin Rashid Maktoum. The price—$3,372,490—was far and away the highest ever for a yearling sold at auction in Europe. When Authaal won the Irish St. Leger by five lengths in 1986, he became the first Group 1 winner in England, Ireland, or France for Sheikh Mohammed.

Maysoon, a daughter of the High Top mare Triple First, won the Gainsborough Stud Fred Darling Stakes (Group 1), ran second in the One Thousand Guineas (Group 1) and third in the Epsom Oaks (Group 1), and placed in three other Group races. She was the top-weighted older mare over eleven to fourteen furlongs on the English Free Handicap in 1987. Maysoon was Shergar's leading earner, with a career total of $156,963.

Tashtiya, a daughter of the Silver Shark mare Tremogia, won the Princess Royal Stakes (Group 3) at Ascot.

Dolka, a daughter of the Kashmir II mare Dumka, and Tisn't, a son of the Clouet mare Zarabella, also won stakes.

Stakes-placed runners from Shergar's first crop were Sherkraine, a filly from the Targowice mare Ukraine Girl, and Shibil, a son of the Pago Pago mare Hilo Girl. Shibil was Shergar's first foal, born six days before the stallion was stolen from Ballymany Stud. He placed in the Derby Italiano (Group 1).

Shergar's only crop included four stakes winners and a colt that set auction records as a weanling and again as a yearling. Perhaps not a disappointing first crop, but certainly below expectations for a horse with Shergar's racing prowess.

Sadly, Michael Church may be correct when he suggests that "although Shergar is the biggest-margin Derby winner, I think his fame now is more to do with his kidnapping."[11]

Shergar was the first Epsom Derby winner—but not the last—for his owner and breeder, his trainer, and his jockey.

Through 2017, five homebreds from the Aga Khan Studs have won the Epsom Derby: Shergar (1981), Shahrastani (1986), Kahyasi (1988), Sinndar (2000), and Harzand (2016). The only breeder with more Epsom Derby winners to his credit is the third Earl of Egremont, with six winners from 1789 through 1831. There is no reason to think that the Aga Khan will not advance to the top of that list in the near future. "With the Aga's families," Sinndar's trainer John Oxx said, "you always feel entitled to believe that anything is possible."[12]

Michael Stoute became Sir Michael in 1999 when he was knighted by Queen Elizabeth II for his work promoting horse racing in his native Barbados. Sir Michael has trained five Epsom Derby winners: Shergar, Shahrastani (bred and owned by the Aga Khan and ridden by Shergar's jockey Walter Swinburn), Kris Kin (2003), North Light (2004), and Workforce (2010). Noted as England's leading trainer ten times, Sir Michael is the only trainer to win a classic race in each of five decades during the twentieth century.[13]

Nicknamed the Choirboy for a youthful appearance that he never really lost, Walter Swinburn rode three Epsom Derby winners: Shergar and Shahrastani for the Aga Khan and Stoute, plus Lammtarra (1995).

Plagued by weight problems throughout a stellar career, Swinburn was sidelined for months after a serious fall when his mount Liffey River crashed through the rail at Sha Tin Racecourse in Hong Kong. His comeback stalled and he put away his tack for good in 2000. Swinburn worked as a trainer after retirement as a rider, sending out more than 250 winners, and as a television commentator.[14]

Swinburn died on December 12, 2016, from head injuries resulting from a fall at his London home. The retired jockey suffered from epilepsy and his family speculated that he fell from an upper-story bathroom while trying to close a window after suffering a seizure. He was fifty-five years old.[15] Sir Michael Stoute called Swinburn "one of the great talents with the best hands of any of them."[16]

Of Shergar, Swinburn once said: "I was just a passenger on a very good horse."[17]

In addition to his five Epsom Derby winners, through the 2017 season Stoute sent out the winners of the Irish Derby (three times), the Irish Oaks (six times), the St. Leger, the Two Thousand Guineas (five times), the Irish Two Thousand Guineas, the One Thousand Guineas (two times), the King George VI and Queen Elizabeth Diamond Stakes (five times), the Japan Cup (two times), the Dubai World Cup, the Prix de l'Arc de Triomphe, and three Breeders' Cup races.

Although the Aga Khan IV enjoyed success with both Richard Fulke Johnson Houghton and Michael Stoute, especially the latter, relationships with both trainers ended abruptly.

After Stoute won the 1989 Gold Seal Oaks with the Aga Khan IV's Aliysa, the Jockey Club claimed that a post-race drug test had been positive for 3-hydroxycamphor, a metabolite of camphor, a prohibited substance. The Aga Khan, who had been critical of drug-testing procedures for years, assembled a cadre of experts to contest the findings. His team, which included the chief of drug testing for the Montreal Olympic Games, determined that 3-hydroxycamphor also could be a metabolite for common substances such as wood chips and carrots.

The Jockey Club did not accept the conclusions of the Aga Khan's experts and the disqualification of Aliysa stood. A few weeks later, during a press conference held at the Savoy Hotel in London, the Aga Khan IV announced that he would no longer race in England until drug-testing procedures there were improved.[18] A total of ninety horses were removed from the training yards of Stoute and Luca Cumani and sent to France and Ireland. Stoute said the Aga Khan IV was "irreplaceable as an owner" and that losing his horses was a "great disappointment."[19]

Four years later, satisfied that changes by the Jockey Club brought the country's drug-testing procedures up to par, the Aga Khan IV resumed racing in England.[20]

The Aga Khan IV and Houghton later parted company because the owner and trainer "didn't see eye-to-eye over jockeys."[21]

Lester Piggott rode Shergar in both his races as a two-year-old and to a win in the 1981 Irish Derby when Walter Swinburn was sitting out a suspension. During a career that spanned four decades, Piggott rode nearly fifty-two hundred winners. They included nine winners of the Epsom Derby and twenty other English classics. Piggott was unplaced on second-choice Shotgun in Shergar's Epsom Derby.[22]

Sheshoon was the first Irish farm purchased by the Aga Khan III (in 1923); Ballymany Stud was the second (in 1926). When the Aga Khan IV assumed control of the family's racing and breeding operations upon the death of his father, Prince Aly Khan, in 1960, he inherited six farms in Ireland: Sheshoon, Ballymany, Ongar, Gilltown, Sallymount, and Williamstown. In a move to consolidate the landholdings, the Ongar and Williamstown farms were sold in the 1960s and Gilltown and Sallymount were sold to Bertram and Diana Firestone a decade later.

The Aga Khan bought back Gilltown and Sallymount in 1989. He sold Ballymany to Sheikh Mohammed bin Rashid Maktoum the same year. The Gilltown purchase generated a flurry of lawsuits and counter-suits involving the Aga Khan, a Japanese businessman named Yoshika Akazawa, and Mr. and Mrs. Firestone. According to a report in the *New*

*York Times,* the Aga Khan said that he purchased Gilltown for $14.2 million in 1989. Akazawa, on the other hand, claimed that he had an agreement to buy the property from Bertram Firestone.[23]

An Irish court finally ruled in July 1991 that the Aga Khan's purchase of Gilltown had priority over the agreement between Akazawa and the Firestones. Akazawa exercised his right of first refusal for Gilltown in January 1990, the court explained, but proceedings for the Aga Khan to purchase the property had started earlier, on November 27, 1989.

The relationship between the Aga Khan and Ghislain Drion ended badly, with allegations of misconduct leveled against the farm manager.[24] After leaving the employ of the Aga Khan in 1998, Drion became a successful breeder of flat runners and jumpers. He died at his home in France in 2007 at the age of sixty-four.[25] Three of Drion's sons have successful careers in the Thoroughbred industry: Etienne Drion and his wife, Anna, are breeders and bloodstock agents in France; François Drion owns Taroka Stud in Ireland; and Nicky Drion manages Indian Creek Farm near Lexington, Kentucky.[26]

The theft of Shergar marked the beginning of a dismal year of misfortune for Epsom Derby winners.

Three months after Shergar was stolen, in May 1983, Derby winner Troy died of acute peritonitis midway through his fourth season at stud at Highclere Stud in England.[27] Winner of the two hundredth running of the Derby in 1979, Troy had been syndicated for a then-record £7.2 million.[28]

Thirteen months after Shergar went missing, Epsom Derby winner Golden Fleece died after suffering what was described in a Coolmore Stud press release as "peracute colic as a result of a bowel perforation." Emergency surgery at Troytown Hospital in Kildare was unsuccessful. Golden Fleece won the 1982 Derby in the colors of Robert Sangster, but contracted a virus and did not race again. The horse fell ill again after standing his first season at Coolmore and had been in poor health for several weeks prior to his death. One press report called the death of

The Shergar Cup, first run at Goodwood Racecourse before being relocated to Ascot, honors the 1981 European Horse of the Year. (Courtesy of Ascot Racecourse)

Golden Fleece a "bitter blow to breeders in Ireland and indeed Europe" and a "major blow in the insurance world."[29]

Speculation about the impact of Shergar's theft in the days after the horse was stolen predicted dire consequences: "The kidnapping of the champion racehorse Shergar from an Irish stud has cast a cloud over the Irish bloodstock industry, a bright spot in an otherwise lackluster economy."[30] "There is no doubt that if Shergar is not found, and found totally unharmed, very quickly indeed that the Irish breeding industry will have suffered a blow from which it may have great difficulty in recovering."[31] Chief Superintendent James Murphy, at a press conference, said that a failure to recover Shergar would "do an amount of damage to the industry."[32] Lord Killanin, former president of the International Olympic Committee and head of an official inquiry into the security at Irish stud farms, called the theft "a severe setback" for the industry.[33]

A year later, however, despite the losses of Shergar, Troy, and Golden Fleece in rapid succession, it already was clear that the projections of doom were overstated. Veterinarian Stan Cosgrove maintained,

"Ireland is the top breeding country for horses in the world. Syndicates from all over the world buy here and will continue to do so despite these setbacks."[34]

Cosgrove was correct. The Aga Khan's confidence in Ireland never wavered despite the theft of Shergar, Sheikh Mohammed bin Rashid Maktoum invested millions to become a major player in Irish racing and breeding, and the predicted defection of breeders from Ireland never materialized.

"Ireland was a very, very unhappy country at the time," the Aga Khan said later. "I don't think you can hold the people of a country responsible for criminal behavior. It is ethically wrong. In addition to which, Ireland had a great tradition of breeding great Thoroughbreds. My grandfather was there, my father was there, I'm there and I hope my children will be there."[35]

Reporting on the status of the horse industry in Ireland in 2016, Horse Racing Ireland's chief executive said that "2016 represented a seventh consecutive year of growth in sales, with the value of Irish bloodstock sold at public auction being €164.2 million, up 7.7% on the 2015 figures. Irish-bred horses continue to dominate at the highest levels internationally and the value of Irish-foaled exported horses sold through public auction grew to €272.9 million. This was a 1.9% increase on the previous year and Irish horses were exported to 36 different countries."[36]

Captain Sean Berry lives a quiet life in County Kildare. He served as technical advisor for a 1984 British Broadcasting Corporation documentary about the theft of Shergar, where his duties for the project included "helping the BBC to acquire for the purposes of filming a Shergar lookalike and a stud which resembles Ballymany."[37] For years Berry fielded annual interview requests from journalists each time the anniversary of the day that Shergar went missing came around. That interest has waned in recent years.

Jonathan Irwin, who manned the negotiation telephones when his friend Captain Berry, was out of town, no longer is involved in horse racing. After he retired from Goffs bloodstock sales, where he served as

CEO for many years, Irwin worked with Ryanair during the formative years of the airline, served as head of the Dublin Sports Council, and was one of the people who brought a stage of the Tour de France bicycle race to Ireland for the first time. The death of Irwin's young son, Jack, and the lack of adequate state services to help families in similar situations led him to establish the Jack & Jill Children's Foundation. He remains a critic of the lack of state-supported assistance for critically ill children and their families.[38]

Sporadic "sightings" of Shergar were reported for years after he was stolen. In March 1991, for example, Shergar supposedly was seen grazing in a pasture in the Channel Islands, an archipelago off the coast of Normandy in the English Channel. Steve Chappell, deputy of the Bloodstock Committee at Lloyd's of London, said at the time that although he could confirm the report, he thought "the whole thing is probably a wild-goose chase and has probably been blown out of all proportion. I can tell you that the people who claim to have found the horse are trying to negotiate a finder's fee but Lloyds will not be paying out any money."[39]

The theft of Shergar generated several books, a few documentaries, and a feature film, *Shergar: Discover the Heart of a Champion,* written and directed by Denis C. Lewiston and starring Mickey Rourke and Ian Holm. The film opened in a single theater and according to one reviewer was "unspeakably bad."[40]

Sean O'Callaghan never responded to requests for an interview for this book. The IRA man who switched sides to become a confidential informant for the Garda died in late August 2017, in a swimming accident in Jamaica where he was visiting family.[41]

Despite being implicated in Shergar's theft by Sean O'Callaghan, Kevin Mallon has consistently denied any involvement. He was neither arrested nor charged by the authorities in connection with the theft and now lives a quiet life in a Dublin suburb. According to the British tabloid *The Sun*, Mallon now passes his afternoons frequenting local betting shops.[42]

Perhaps the final word on the disappearance of Shergar comes from the Jockey Club in England. In volume 50 of the *General Stud Book*, on page 2278 under "Obituary of Stallions," this notation describes Shergar: "Fate unknown, no foals recorded since 1983."[43]

Statue of Shergar on the grounds of Gilltown Stud in Ireland. (Sarah Farnsworth, courtesy of the Aga Khan Studs)

# Acknowledgments

What remains to be said about the taking of Epsom Derby winner Shergar, whose theft some thirty-odd years ago was widely reported by the racing press and general interest media at the time it happened?

Quite a lot, as it turns out.

Was the theft a calculated political act or something more random? Why was the horse in Ireland in the first place when there were more lucrative syndication offers from America? Why did an intensive search across the Republic of Ireland fail to turn up anything useful? What were the legal ramifications? Was the Provisional Irish Republican Army responsible, or was one of the alternative conspiracy theories the true story? What about the psychics recruited by the Garda and by others?

Making sense of Thoroughbred racing's most famous cold case required the help of a small army of people. My initial contacts had much to say about Shergar and then directed me to a cast of characters I never would have known about otherwise. They all deserve my enduring thanks for helping make this book much better than it otherwise would have been.

Dr. Peter Timoney, a family friend of long standing from the Maxwell H. Gluck Equine Research Center at the University of Kentucky in Lexington, shared his recollections of Shergar and also directed me to Captain Sean Berry. Head of the Irish Thoroughbred Breeders Association when Shergar went missing, Berry recorded his experiences in the post-theft days by making notes on dozens, probably hundreds of bits of paper. With the help of a friend, Jack O'Connell, Berry reduced those notes to eighteen dense pages of commentary, which he gave me during one of my research trips to Ireland. His contacts with men who claimed to have Shergar were the focus of "Taking Shergar: Horse Racing's Most Famous Cold Case," an award-winning long-form article I wrote for the *Blood-Horse*.

Tom Dixon, a retired insurance adjuster best known for his investigation into the death of Alydar, put me in touch with Julian Lloyd. An insurance man who was boots-on-the-ground in Ireland representing the underwriters at Lloyd's of London who covered Shergar, Julian experienced firsthand the frenzy in the days after the theft. Julian also put me on the track of the Mobius Group, which mounted the last organized search for Shergar.

It took months to track down Stephan A. Schwartz, who was chairman and research director of the Mobius Group before it disbanded, but the search was worth the effort. Stephan and his wife, Ronlyn, were kind enough to put me up for a few days while Stephan shared his extensive files about the stallion probes. Stephan recounted a story that no one outside a small circle of people had ever heard, the story of a remote viewing search for Shergar. Randall J. De Mattei, executive director of Mobius at the time, was also helpful in providing information about the probes and the on-site investigation.

Tom Dixon was an invaluable intermediary for interviews with Terry Hall, the lead equine underwriter at Lloyd's of London when coverage was written for Shergar. Terry patiently explained the complicated workings of Lloyd's. Thanks also to Terry's son Simon, who gave me an insider's tour of the fantastic Lloyd's building.

Leo Powell, editor of the *Irish Field,* proved to be a valuable contact in Dublin. He also introduced me to David Horgan, who worked for years trying to convince an insurance company to pay a mortality claim for Shergar filed by Stan Cosgrove. Although David's efforts on behalf of Cosgrove were unsuccessful, in the process he assembled a massive amount of research about the theft and fate of Shergar. He shared that research for this book, including what may be the most authoritative—albeit quasi-official—statement by a member of the Garda.

Dr. Emma Adam, a veterinarian, PhD, and family friend for years, introduced me to Sir Michael Stoute, who trained Shergar at his yard in Newmarket. Sir Michael spent a morning with me talking about training his first Epsom Derby winner and about Shergar's riderless jaunt across the Lime Kiln gallop, past the Boy's Grave, and down the road toward Henry Cecil's training yard.

Chris Adam, Emma's mother, recommended Jean Bucknell as a guide during my two trips to Newmarket. Jean apparently knows everyone with any connection to racing and she provided invaluable assistance in arranging interviews with Cliff Lines, Dave Goodwin, and Dickie McCabe, the lads who took care of Shergar while he was in training with Sir Michael. The lads shared interesting perspectives about working with the Derby winner.

Jonathan Irwin was head of Goffs sales during the early 1980s. I met Jonathan years ago when I was working for the *Blood-Horse* and he was buying yearlings for the British Bloodstock Agency (Ireland). He talked with me during a busy day as head of the Jack & Jill Children's Foundation, which raises money and advocates on behalf of special-needs children in Ireland.

Dr. James MacLeod from the Gluck Center introduced me to John M. Flynn, who worked at Weatherbys Ireland blood-typing laboratory. Flynn helped me understand the state of the art for horse identification during the early 1980s, and in the process debunked one of the many conspiracy theories generated by the theft of Shergar.

I was especially interested in the syndication of Shergar and in the legal wrangling that arose after he was stolen. Michael Drake from the Newmarket law firm of Rustons & Lloyd walked me through drafting the syndication agreement. Michael Payton, chairman of Clyde and Co. in London, discussed the post-theft legal issues and his involvement in the Mobius Group's investigation.

James Keogh, a successful bloodstock agent in central Kentucky with roots in Ireland, shared his perspectives on the theft of Shergar and the political situation in Northern Ireland that led to the Troubles. His wife, Anne Eberhardt Keogh, a wonderful equine photographer for *Blood-Horse* and a longtime friend, helped track down images for my article "Taking Shergar: Horse Racing's Most Famous Cold Case." The article won national awards from the American Society of Journalists and Authors and American Horse Publications, honors I'm happy to share with Anne and her *Blood-Horse* colleagues Eric Mitchell and Claire Novak.

It's almost impossible to imagine researching a book about Thoroughbred racing without the help of Director Becky Ryder, Cathy Schenck, and Roda Ferraro at the Keeneland Library in Lexington, Kentucky. Becky keeps the ship afloat while reminding everyone who will listen about the importance of a reference library like the one at Keeneland. Cathy, who retired in 2017, will be missed. Roda, now Keeneland's head librarian, spent time in Belfast researching how libraries and museums can remain neutral in the face of a conflict like the Troubles. She answered numerous questions, shared books and scholarly articles, helped with research, and provided constant encouragement while I was writing. Multiple Eclipse Award winner Mary Simon and talented editor and writer Kim Brown, both great friends, provided valuable feedback on the manuscript.

Edward L. Bowen, my editor at the *Blood-Horse* when Shergar was stolen and now president of the Grayson-Jockey Club Equine Research Foundation, was a midwife of sorts for this book. Over lunch in fall 2016 at the Thoroughbred Club of America, a stone's throw from Keeneland Racecourse, Ed suggested that the University Press of Kentucky might be interested in Shergar's story. Thanks, Ed. You were right.

Anne Dean Dotson and Patrick O'Dowd at the University Press of Kentucky were wonderful partners in the creation of this book. They answered questions and provided suggestions and support throughout the publishing process. The book is better because of their guidance. Thanks also to Frederick McCormick, Jackie Wilson, Ila McEntire, and the rest of the University Press staff.

Few things are as humbling to a writer as turning over what you thought was a clean, consistent, and cohesive manuscript to a talented copyeditor. Robin DuBlanc is one of those copyeditors and she deserves special thanks for her work on the manuscript.

Sources for photographs include John Crofts, Ed Byrne, George Selwyn, Laurie Morton, Nicholas Nugent at Goffs in Ireland, Ascot Race Course in England, the Keeneland Library, Lucie Cash at the Royal Mail in London, and Aline Giraud at the Aga Khan Studs.

While wrapping up research and writing, I made the acquaintance of Alison Millar, an award-winning documentary filmmaker from Belfast. Alison was working on a documentary about Shergar for the British Broadcasting Company at the time, and we spent a few days touring central Kentucky and sharing what we had learned while working on our respective projects. She played the "wee Irish lass" card with great success in and around Kildare to film a few individuals who were not interested in talking with me, since I'm neither wee nor Irish nor a lass. Alison's film was scheduled for broadcast by the BBC during spring 2018.

Many other friends, both old and new, contributed to the book. Although not identified for one reason or another, you know who you are and you have my thanks.

Thanks most of all to my wife, Roberta, whose support and encouragement never wavered, not even when a years-long book project finally outgrew my office and took over our dining room—and a significant portion of our lives.

# Appendix 1

Shergar's Pedigree

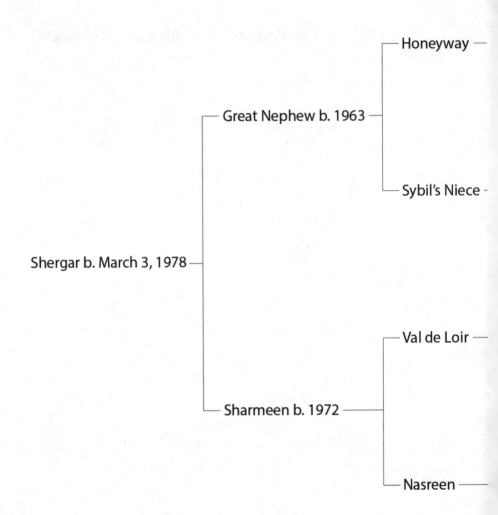

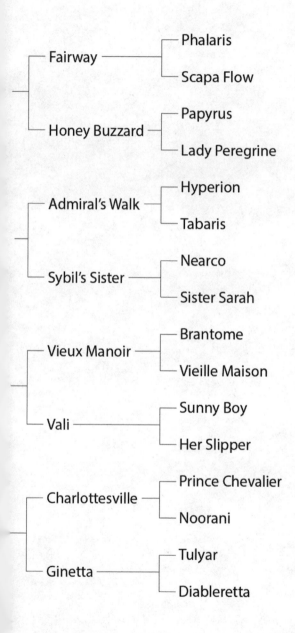

- Fairway
  - Phalaris
  - Scapa Flow
- Honey Buzzard
  - Papyrus
  - Lady Peregrine
- Admiral's Walk
  - Hyperion
  - Tabaris
- Sybil's Sister
  - Nearco
  - Sister Sarah
- Vieux Manoir
  - Brantome
  - Vieille Maison
- Vali
  - Sunny Boy
  - Her Slipper
- Charlottesville
  - Prince Chevalier
  - Noorani
- Ginetta
  - Tulyar
  - Diableretta

Mumtaz Mahal, the seventh dam of Shergar, was a brilliant racehorse and the foundation mare for one of the Aga Khan's most influential families. The Aga Khan III purchased Mumtaz Mahal for 9,100 guineas in 1922.

# Appendix 2

## Shergar's 1980–1981 Racing Record

### Kris Plate

Newbury; September 19, 1980; 1 mile

| | |
|---|---|
| 1st | Shergar, Piggott |
| 2nd | Chief Speaker, Cochrane |
| 3rd | Jungle Jim, Starkey |

Winning margin: 2½ lengths
Time: 1:38.71
23 starters

### William Hill Futurity Stakes (G1)

Doncaster; October 25, 1980; 1 mile

| | |
|---|---|
| 1st | Beldale Flutter, Eddery |
| 2nd | Shergar, Piggott |
| 3rd | Sheer Grit, Johnson |

Winning margin: 2½ lengths
Time: 1:43.53
7 starters

## Guardian Newspaper Classic Trial (G3)

Sandown; April 25, 1981; 1¼ miles

| | |
|---|---|
| 1st | Shergar, Swinburn |
| 2nd | Kirtling, Hide |
| 3rd | King's General, Starkey |

Winning margin: 10 lengths
Time: 2:09.35
9 starters

## Chester Vase (G3)

Chester; May 5, 1981; 1¼ miles

| | |
|---|---|
| 1st | Shergar, Swinburn |
| 2nd | Sunley Builds, Cook |
| 3rd | Six Mile Bottom, Carson |

Winning margin: 12 lengths
Time: 2:40.47
10 starters

## Derby Stakes (G1)

Epsom, June 3, 1981, 1½ miles

| | |
|---|---|
| 1st | Shergar, Swinburn, Stoute |
| 2nd | Glint of Gold, Matthias, Balding |
| 3rd | Scintillating Air, Baxter, Hobbs |
| 4th | Shotgun, Piggott, Thornton |
| 5th | Church Parade, Carson, Hern |
| 6th | Sheer Grit, Mercer, Brittain |
| 7th | Silver Season, Johnson, Brittain |

| | |
|---|---|
| 8th | Riberetto, Eddery, Boss |
| 9th | Sunley Builds, Waldron, Hunter |
| 10th | Kings General, Taylor, Harwood |
| 11th | Sass, Reid, Kelleway |
| 12th | Krug, Raymond, Mellor |
| 13th | Kalaglow, Starkey, Harwood |
| 14th | Robellino, Cook, Balding |
| 15th | Golden Brigadier, Bradwell, Brittain |
| 16th | Kind of Hush, Cauthen, Hills |
| 17th | Al Nasr, Gibert, Fabre |
| 18th | Waverly Hall, Crossley, Simpson |
| | |
| DNS* | Lydian, Head, Head |

Winning margin: 10 lengths (new record)
Time: 2:44.21
*DNS = Did not start

## Irish Sweeps Derby (G1)

The Curragh Racecourse; June 27, 1981, 1½ miles

| | |
|---|---|
| 1st | Shergar, Piggott |
| 2nd | Cut Above, Carson |
| 3rd | Dance Bid, Whitman |

Winning margin: 4 lengths
Time: 2:32.07
12 starters

## King George VI and Queen Elizabeth Diamond Stakes (G1)

Ascot; July 25, 1981; 1½ miles

| | |
|---|---|
| 1st | Shergar, Swinburn |
| 2nd | Madam Gay |
| 3rd | Fingal's Cave |

Winning margin: 4 lengths
Time: 2:35.04
7 starters

## St. Leger Stakes (G1)

Doncaster; September 12, 1981; 1 mile, 6 furlongs, and 127 yards

| | |
|---|---|
| 1st | Cut Above, Mercer |
| 2nd | Glint of Gold, Matthias |
| 3rd | Bustomi, Piggott |
| 4th | Shergar, Swinburn |

Winning margins: 2½ lengths, 4 lengths, 5 lengths
Time: 3:11.60
7 starters

# Appendix 3

## The Shergar Syndicate

**Report of Syndicate Committee to Shareholders of Shergar Syndicate**

3rd February 1984

### Introduction

1. On 8 February 1984 it will be one year since Shergar was kidnapped from his stable in Ballymany Stud, Curragh, Co. Kildare. During this time it has been the firm policy of the Committee to maintain strict confidentiality about all aspects of the case. This policy has been pursued on the firm advice of, among others, the Irish Police and the Irish Government. The objective of the policy has been to avoid jeopardizing any possibility of achieving the safe return of the stallion. The kidnapping attracted a remarkable degree of interest in the world's press, and there was every chance that any publicity of anything being done would have prejudiced freedom of manoeuvre and would have foreclosed on some of the options that were open. Therefore, even in respect of you, the shareholders, the Committee have heretofore only made sporadic reports and requested absolute discretion towards the Press.

2. The Committee now feel that the time is right to report more fully in writing to the Shareholders and in due course to make this report available to the media on a selective basis. They feel a duty to do so towards the shareholders but also in the wider interests of the bloodstock industry in general which needs to know what happened and how it happened; and also in the interest of putting the record straight with

regard to some of the more grossly inaccurate and speculative reporting that has taken place. The Committee now feel free to do so because the chances of Shergar still being alive are remote; because they accept the reports, recently attributed to the Irish police, to the effect that the stallion was kidnapped by the IRA and died shortly afterwards, as being probably correct; and because the requirement for secrecy no longer exists in view of the long period in which nothing has been heard from the gang responsible.

## The Incident

3. The kidnapping took place during the evening of Tuesday, 8 February 1983. At about 2040 hours a young son of groom, James FitzGerald, answered the door at their house, in the centre of Ballymany Stud, which is located alongside the Curragh in Co. Kildare. He was forced inside by armed men and Mr. FitzGerald himself came downstairs to find his son pinned to the floor. The men put Mr. FitzGerald's family in one room before taking him and his wife to the kitchen. They were calm and well-behaved after their initial violent intrusion. Mr. FitzGerald was then forced to take the men to Shergar's stall and to assist in loading the horse into a double horsebox which they summoned up the drive from the main road by two-way radio. At least one of the gang was familiar with handling horses. The horsebox, towed by what is believed to have been an old brown Hillman Hunter or Vauxhall car, left the Stud at about 2100 hrs.

Mr. FitzGerald was taken back to his house and held until about 2200 hrs. at which time he was put into a van and driven to the outskirts of Kilcock, some 20 miles north of Ballymany. The men told him they required a ransom of £2 million, made dire threats of what they would do if Mr. FitzGerald spoke to the police, and then told him the direction in which to walk to Kilcock. He did so, and telephoned from a callbox to ask his brother to collect him. The brother did so, drove him back to Ballymany, and dropped him on the main road near the main gate of the Stud. He walked the short distance to his house and telephoned M. Ghislain Drion, the Stud Manager, at about 0115 hrs. (Wednesday, 9 February 1983). M. Drion drove to Ballymany from his home a short distance away and was urged by Mr. FitzGerald on arrival not to tell the police.

4. Mr. Drion discussed the problem with the Syndicate Veterinary Surgeon, who lives nearby, before telephoning His Highness, The Aga Khan, in Switzerland at around 0300 hrs. Irish time. M. Drion sought the Aga Khan's views as owner of the Stud and previous owner of Shergar (he retained six of the forty shares when the stallion was syndicated) on whether it should be envisaged to pay the ransom and recover the horse without putting the matter in the hands of the Irish police as the kidnappers had ordered, or whether the matter should be put forthwith into the hands of the authorities at the highest possible level immediately. It was clear that it would be inappropriate and socially irresponsible for the Syndicate to attempt to deal with such a criminal matter without doing so; such an incident could not for long be kept from the police and media; the complexity of handling such a matter on behalf of a Syndicate of 34 shareholders would be so difficult; and, the Syndicate could not be sure if it paid a ransom swiftly that the money would go to the genuine kidnappers or that the horse would be returned unharmed. M. Drion then called the Minister for Finance, Mr. Alan Dukes, at about 0400 hrs., and the Minister confirmed that he would immediately initiate appropriate steps. He did so by passing the matter forthwith to the Minister for Justice, Mr. Michael Noonan, who in turn informed the police.

5. Full details of the incident took some time to establish. Mr. FitzGerald is a man of about 50 years of age and undoubted loyalty, who was born on Ballymany Stud, but he was understandably terrified to give details of what took place for fear of the threatened retribution on him and his family.

6. At least six men in three vehicles took part in the kidnapping. They were armed with at least a rifle, a sub-machine gun and a revolver, and they were equipped with two-way radios. They were more than strong enough to overwhelm any security measures that could have been in effect, and the advantage of surprise was on their side in that such an armed attack on a stud farm was unprecedented in the world as a whole, and unique in Ireland.

7. Visitors to the Stud who left at around 2040 hrs. gave descriptions of three men loitering at the gate, from which identikit pictures were made up by the police, and were subsequently published in the press. No progress was made from these pictures.

## The Committee and Shareholders

8. Considerable complexities were imposed on the handling of the case by the form of ownership. Some 34 shareholders from 9 countries owned the 40 shares in the Syndicate. They were represented by 5 Committee members from 4 countries who had wide-ranging powers under the Syndicate Agreement to make decisions on behalf of the Syndicate members. In the immediate aftermath of the kidnapping, a full spectrum of attitudes was shown by the shareholders, ranging from those who considered the importance of the stallion to be such that they were prepared to make a deal with the kidnappers, to those who were implacably opposed to any payment of any ransom whatsoever. Individual positions were complicated by insurance arrangements and the prospect of greater or lesser loss depending on those arrangements. Throughout, the Committee were mindful of their wider responsibility to society in general and the bloodstock industry in particular, as well as being mindful of the fact that there was a potential claim by the Syndicate for compensation under the Irish Malicious Injuries Act 1981.

9. The Committee was contacted immediately by M. Drion, met during the year when it was considered necessary, gave authority for all major actions and were regularly briefed and updated on all that was happening. Shareholders, unfortunately, had to be less well briefed in the interest of security but were eventually given a full briefing in Paris the day before the Prix de L'Arc de Triomphe, on 1 October 1983, with the opportunity to consult the record of that meeting thereafter.

## The Authorities

10. The fullest co-operation was given by the Committee and its representatives to the Irish authorities at all times. Close liaison was

maintained with the police, their advice sought on all actions, and every assistance given to anything that they wanted. The enquiries of the Committee were meanwhile pursued in the United States, France, the United Kingdom, Northern Ireland and the Republic of Ireland. All the many leads available to the Committee were followed up.

## Insurance and Malicious Injuries Claim

11. The actions of the Committee were often circumscribed by insurance considerations. As insurance was a matter for individual shareholders, individual arrangements were not formally known by the Committee. A substantial proportion of the syndicated value of the stallion was however covered in around 30 Lloyds' syndicates and 30 external companies. Furthermore, legal advice was obtained at an early stage to the effect that a preliminary notice of a claim under the Irish Malicious Injuries Act should be filed by the Syndicate with the Kildare County Council. The Committee therefore felt obliged, in order to safeguard shareholders' interests, to instruct solicitors to file such a preliminary notice with a claim for Ir.£20 million within the required fourteen day period.

## Hoax Incidents

12. A. Some confusion existed after the kidnapping as the press reacted to every unlikely speculation and as countless cranks, hoaxers, and people genuinely concerned to help provided a mass of information from across the world. The best known example of such ill-placed though no doubt well-intentioned press enthusiasm was when three racing journalists, John Oaksey, Peter Campling and Derek Thompson, were the subject of a hoax when they flew to the stables of horse trainer Jeremy Maxwell in Northern Ireland supposedly to negotiate with the kidnappers for the return of Shergar.

B. This was far from the only such incident encountered during the months that followed. Apparently the Syndicate Vet was the subject of a hoax in which he was widely reported to have lost some Ir.£80,000 in July 1983. This apparent hoax was reported to have involved a detective and a Co. Clare farmer. The Committee await with interest the outcome of the police inquiry into this matter, which was convened last November.

## Contact with Kidnappers

13. Contact was made swiftly with the real kidnappers by telephone after the stallion was kidnapped (at around 2040 hrs. on the evening of Tuesday, 8 February), with the same anonymous Irish male voice always speaking for the kidnappers thereafter.

A. The first telephone call from the kidnappers came on the morning of Wednesday, 9 February, when M. Drion's wife received a call at their home from the anonymous caller asking to speak to M. Drion. She referred him to Ballymany Stud.

B. The next call was at 1545 hrs. the same day when the caller to Ballymany Stud demanded to speak to M. Drion. He was not there, so one of the girls in the office was instructed to get him to the telephone 20 minutes later. She did so and a conversation took place between M. Drion and the same caller at about 1605 hrs. M. Drion, who has a pronounced French accent, had difficulty in understanding what was being said, and the caller gave up after a few minutes. He called back again at 1745 hrs. and demanded a telephone number in France and repeated the ransom demand made to Mr. FitzGerald of £2 million. At 1620 hrs. the next day, Thursday, 10 February, one of the girls in the Ballymany Stud office received a call from the same Irish person with an order to man the telephone number that M. Drion had given them in Paris. This was done and at about 2100 hrs. the same evening a fairly long conversation took place to the Paris number, when the ransom demanded by the kidnappers was repeated and a counter demand was made to them to produce proof that they did indeed hold the horse. At 2200 hrs. the next day, Friday, 11 February, a call was received to the Paris number giving instructions to collect proof of the fact that the caller held the stallion at 0900 hrs. the following morning from the Crofton Airport Hotel in Dublin. A demand of £2 million was repeated. A representative of the Committee went to the Hotel as instructed the following morning (Saturday, 12 February) and awaited the arrival of the proof, but in the absence of its arrival eventually gave up and left.

C. The kidnappers again called the Paris number at around 1115 hrs. the same morning, Saturday, 12 February, and complained vigorously that there had been nobody at the hotel. They were told they were mistaken and eventually gave instructions to repeat the exercise one hour later.

D. In fact they called again and had a long conversation at about 1515 hrs. in which they said that the proof had been handed in at the Rosnaree Hotel on the Dublin/Belfast Road, and also directed that the Committee representative in Paris was to get full power to deal with the case. They were becoming unhappy at this stage, and said that they would ring back in one hour by which time they expected the man on the telephone to have full power to pay over £2 million.

E. They rang again for a long conversation at 1700 hrs. and demanded a commitment to pay or the stallion would be killed. The Committee representative attempted to explain the impossibility of making such a decision swiftly on behalf of 34 shareholders, and attempted to obtain a further delay in the proceedings.

F. During this time proof had indeed been collected from the Rosnaree Hotel consisting of several polaroid photographs of Shergar, some including the Friday, 11 February, issue of the "Irish News," a Belfast newspaper. The Committee were therefore satisfied that the stallion was alive on 11 February and almost certainly in Ireland. They were not of course sure that he had not been injured, nor that the kidnappers would indeed hand him over if a ransom was paid.

G. The final conversation took place at about 2240 hrs on the Saturday night after proof had been collected. A very brief conversation took place in which the caller asked if the money was ready, and when told that the Committee were not yet satisfied ended with the final words: "If you are not satisfied, that's it." The caller then hung up the telephone and nothing has been heard from the kidnappers since. This was only some four days after Shergar was kidnapped.

14. Soon after this final conversation a recorded message was put

on the appropriate telephone in Paris to the effect that the Committee were keen to reopen the dialogue with the kidnappers. Nevertheless, the kidnappers were never heard from again. It should be emphasized that throughout this period the Committee were in the closest liaison with the Irish police, who agreed fully with everything that was done. Recordings of all these telephone conversations are held by the Committee.

15. The demands of the kidnappers were to a great extent unreasonable and illogical, to the extent that they raised the question as to whether they seriously wanted or expected to receive a ransom or whether they were satisfied with the confusion and publicity they achieved. For example, at various times:

A. They demanded a ransom including 100 pounds sterling notes, which of course do not exist.

B. They demanded at 1745 hrs one evening that M. Drion should personally deliver £2 million in Paris at 1200 hrs the next morning. He was in Ballymany at the time, but they were unconcerned about the impossibility of the demand.

C. They ordered the representative in Paris to get authority from shareholders to pay the ransom within one hour, but forbade him to telephone Ireland to speak to shareholders there.

D. At 1700 hrs on Saturday, 12 February, they demanded that the representative in Paris should get £2 million before the end of the night. The representative protested the impossibility of doing so. The called again for the last time at 2240 hrs. some 5 ½ hours later.

E. Their demands moved too fast for a proper response to be possible.

F. They never reduced their demand of £2 million and terminated the dialogue after some four days.

16. After contact was broken, the Committee continued to make efforts to signal a wish to restore it:

A. A recorded message was left on the appropriate Paris telephone line, and other likely telephones were manned.

B. Articles were placed in the press implying a wish to talk, in particular on the 5 March 1983.

C. In addition one of the Irish shareholders was featured in a full-page article in an Irish newspaper on the 11 April, in which, in his reported remarks, he came close to saying that he would organize a ransom payment if approached. The Committee had not known of this interview in advance and had not authorized it in any way, but it is interesting that no response was received from the genuine kidnappers. If the horse had been alive at that stage, there would have been a great incentive for the kidnappers to deal with an Irishman in Ireland.

## Reward Offers

17. Substantial rewards were offered for the safe return of the stallion. A reward of £10,000 was offered initially by the 'Sporting Life' racing newspaper, and the Irish Bloodstock Breeders' Association then offered a substantial but unspecified reward which was subsequently reported to be £50,000. Finally, in November, a group of shareholders went on record with an offer of £250,000. These reward offers generated a number of letters and telephone calls in response, all of which were followed up, but none of which in the event were helpful.

## No Payments by Syndicate

18. The Committee wish to reconfirm that neither they, nor the Aga Khan (who is not a member of the Committee, but who has been involved in the case as former owner of the stallion and owner of Ballymany Stud), have made any payments themselves, or have been party in any way whatsoever to any payments by any other individual or group of individuals to any genuine or hoax kidnappers. Any statements published in the past or to be published in the future to the contrary are totally untrue. They have cooperated fully with the authorities throughout, and have always remained conscious of their wider responsibilities to society.

## Conclusions

19. The general belief of informed observers since soon after the time of the kidnapping was that it was carried out by the IRA. Mean-

while, however, much speculation and rumour about the motivation of the kidnappers has been printed in the press, in particular to the effect that this stemmed from a personal vendetta against the Aga Khan. A prominent article to this effect appeared, for example, in a 3-day 'Exclusive Super Series' in the English "Daily Star" newspaper commencing on 8 November 1983. This theory had been examined by the Committee at some length very early on but absolutely no evidence was found to support the theory. The conversations with the kidnappers contained no reference whatsoever to the Aga Khan or his personal interests. The kidnappers did demand a telephone number in France, but it was indeed France they asked for and not Paris in particular. That was the choice of M. Drion and it is probable that the kidnappers chose France because they had a substantial connection with that Country and therefore probably felt that France would be a convenient and relatively safe location for this operation. The Committee were of the firm opinion after careful consideration and analysis that the motivation of the kidnappers was strictly that of financial gain or publicity, or both.

20. The Committee were satisfied from a very early stage that they were dealing with the IRA, and today one year later remain firmly of that view. They are further of the view that the operation was organized by a senior member of the organization who remained in charge and took a personal interest throughout. Their investigations further indicate that Shergar never left the Republic of Ireland and, though this is not certain, such evidence as is yet available suggests that he was killed soon after he was kidnapped by men who had no regard for the horse or their country.

21. The Committee note recent reports to the effect that the Irish police believe that elements of the same gang that kidnapped Shergar were involved in the failed attempt to kidnap Mr. Galen Weston and the initially successful kidnap of Mr. Don Tidey. The Committee believe these reports to be true.

22. Hindsight leads to the conclusion that the kidnapping of Shergar was the start of another kidnap campaign by the IRA and underlines the question which was first considered in the early days of the case, of

how serious and determined the kidnappers were in seeking a ransom for the stallion. The Committee believe that the kidnappers did not respond in the way they would have done with a human victim because:

A. The criminal records of the men involved are likely to be such that the penalties for maliciously stealing and killing a horse would be of little concern to them.

B. It is reasonable to conclude that the kidnappers regarded the Shergar kidnap as the start of an even more unpleasant campaign of kidnapping human beings, and they therefore wished to extort £2 million from the Syndicate very quickly or otherwise they were quite prepared to kill the stallion in order to create an atmosphere and a psychology that they envisaged would assist their later endeavours.

23. The Committee believe (and know that the overwhelming majority of Irish people believe) that both the solving of this crime and the conviction of those responsible are of vital interest to Ireland in general and to the Irish bloodstock industry in particular. The Committee will continue to urge the Irish authorities to redouble their efforts to reach and make public a conclusion.

## Initial Shareholders in the Shergar Syndicate

| | |
|---|---|
| Aidridge Ltd. | 4 shares |
| Ardenode Stud Ltd. | 1 share |
| Sir John Jacob Astor | |
| & Hon. Lord Howard De Walden | 1 share |
| Bluefield Farm Corp. | 1 share |
| Brolon Investments | ½ share |
| Claiborne Farm | 1 share |
| The Earl of Derby | 1 share |
| Dirgai Co. | 1 share |
| Bertram R. Firestone | 1 share |
| John R. Gaines | 1 share |
| Hascombe & Valiant Studs | 1 share |
| Herkimer Ltd. (the Aga Khan IV) | 6 shares |

| | |
|---|---|
| Juddmonte Farms | 1 share |
| G. W. Leigh | 1 share |
| Lockridge Farm | 1 share |
| Edmund Loder | 1 share |
| Mrs. Harry A. Love | ½ share |
| John Magnier | 1 share |
| Hamdan Al Maktoum | |
| & Maktoum Al Maktoum | 1 share |
| Maylands Stud Ltd. | 1 share |
| Sir Robin McAlpine | 1 share |
| Patrick W. McGrath | 1 share |
| Paul Mellon | 1 share |
| Moreton Bloodstock Management Ltd. | 1 share |
| Stavros S. Niarchos | 1 share |
| M. Vincent O'Brien | 1 share |
| Oldtown Stud | 1 share |
| Pantheon Ltd. | 1 share |
| Capt. A. D. D. Rogers | 1 share |
| Robert Sangster | 1 share |
| Jacques Wertheimer | 1 share |
| White Lodge Stud | 1 share |
| Windfields Farm Ltd. | 1 share |
| Total | 40 shares |

# Notes

## Author's Note

1. There is no familial relationship between Julian and Lloyd's of London, although a mutual acquaintance suggests that Julian does not discourage clients from believing otherwise.

2. Sergeant Jim Malloy, Garda Press & Public Relations Office, email to author, January 20, 2016.

3. Ireland's Department of Foreign Affairs also apparently maintains a file on the Shergar theft from the country's embassy in London, but refuses to release the information to the public. Justification for the refusal is that the information "might cause distress or danger to living individuals or . . . might lead to a defamation action." Elaine Edwards, "Shergar and Phone Tapping Files Withheld from Public," *Irish Times,* September 21, 2015.

4. The committee representing the syndicate that owned Shergar came to the conclusion that the theft was an IRA operation, "Report of the Syndicate Committee to Shareholders of Shergar Syndicate," February 3, 1984. Sean O'Callaghan, a highly placed Garda informer who worked in the IRA hierarchy for many years, named the Provos who organized and carried out the theft of Shergar in his memoir, *The Informer: The Real Life Story of One Man's War against Terrorism,* (London: Corgi Books, 1999), 193–95. Numerous interviews conducted by the author also reflect a general agreement there was an IRA connection.

## Introduction

1. Richard Baerlein, *Shergar and the Aga Khan's Thoroughbred Empire* (London: Michael Joseph, 1984), 146–47.

2. A major player in the Shergar story, Stan Cosgrove is one of Ireland's most respected veterinary surgeons. Founder of Troytown Equine Hospital in Kildare and cofounder of the Racing Academy and Centre for Education, Cosgrove received the Irish Thoroughbred Breeders' Association's highest award when he was named to the ITBA Hall of Fame in 2003. He also managed Moyglare Stud for many years.

3. Almost from the night he received the calls from Stan Cosgrove, Sean Berry began making notes on small scraps of paper setting out his substantial involvement in the Shergar story: a record "from A to Z," he said. With the assistance of the late Jack O'Connell, a friend and bookstore owner, Berry

214 Notes to Pages 2–6

later compiled those notes into a comprehensive account. He kindly shared that information with the author. References to Berry throughout this book are based primarily on his notes and on two lengthy conversations that the author had with him at his home on May 7, 2015 and March 10, 2017. Other sources will be referenced as necessary.

4. An Garda Síochána is the Republic of Ireland's national police force. Chief Superintendent Murphy soon would take charge of the search for Shergar.

5. Automatic weapons were, and still are, difficult to obtain by civilians in the Republic of Ireland. Their use by the gang that took Shergar was an early indication of Provisional Irish Republican Army involvement in the theft. Further confirmation, set out in chapter 12, includes the discovery on the grounds of Ballymany of a magazine with more than two dozen rounds of ammunition that was manufactured for a type of automatic weapon known to be used by the IRA.

6. Ironically, the largest military installation in the country is the Curragh Camp, located just across the M7 and R445 highways and almost within sight of The Curragh Racecourse and the Aga Khan's Ballymany Stud.

7. The current Aga Khan, with the designation "IV," since 1957 has been the spiritual leader of millions of Ismaili Muslins around the world. His grandfather, the Aga Khan III, and his father, Prince Aly Khan, were prominent Thoroughbred breeders and owners and the Aga Khan IV has successfully carried on the family tradition. When the context might lead to confusion, the current Aga Khan and his grandfather are identified as either "IV" or "III."

8. Ulrich Boser, *The Gardner Heist: The True Story of the World's Largest Unsolved Art Theft* (New York: HarperCollins, 2010), 164–66.

9. Peter Fearon, "Art Becomes Artillery: 'Real IRA' Swaps Stolen Paintings for Guns," *New York Post,* July 2, 2001.

10. Gloria Millner and Jim Jordan, "Theft of Shergar No Big Surprise Here," *Lexington Herald,* February 10, 1983; Clive Gammon, "The $40,000,000 Horse," *Sports Illustrated,* August 3, 1981.

## 1. Birth of an Empire

1. R. C. Lyle, *The Aga Khan's Horses* (London: Putnam, 1938), 73.

2. A good account of Blenheim's unlikely win in the 1930 Epsom Derby can be found in Abram S. Hewitt, *Sire Lines,* rev. ed. (Lexington, KY: Eclipse, 2006), 83–88.

3. The title "Aga Khan" was bestowed upon the Aga Khan III's grandfather by the emperor of Persia during the 1830s; the appellation "His Highness" was added by Queen Victoria in 1886. Upon the death of the first Aga Khan in 1881, his eldest son, Aqa Ali Sham, assumed the title. The Aga Khan II lived only four years. Following his untimely death, his son, Sultan Mohamed Shah, became the Aga Khan III at the age of eight. Philip Jodidio, *A Racing and Breeding Tradition: The Horses of the Aga Khan,* 2nd ed. (London: Prestel,

2011), 45. Unless otherwise noted, references to the Aga Khan in this chapter refer to the Aga Khan III.

4. "What Is the Difference between Sunni and Shia Muslims?" *Economist,* May 29, 2013. Following the death of the Prophet Muhammad in 632, his followers disagreed about who should be his successor. The majority favored Abu Bakr, father-in-law of the founder of Islam. The dissenters thought a blood relative of Muhammad was the better choice and claimed that Ali, his cousin and son-in-law, was the legitimate successor. The backers of Ali became known as the Shia, the "partisans of Ali."

5. For a thorough discussion of the decision and its implications, see Teena Purhoit, *The Aga Khan Case* (Boston: Harvard University Press, 2012). For contemporaneous reporting of the case, see "Judgment Delivered Nov. 12, 1886 on the 'Khoja Case' (Aga Khan Case)," *Bombay Gazette Steam Press,* November 12, 1886, http://ismaili.net/heritage/node/27983.

6. In a rare error of judgment made a few months after being elected to head the League of Nations, the Aga Khan embraced the philosophy of Adolf Hitler. The two men met in Berlin on October 20, 1938. According to sportswriter Quintin Gilbey, who became friends with the Aga Khan during the 1930s, the Aga Khan initially saw Hitler as a "firm pillar of peace." That assessment was wrong, of course, as the Aga Khan realized when the Nazi army marched into Austria in 1938. "Hitler Receives Aga Khan," *New York Times,* October 21, 1938; Quintin Gilbey, *Fun Was My Living* (London: Hutchinson, 1970), 240; James C. Nicholson, *Never Say Die: A Kentucky Colt, the Epsom Derby, and the Rise of the Modern Thoroughbred Industry* (Lexington: University Press of Kentucky, 2013), 77.

7. Gilbey, *Fun Was My Living,* 259.

8. James Reginato, "The Aga Khan's Earthly Kingdom," *Vanity Fair,* February 2013, http://www.vanityfair.com/style/2013/02/aga-khan-spiritual-leader-multi-billionaire. See also "Aga Khans Jubilee Celebrations in India," https://www.youtube.com/watch?v=XxtcOHG70zE; "Aga Khan 3 Weighed in Diamonds," https://www.youtube.com/watch?v=uMWKovxkWHU; and "A Tribute to Sultan Muhammad Shah Aga Khan 3," https://www.youtube.com/watch?v=XxtcOHG70zE, for newsreel coverage of the Aga Khan III's Golden, Diamond, and Platinum Jubilee celebrations.

9. Nimira Dewji, "Legacy of Jubilees of Imam Sultan Mohamed Shah," *Ismailimail,* September 12, 2016, https://ismailimail.wordpress.com/2016/09/12/legacy-of-jubilees-of-imam-sultan-mohamed-shah/.

10. Naoroji M. Dumasia, *The Aga Khan and His Ancestors: A Biographical and Historical Sketch* (New Delhi: Readworthy, 2008), chapter 26, "The Aga Khan, Sportsman." This electronic work is a reproduction of a book originally published in Bombay by the Times of India Press in 1939.

11. Richard Baerlein, *Shergar and the Aga Khan's Thoroughbred Empire* (London: Michael Joseph, 1984), 26.

12. British Pathé newsreel coverage of the 1930 Epsom Derby included a few seconds of stock footage showing Prince Monolulu: http://www.british-pathe.com/video/the-derby-1930/query/epsom+derby.

13. Episode #56-28 of *You Bet Your Life*, first broadcast April 4, 1957, https://www.youtube.com/watch?v=0n8dI8F2H10

14. Prince Monolulu told various stories about his past over the years, many contradictory, some true. In reality, the prince was Peter Carl Mackay, an actor who hailed from the Caribbean rather than from Africa. His flamboyant presence at British racecourses for a time arguably made him one of the most recognizable black men in the country. He was a fixture on the streets of Newmarket, where the National Horseracing Museum holds memorabilia relating to his life and times. Jon Wright, "Newmarket Memories of Racing Tipster Prince Monolulu," *A History of the World*, BBC Suffolk, February 1, 2010. His autobiography as told to Sidney White, *I Gotta Horse: The Autobiography of Ras Prince Monolulu* (London: Hurst & Blackett, 1955), is out of print.

15. This account of Prince Monolulu's bizarre death is based on Graham Lord's biography of Bernard, *Just the One: The Wives and Times of Jeffrey Bernard, 1932–1997* (CB Creative Books, Kindle ed., 2013), chapter 9, "Beau Bernard."

16. Blenheim became Blenheim II after he was imported to the United States, the suffix indicating that another horse with the name had already been registered with the Jockey Club in America. The first Blenheim, also a son of Blandford, had been imported to the United States in utero. He was a stakes winner but failed at stud.

17. Blenheim was sired by Blandford, out of the Charles O'Malley mare Malva. Blandford had already sired one Epsom Derby winner, Trigo, in 1929, and would sire two more after Blenheim: Windsor Lad in 1934 and Bahram, winner of the English Triple Crown, for the Aga Khan in 1935.

18. Dumasia, *The Aga Khan and His Ancestors*, 335.

19. Ferdinand Kuhn Jr., "Blenheim, 18-1 Shot, Wins English Derby," *New York Times*, June 5, 1930.

20. Edward L. Bowen, "Highclere," *Blood-Horse*, June 6, 1977, 2376–82.

21. Kuhn, "Blenheim, 18-1 Shot, Wins English Derby."

22. The Aga Khan already had a reputation as a breeder of good horses by the time Blenheim won the 1930 Epsom Derby, and he is sometimes erroneously credited as both the breeder and owner of the colt. His press luncheon prediction that he would breed the winner of the 1930 Epson Derby thus was only partially correct.

23. Hewitt, *Sire Lines*, 83.

24. After nearly two decades spent studying pedigrees while he had "neither the means nor the time" to follow the advice of Ireland's Lord Wavertree to establish a racing stable, the Aga Khan began buying yearlings in 1921. Lyle, *The Aga Khan's Horses*, 3–4. George Lambton was the Aga Khan's first choice to

train his horses, but Lambton was occupied with the stable of Lord Derby and could not accept the job. He agreed, instead, to help the Aga Khan buy horses for a friend, Dick Dawson, to train. The plan was for the Aga Khan to mark sales catalogues based on breeding and Lambton to make the final selections based on conformation. Richard Baerlein, *Shergar and the Aga Khan's Thoroughbred Empire* (London: Michael Joseph, 1984), 17–19.

25. Bowen, "Highclere," 2382.

26. For a comprehensive review of Gallant Fox and his Triple Crown, see William H. P. Robertson, *The History of Thoroughbred Racing in America* (New York: Prentice-Hall, 1964), 275–83; for past performances, see *Champions: The Lives, Times, and Past Performances of America's Greatest Thoroughbreds,* rev. ed. (New York: Daily Racing Form Press, 2005), 58.

27. Charles Hatton, a columnist for *Daily Racing Form,* is often credited with coining the term *Triple Crown* after Gallant Fox swept the classics, but the term was used by a *New York Times* writer as early as 1923. By 1935, when Omaha (a son of Gallant Fox) won all three of the classics, writers were using "Triple Crown" to describe the rare feat as a matter of course. Bennett Liebman, "Origins of the Triple Crown," *New York Times,* April 24, 2008, https://therail.blogs.nytimes.com/2008/04/24/origins-of-triple-crown/. For more information on the American classic races, see Richard Sowers, *The Kentucky Derby, Preakness and Belmont Stakes: A Comprehensive History* (Jefferson NC: McFarland, 2014).

28. In May 1931, William Woodward Sr. embarked on a two-month journey around Europe. The first entry of a dairy he kept on the trip, dated May 20, read: "Starting on rather an adventure—off to win the Epsom Derby—if possible—a difficult task—it is only done by the grace of the Gods of good fortune—but their lightning bolts do strike once in a while." Cindy Deubler, "Maryland's Thoroughbred Man: Belair Stud's Woodward Gets Nod as Pillar of the Turf," *Mid-Atlantic Thoroughbred,* n.d., http://midatlantictb.com/cms/index.php/features/34-hall-of-fame/668-maryland-s-thoroughbred-man-belair-stud-s-woodward-gets-nod-as-pillar-of-the-turf.

29. Readers looking for more information about Never Say Die should read Nicholson, *Never Say Die.*

30. Hewitt, *Sire Lines,* 85–88.

31. "Blenheim," *Blood-Horse,* July 11, 1936, 42–43.

32. Dorothy Ours, *Battleship: A Daring Heiress, a Teenage Jockey, and America's Horse* (New York: St. Martin's, 2013) 216–18, 222.

33. "Blenheim," 42.

34. More information about Whirlaway's Triple Crown can be found in John Hervey ("Salvator"), *American Race Horses, 1941* (New York: Sagamore, 1941), 133–45.

35. Hewitt, *Sire Lines,* 87.

36. "Blenheim II in the News Again," *Blood-Horse,* November 28, 1936,

593. The crux of the complaint was that the Aga Khan told Dale and Dai-ziell that the deal was canceled and therefore no commission was due, but then negotiated the sale directly with the syndicate. The Aga Khan reportedly offered to settle the case when it was revealed that the dispute was the result of a miscommunication between the seller and the agents. Based on the typi-cal agent's commission of 10 percent, the claimed commission (£4,500) put the price for Blenheim at £45,000, roughly $4.84 million in 2017. Eric W. Nye, *Pounds Sterling to Dollars: Historic Conversion of Currency,* http://www.uwyo.edu/numimage/currency.htm.

37. Hewitt, *Sire Lines,* 87.

38. "The Battle of Blenheim, *Blood-Horse,* August 1, 1936, 113.

39. "U.S. Syndicate Buys Blenheim," *Morning Post,* July 7, 1936.

40. The English Triple Crown, like its American counterpart, consists of three races for three-year-olds contested over varying distances at three dif-ferent racecourses: the one-mile Two Thousand Guineas at Newmarket, the one-and-a-half-mile Derby at Epsom, and the one-and-three-quarters-mile St. Leger at Doncaster. The last winner of the English Triple Crown was Nijinsky II in 1970. "The English Triple Crown in Focus," *Blood-Horse,* September 13, 2012, updated June 2, 2016.

41. Before selling Mahmoud and Bahram for export to America, the Aga Khan offered all of his horses first to the British National Stud and then to the government in Italy. The British Ministry of Agriculture refused the offer. It was a decision the Aga Khan said he "never could understand" because the asking price was less than one-tenth of the market value of the horses. Mus-solini subsequently vetoed the sale of the Aga Khan's horses to the Italian government. Sultan Muhammad Shah, the Third Aga Khan, *The Memoirs of Aga Khan: World Enough and Time* (New York: Simon & Schuster, 1954), 289–326.

42. Nicholson, *Never Say Die,* 77.

43. "Aga Khan's Tulyar Sold for $700,000," *New York Times,* February 6, 1953.

44. Humphrey S. Finney, "Already the Home of Two Costly and Aristo-cratic Stallions Who Flew in from Europe This Month, the U.S. Now Bids a Welcome to Tulyar," *Sports Illustrated,* July 30, 1956.

45. See Hewitt, *Sire Lines,* 139–46, for a discussion of Nasrullah as a race-horse and as a sire.

46. John Randall, "Richards Is in a Class of His Own," *Racing Post,* May 17, 1999. Travel restrictions in England during World War II limited Nasrul-lah's racing to Newmarket in Suffolk. Baerlein, *Shergar and the Aga Khan's Thoroughbred Empire,* 31.

47. Hewitt, *Sire Lines,* 145.

48. Jodidio, *A Racing and Breeding Tradition,* 64.

49. See Butters's profile at "Horseracing History Online" from the National

Horseracing Museum in Newmarket: http://www.horseracinghistory.co.uk/hrho/action/viewDocument?id=892.

50. Sultan Muhammad Shah, *The Memoirs of Aga Khan,* 212.

51. "Trainer for Aga Khan's Stable Injured by Auto," *St. Louis Post-Dispatch,* October 18, 1949.

52. Baerlein, *Shergar and the Aga Khan's Thoroughbred Empire,* 35–37.

## 2. Families

1. Philip Jodidio, *A Racing and Breeding Tradition: The Horses of the Aga Khan,* 2nd ed. (London: Prestel, 2011), 64.

2. Richard Baerlein, *Shergar and the Aga Khan's Thoroughbred Empire* (London: Michael Joseph, 1984), 38.

3. Peter Willett, "Obituary of Prince Aly Khan," in *Bloodstock Breeders Review* (London: British Bloodstock Agency, n.d.), 215.

4. "The Year of Prince Aly Khan," in *Aga Khan Studs History,* chapter 7, http://www.agakhanstuds.com/History/FamilyTradition/7/en.

5. "Aly Khan's Son, 20, New Aga Khan," *New York Times,* July 13, 1957.

6. The portion of the Aga Khan III's will dealing with succession can be found at http://ismaili.net/timeline/1957/195707/11will.html.

7. Gilbey acknowledged that he was speculating when he wrote that Prince Aly's divorce from actress Rita Hayworth and subsequent affair with "beautiful actress Gene Tierney" were among the factors that ultimately led to the Aga Khan III's decision to choose his grandson as the next Aga Khan. Quintin Gilbey, *Fun Was My Life* (London: Hutchinson, 1970), 242.

8. "An Imam from Harvard," *New York Times,* July 13, 1957.

9. Paul Evan Ress, "Prince Karim Aga Khan," *Sports Illustrated,* August 10, 1964.

10. Baerlein, *Shergar and the Aga Khan's Thoroughbred Empire,* 18. Readers interested in the Aga Khan's own recollections of his time as an owner and breeder are referred to *Memoirs of the Aga Khan: World Enough and Time* (New York: Simon & Schuster, 1954), chapter 10, "A Respite from Public Life."

11. "The Aga Khan Tradition Continues," in *Aga Khan Studs History,* chapter 8, http://www.agakhanstuds.com/History/FamilyTradition/8/en.

12. Baerlein, *Shergar and the Aga Khan's Thoroughbred Empire,* 44–48.

13. Ibid., 76.

14. Ibid., 77.

15. The English Jockey Club eventually dropped its ban on licensing female trainers in 1966 after a protracted legal battle with Florence Nagle. Helen Johnson Houghton's obituary noted that she was the first woman to train a classic winner in Britain. "Johnson Houghton Dies, Aged 102," *Scotsman,* December 6, 2012.

16. George Selwyn, "The Stoute Way to Make It Big," *Pacemaker,* September 1983, 112–18; Michael Stoute Epsom Derby Profile, http://www.epsom-derby.net/michael-stoute.html.

17. Sir Michael Stoute, conversation with author at Freemason Lodge, Newmarket, May 4, 2015.

18. A note about group and graded races: Many of the Thoroughbred races mentioned herein are designated as either Group 1, Group 2, or Group 3 events in Europe or Grade I, Grade II, or Grade III events in the United States. These designations simplify the process of assessing racing class by identifying a country's best races with the highest-quality fields. Grading races in Europe began in the mid-1960s, and in the United States in 1973. For example, the races that comprise the American Triple Crown (the Kentucky Derby, the Preakness Stakes, and the Belmont Stakes) all are designed Grade I events. In England and Ireland, both countries' Two Thousand Guineas, the English Epsom Derby, the Irish Derby, and the English and Irish St. Legers are classified as Group 1 events. Shergar's Group 1 races were the 1980 William Hill Futurity, in which he finished second; the 1981 Epsom Derby, Irish Derby, and King George VI and Queen Elizabeth Diamond Stakes, all of which he won; and the 1981 St. Leger, in which he finished fourth. Shergar also won the 1981 Guardian Newspaper Classic Trial and the Chester Vase, both Group 3 races. Unless otherwise noted, the designations for group and graded races are not included in the text.

19. Information about Shergar's races is taken from *Racehorses of 1980,* a Timeform publication compiled and produced by Phil Bull and Reg Griffin (Halifax, UK: Portway, 1981).

20. Stoute, conversation with author.

21. Lester Piggott added a ninth Epsom Derby winner in 1983, with Teenoso. His record of nine winners in the classic has never been equaled. For information about Piggott's remarkable career, see Dick Francis, *Lester: The Official Biography* (London: Michael Joseph, 1986).

22. Emma Jacobs, "Walter Swinburn, Jockey, 1961–2016," *Financial Times,* December 16, 2016.

23. Ibid., 44–49. For more about Never Say Die, see James C. Nicholson, *Never Say Die: A Kentucky Colt, the Epsom Derby, and the Rise of the Modern Thoroughbred Industry* (Lexington: University Press of Kentucky, 2013).

## 3. Black Swans

1. Black Swan Events, "About," http://blackswanevents.org/?page_id=26.

2. Taleb defined Black Swan events as having "rarity, extreme impact, and retrospective (although not prospective) predictability," and he argued that a few such events "explain almost everything in our world, from the success of ideas and religions, to the dynamics of historical events, to elements of our own personal lives." Nassim Nicholas Taleb, *The Black Swan: The Impact of the Highly Improbable* (New York: Random House, 2010), xxii.

3. For the thefts of Canadian champion Fanfreluche from Claiborne Farm in Kentucky and Nelson Bunker Hunt's Carnauba in Italy, see chapter 9.

4. While Ireland has been marred by political and religious strife for hundreds of years, the "Troubles" generally refers to a specific period running from 1969 through the late 1990s. Some thirty-seven hundred people died during that time as armed factions fought over the British presence in Northern Ireland. For a thorough history of the Troubles, see David McKittrick and David McVea, *Making Sense of the Troubles: The Story of the Conflict in Northern Ireland* (Chicago: New Amsterdam Books, 2002).

5. Ed Moloney, *A Secret History of the IRA* (New York: Norton, 2002), 150.

6. The "Celtic Tiger" refers to a rapid economic boom across Ireland. A survey of Ireland published by the *Economist* in 1988 concluded that the country "was headed for catastrophe," mainly due to the creation of a welfare state that was not sustainable. A decade later, however, Ireland was featured on a cover of the publication as "Europe's shining light." In some years during the Celtic Tiger time frame—generally considered to run from the mid-1990s through the mid-2000s—the Irish economy grew by as much as 10 percent annually. "The Luck of the Irish," *Economist,* October 14, 2004, http://www .economist.com/node/326107.

7. *Day of the Jackal* author Frederick Forsyth, who lived with his family in Dublin at the height of the Troubles, described the dichotomy between life in Northern Ireland and the Republic in his memoir: "In the north, the guerrilla campaign of the IRA against the Belfast government and the British armed forces posted there was at its height, but in the south, the Republic of Ireland, all was quiet and immensely sociable. There were tales of Brits who had to leave because they could not take the partygoing, so they took their damaged livers back home." Frederick Forsyth, *The Outsider: My Life in Intrigue* (New York: G. P. Putnam's Sons, 2015), 277.

8. The civil rights struggle in Northern Ireland stretched back at least a century before the explosion of the Troubles, to a time when Daniel O'Connell began organizing large peaceful protests in an effort to convince the British government to drop laws that discriminated against Catholics. By the mid-1960s, protesters in Northern Ireland were emulating civil rights demonstrations by African Americans in the United States, evoking similar violent responses from the authorities. Jack Holland, *The American Connection: U.S. Guns, Money, and Influence in Northern Ireland* (Niwot, CO: Roberts Rinehart, 1999), 27. For a comprehensive review of the early years of the Troubles, see Richard Clutterbuck, *Protest and the Urban Guerrilla* (London: Cassell, 1973), "Part II, Northern Ireland—A Violent Contrast," 47–140.

9. Comprehensive discussion of Northern Ireland's history, the rise of the Provisional Irish Republican Army, and the Troubles is far beyond the scope of this book. Good sources for general history of Northern Ireland are: Richard Bourke and Ian McBride, eds., *The Princeton History of Modern Ireland* (Princeton: Princeton University Press, 2016), chapter 5; and Thomas Bartlett, *Ireland: A History* (Cambridge: Cambridge University Press, 2010), chapters 6 and 7.

For more information about the Irish Republican Army, see Moloney, *A Secret History of the IRA*, and Brendan O'Brien, *The Long War: The IRA and Sinn Féin* (New York: Syracuse University Press, 1990).

10. Clutterbuck, *Protest and the Urban Guerrilla*, 88.

11. Bartlett, *Ireland*, chapter 6, "The Making of the Two Irelands," 377–467; "Why Is Northern Ireland Part of the United Kingdom?" *Economist*, November 7, 2013.

12. As used herein, the term *republican* refers to a political movement favoring a united Ireland, with the six counties in Northern Ireland back in the fold.

13. According to Ed Moloney, who wrote one of the most comprehensive accounts of the Troubles that erupted in Northern Ireland in 1969, at least four groups over the years have claimed to represent the Irish Republican Army. They include the "Provisional" Irish Republican Army, which split from the "official" Irish Republican Army at the start of the Troubles. Better known as the "Provos," the Provisional Irish Republican Army often is abbreviated as the PIRA. For consistency and unless otherwise noted, references to the "IRA" refer to the Provisional Irish Republican Army. Moloney, *A Secret History of the IRA*.

14. Clutterbuck, *Protest and the Urban Guerrilla*, 59.

15. Bourke and McBride, *The Princeton History of Modern Ireland*, 397.

16. Kidnappings in the Republic of Ireland violated at least the spirit, and maybe the letter, of IRA General Army Order No. 8, dated October 1973, which prohibited "any military action against 26 county forces under any circumstances, whatsoever." O'Brien, *The Long War*, appendix 2, 407. Stealing property, such as a horse, to finance the campaign against the British likely was not subject to any general prohibition of IRA activity in the Republic.

17. Joan S. Howland, "Let's Not Spit the Bit in Defense of 'The Law of the Horse': The Historical and Legal Development of American Thoroughbred Racing," *Marquette Sports Law Review* 14 (Spring 2004): 473n43.

18. James E. Clarity, "Charles Haughey Dies at 80; an Irish Leader with Energy and Expensive Tastes," *New York Times*, June 14, 2006.

19. The 1970 "Arms Trial" in Dublin was widely reported and followed, both in Ireland and abroad, in the same way the O. J. Simpson murder trial occupied the attention of just about everyone in the United States a quarter-century later. Brenda O'Connor, "The Idiot's Guide to the Arms Trial," *Independent*, May 6, 2001. For a time, Haughey also was given at least some credit for the creation of the Provos by fomenting a split in the ranks of the official IRA. According to investigative journalist Ed Moloney, however, the divide-and-conquer policy was approved by Prime Minister Jack Lynch and his cabinet months before the official IRA and the Provos parted ways. Moloney, *A Secret History of the IRA*, 265–66.

20. Forsyth, *The Outsider*, 281.

21. "Taoiseach" is the official title for the prime minister of the Republic

of Ireland. With roots in the Irish language, the word translates as "leader," https://en.oxforddictionaries.com/definition/Taoiseach.

22. Lynch was head of Fianna Fáil, the political party most sympathetic to the republican movement in the south. McKittrick and McVea, *Making Sense of the Troubles*, 66.

23. "Irish Tax Breaks a Proven Thoroughbred Idea," *Scotsman*, March 6, 2005.

24. "Obituary: Robert Sangster," *Daily Telegraph*, April 9, 2004.

25. An excellent discussion of The Minstrel's racing career can be found in Tony Morris, "Little Bundle of Class Who Proved Doubters Wrong," *Racing Post*, June 11, 2011.

26. Winston Collins, "The Nine Million Dollar Horse," *Windsor Star*, February 11, 1978.

27. P. J. Timoney, "Horse Species Symposium: Contagious Equine Metritis; An Insidious Threat to the Horse Breeding Industry in the United States," *Journal of Animal Science* 89 (2011): 1552–60, https://www.aphis.usda.gov/publications/animal_health/content/printable_version/fs_CEMrev09.pdf. For general information about CEM, see APHIS Fact Sheet, "Contagious Equine Metritis," May 2014, https://www.aphis.usda.gov/publications/animal_health/content/printable_version/fs_CEMrev09.pdf.

28. While Haughey's tax break was a godsend for Ireland's Thoroughbred industry, the idea did not set well with horsemen in other European Union countries who saw the incentive as unfair state-sponsored competition for racing's euros. The *Economist* called the tax exemption a "scandal," and in the mid-2000s the European Commission initiated an investigation to decide whether the incentive amounted to illegal state aid. "Horses for Courses," *Economist*, October 14, 2004. The tax exemption ended on July 31, 2008. "Finance Bill 2007: Current Tax Exemption on Stud Fees Ends in July 2008; New Tourism VAT Break," Finfacts Ireland, http://www.finfacts.ie/irishfinancenews/article_10008917.shtml.

29. Sam McAughtry, "Wonder-Horse Shergar Gets a Hero's Welcome," *Irish Times*, October 12, 1981.

## 4. Assassination

1. William Borders, "Lord Mountbatten is Killed as His Fishing Boat Explodes; I.R.A. Faction Says It Set Bomb," *New York Times*, August 28, 1979.

2. Richard Hough, *Mountbatten: Hero of Our Time* (London: Pan Books, 1981), 3.

3. Gelignite is a nitroglycerine-based explosive invented by Alfred Nobel, who also invented dynamite, blasting gelatine, and gelatin dynamite. Its manufacture involves adding guncotton to nitroglycerine along with an antacid for stability and wood pulp to improve the sensitivity of the explosive. "Gelatin," *Explosives-Compositions*, http://www.globalsecurity.org/military/systems/

munitions/explosives-compositions.htm. The bomb that destroyed the *Saturn V* reportedly was a seventeen-inch plastic tube containing five pounds of gelignite and a detonator that could be operated by remote control. Hough, *Mountbatten,* 4. Later in its campaign against the British, the IRA would rely more for its bombs on Semtex, a powerful explosive manufactured in Czechoslovakia that came to Ireland by means of a smuggling route through Libya. In the mid-1980s, the IRA took delivery of more than 120 tons of weapons from Libya, including a ton of Semtex. According to some estimates, three pounds of Semtex is sufficient to demolish a two-story building. "Semtex," *Explosives-Composition.*

4. John Courtney, *It Was Murder! Murders and Kidnappings in Ireland: The Inside Story* (Dublin: Blackwater, 1996), 15.

5. "Statement by I.R.A.," *New York Times,* August 31, 1979.

6. John Courtney retired from the Garda in 1991 after some forty-five years of service. This account of the Garda investigation into the assassination of Lord Mountbatten is taken primarily from Courtney's memoir, *It Was Murder!* and from an interview with the author conducted by telephone on January 27, 2017.

7. "Top Irish Detective Leads Search for Stolen Horse," *New York Times,* February 13, 1983.

8. Courtney, interview.

9. Hough, *Mountbatten,* 356–58.

10. R. W. Apple Jr., "Conservatives Win British Vote; Margaret Thatcher First Woman to Head a European Government," *New York Times,* May 4, 1979.

11. Joseph R. Gregory, "Margaret Thatcher, 'Iron Lady' Who Set Britain on New Course, dies at 87," *New York Times,* April 8, 2013.

12. Not everyone agrees that the IRA relied heavily on money and arms from the United States. Kevin Cullen, a respected journalist and winner of an Overseas Press Club of America Citation of Excellence for his reporting from Northern Ireland, said that "contrary to popular belief, the IRA didn't rely on American money or weapons." Cullen argued in a *Frontline* series that American influence on the British to negotiate a ceasefire with the IRA was a more important asset held by the United States. "America and the Conflict," *The IRA & Sinn Fein, Frontline* on PBS, http://www.pbs.org/wgbh/pages/frontline/shows/ira/reports/america.html.

13. Ed Moloney, *A Secret History of the IRA* (New York: Norton, 2002), 16.

14. Following the assassination of Lord Mountbatten, the FBI "changed their neutralist policy" toward IRA activity in the United States and "agreed to cooperate with British intelligence" to curb domestic IRA political activity. Colin P. Clark, *Terrorism, Inc.: The Financing of Terrorism, Insurgency, and Irregular Warfare* (Santa Barbara, CA: Praegar Security International, 2015), 45.

15. In an address to Congress in February 1985, the first time that body

was addressed by a British prime minister since a speech by Winston Churchill more than thirty years earlier, Prime Minister Thatcher was still urging Americans to refrain from supporting the IRA. Critical of NORAID, Mrs. Thatcher argued that "money is being used to buy the deaths of Irishmen, north and south of the border—and 70 per cent of those killed by the IRA are Irishmen." "'Don't Buy Irish Deaths,' Thatcher Urges Americans: Raps Gifts to IRA in Talk to Congress," *Los Angeles Times,* February 20, 1985.

16. *Attorney General of the United States v. Irish Northern Aid Committee,* 530 F. Supp. 241, 255 (S.D.N.Y 1981), *aff'd,* 668 F.2d 159 (2d Cir. 1982).

17. Warren Richey, "On the Trail of US Funds for IRA," *Christian Science Monitor,* January 14, 1985; see *United States v. Duggan,* 743 F.2d 59 (2d Cir. 1984) and chapter 7 in this book regarding the federal trial at which Hanratty testified.

18. Robert D. McFadden, "5 Are Acquitted in Brooklyn of Plot to Run Guns to I.R.A.," *New York Times,* November 6, 1982.

19. Various spellings for the Libyan leader emerged over the years. Muammar al-Qadhafi is the spelling used in the *World Factbook,* published by the Central Intelligence Agency, https://wwwcia.gov/library/publications/the-world-factbook/geos/ly.html.

20. Tim Weiner, *Legacy of Ashes: The History of the CIA* (New York: Doubleday, 2007), 382.

21. Moloney, *A Secret History of the IRA,* 16.

## 5. Shergar Ascendant

1. Storm Bird was a son of Northern Dancer–South Ocean, by New Providence. Until 2003, when the sale was discontinued, Sangster often shopped for sons of Northern Dancer at the July select sale held annually at Keeneland in Lexington, Kentucky.

2. Assessing Storm Bird's juvenile season, Timeform compared the colt to Nijinsky II, The Minstrel, and Try My Best (all trained by Vincent O'Brien): "Of these, we rate Storm Bird the highest . . . in our opinion, he's a very worthy favorite to emulate the victories of Nijinsky in the Two Thousand Guineas and of Nijinsky and The Minstrel in the Derby." Phil Bull and Reg Griffin, "Storm Bird," *Racehorses of 1980* (Halifax, UK: Portway, 1981).

3. Raymond Gallagher, "$15 Million Racehorse Security Scare," *Irish Times,* January 23, 1981; "Grudge Led to Storm Bird Attack," *Irish Times,* January 28, 1981.

4. Storm Bird's disastrous three-year-old season is summarized in Tony Morris, "Storm Bird," in *Thoroughbred Stallions* (Swindon, UK: Crowood, 1990), 228–30; Bull and Griffin, "Storm Bird."

5. "Storm Bird Has Cough," *Irish Times,* April 15, 1981.

6. "Storm Bird Goes in Guineas," *Irish Times,* May 7, 1981.

7. Named Ballydoyle, Storm Bird's $3.5-million full brother was a winner

in four starts. The horse should not be confused with a more successful filly also named Ballydoyle, a Group 1 winner three decades later.

8. "Prominent Stallion Storm Bird Dead," *Blood-Horse,* December 12, 2004; "Sangster Sells Storm Bird for $30m," *Irish Times,* July 25, 1981.

9. Gerald Eskenazi, "Spectacular Bid Is Dead at Age 27; Crown Attempt Was Foiled by a Pin," *New York Times,* June 11, 2003.

10. Ashford Stud was purchased by John Magnier during the mid-1980s and now serves as the American division of Coolmore Stud, http://coolmore.com/america/farm/.

11. Statistical information about Storm Cat's record as a stallion was provided by Overbook Farm, where the horse spent his career at stud, and reported by *Blood-Horse* at the time of his death. "Leading Sire Storm Cat Dies at Age 30," *Blood-Horse,* April 24, 2013.

12. A summary of Shergar's three-year-old season may be found here: Phil Bull and Reg Griffin, "Shergar," *Racehorses of 1981* (Halifax, UK: Portway, 1982), 779–88.

13. Readers unfamiliar with common practices in English training yards might find Rebecca Cassidy's ethnological study useful. Rebecca Cassidy, *The Sport of Kings: Kinship, Class and Thoroughbred Breeding in Newmarket* (Cambridge: Cambridge University Press, 2002).

14. David Goodwin, conversation with the author at the National Horseracing Museum, Newmarket, March 15, 2017.

15. Cliff Lines, conversation with the author, Exning, near Newmarket, March 15, 2017.

16. There are various meanings of "walleye," including an eye with a light-colored or white iris or a dense and opaque cornea. *Taber's Cyclopedic Medical Dictionary,* 11th ed. (Philadelphia: F. A Davis, 1969).

17. Dickie McCabe, conversation with the author at the Golden Lion pub, Newmarket, March 15, 2017.

## 6. "You need a telescope to see the rest"

The chapter title is a reference to an iconic race call made by BBC radio commentator Peter Bromley as Shergar drew away from the field in the 202nd Epsom Derby: "There's only one horse in it . . . you need a telescope to see the rest."

1. John Randall and Tony Morris, *A Century of Champions: Horse Racing's Millennium Book* (Halifax, UK, 1999), 80.

2. Tom Richmond, "The Derby Day When Swinburn and Shergar Rode into Legend," *Yorkshire Post,* December 14, 2016.

3. "Beldale Flutter a Shock Winner," *Irish Times,* May 14, 1981.

4. Phil Bull and Reg Griffin, *Racehorses of 1981* (Halifax, UK: Portway, 1982), 114–18.

5. Chris Cook, "Walter Swinburn Obituary," *Guardian,* December 13, 2016.

6. Tom MacGinty, "Shergar Annihilates Field by Ten Lengths," *Irish Independent,* June 3, 1981.

7. Ibid.

8. *Epsom Derby: The Shergar Story,* BBC Sport radio program broadcast on June 1, 2011, notes from broadcast available here: http://www.bbc.com/sport/horse-racing/13593356.

9. "Derby Hero Suspended for Careless Riding," *Irish Independent,* June 18, 1981.

10. Dick Francis, *Lester: The Official Biography* (London: Michael Joseph, 1986), 52–55.

11. The Boy's Grave is a small memorial honoring an unknown gypsy boy who, legend says, hanged himself because he mistakenly thought he had lost one of the family's sheep while tending the flock. There is a simple cross and usually flowers at the grave. http://www.thegranthams.co.uk/paul/graves/gypsyboy.html.

12. "Irish Derby: 1866–2015," in The Curragh Information Guide, http://www.curragh.ie/derby150/1981%E2%80%931990.html.

13. Michael O'Farrell, "Immobile Piggott Pays Supreme Tribute to Super Shergar," *Irish Times,* June 29, 1981.

14. Ibid.

15. Richard Baerlein, *Shergar and the Aga Khan's Thoroughbred Empire* (London: Michael Joseph, 1984), 105–8.

16. Kent Hollingsworth, "The Aga Khan IV," *Blood-Horse,* October 31, 1981, 6856–63.

17. Ibid.

18. Sir Michael Stoute, conversation with the author at Freemason Lodge, Newmarket, May 4, 2015.

19. Hollingsworth, "The Aga Khan IV."

20. Gloria Millner and Jim Jordan, "Theft of Shergar No Big Surprise Here," *Lexington Herald,* February 10, 1983; Clive Gammon, "The $40,000,000 Horse," *Sports Illustrated,* August 3, 1981.

21. A list of the original shareholders in the Shergar syndicate can be found in appendix 3.

22. Michael Drake, conversation with the author at the High Street office of Rustons and Lloyd, Newmarket, March 14, 2017.

23. On July 20, 1982, the Irish Republican Army detonated a massive nail bomb in Hyde Park in London, killing four mounted soldiers and seven of their horses.

24. Gammon, "The $40,000,000 Horse."

25. Shergar's pedigree can be found in appendix 1.

26. Anne Peters, e-mail to author, September 16, 2017.

27. Joanne A. Fishman, "The Aga Khan Lifts Italy's Sales," *New York Times,* August 8, 1983.

28. The author reported extensively on contagious equine metritis in *Blood-Horse* magazine during 1978–79. A good summary can be found here: "Equine Metritis in Kentucky," *Blood-Horse,* March 20, 1978, 1329–33.

29. Hollingsworth, "The Aga Khan IV."

## 7. Guns and Money

1. Ed Moloney, *A Secret History of the IRA* (New York: Norton, 2002), 144.

2. The SS *Claudia* was owned by two West German "gray market" arms dealers and was sailing from Tripoli in Libya to Ireland when the vessel and arms were seized off the Irish coast. "Libya: Supplying Terrorist Weapons," a declassified December 1984 report from the Central Intelligence Agency's Directorate of Intelligence that listed the Provisional Irish Republican Army among recipients of weapons from Libya; the comment regarding weapons shipments from the United States was taken from a declassified February 2, 1983, Federal Bureau of Investigation document obtained through a Freedom of Information Request. Both documents were heavily redacted.

3. Reporter Ed Moloney suggests that at least $3.5 million made its way from Libya to the IRA during the 1970s and that as many as three shipments of arms were moved successfully from Tripoli. Moloney, *A Secret History of the IRA,* 10. For a comprehensive history of American support for the IRA, see Jack Holland, *The American Connection: U.S. Guns, Money, and Influence in Northern Ireland* (Niwot, CO: Roberts Rinehart, 1999).

4. The Libyans reportedly restarted modest cash payments, but no weapons, to the IRA in 1981, mainly because Colonel Qadhafi was impressed by the resolve of the protesters. Moloney, *A Secret History of the IRA,* 12.

5. Sinn Féin is the political—and legal—arm of the Irish republican movement. David McKittrick and David McVea, *Making Sense of the Troubles: A History of the Northern Ireland Conflict* (London: Penguin Books, 2012), 127.

6. This account of Gabriel Megahey's role as arms procurer for the Irish Republican Army in the United States is based on documents from Megahey's conviction and failed appeal in federal court, *United States v. Megahey, et al,* 553 F. Supp. 1180 (E.D.N.Y., 1982), *aff'd sub non United States v. Duggan,* 743 F.2d 59 (2d Cir. 1983); Peter Taylor, *Provos: The IRA and Sinn Fein,* rev. ed. (Bloomsbury, UK, 1998), "Prologue: America"; Sean Boyne, "Uncovering the Irish Republican Army," *Jane's Intelligence Review,* August 1, 1996; and Warren Richey, "Roller Skates and Rifles: How IRA Group Tried to Sneak Arms out of US," *Christian Science Monitor,* January 18, 1985.

7. A long history of violence notwithstanding, the IRA claimed the moral high ground in its long-standing campaign against British rule in the six counties comprising Northern Ireland: "The Irish Republic Army as the legal representatives of the Irish people are morally justified in carrying out a campaign of resistance against foreign occupation forces [the British] and domestic col-

laborators." Extracts from the *Green Book, IRA Training Manual,* reproduced in Brendan O'Brien's *The Long War: The IRA and Sinn Féin,* 2nd ed. (Syracuse: Syracuse University Press, 1999), appendix 1.

8. Backed by the United States, the mujahideen used Redeye missiles successfully against Soviet helicopters in Afghanistan, and subsequent versions (including the Stinger missile system) have seen action on battlefields and been employed against civilian targets around the world. In 2010, the IRA was among the militant groups reported to have SAMs. For a history of the Redeye, see "Man-Portable Air-Defense Systems: A Persistent and Potent Threat," an assessment issued by Stratfor Worldview on February 1, 2010, https://www.stratfor.com/article/man-portable-air-defense-systems-persistent-and-potent-threat.

9. Following the assassination of Lord Louis Mountbatten by an IRA bomb in August 1979 and at the urging of Queen Elizabeth, Prime Minister Margaret Thatcher, and British intelligence, the FBI stepped up its investigation of IRA activities in the United States. Colin P. Clarke, *Terrorism, Inc.: The Financing of Terrorism, Insurgency, and Irregular Warfare* (Santa Barbara, CA: Praegar Security International, 2015). See also Moloney, *A Secret History of the IRA,* 16. Those efforts apparently were successful. J. L. Stone Jr., "Irish Terrorism Investigations," *FBI Law Enforcement Bulletin,* October 1987, 18.

10. *United States v. Falvey,* No. 81 Crim. 423(S-2), United States District Court, E.D.N.Y. (June 15, 1982).

11. Joyce Wadler, "Unbowed, and Unashamed of His I.R.A. Role," *New York Times,* March 16, 2000.

12. O'Brien, *The Long War,* 121.

13. Warren Richey, "On the Trail of US Funds for IRA," *Christian Science Monitor,* January 14, 1983.

14. This action expanded a preliminary investigation into NORAID fund-raising efforts initiated by the FBI a year earlier that revealed "apparent" NORAID ties to "weapons procurement activities for the PIRA." Previously classified memoranda from ADIC, New York to the director of the FBI, dated December 10, 1982 and November 7, 1983. Earlier in 1981, the Irish Northern Aid Committee was declared an "agent" of the Irish Republican Army by a federal district court, a finding later affirmed on appeal. *Attorney General of the United States v. Irish Northern Aid Committee,* 530 F. Supp. 241 (S.D.N.Y., 1981), *aff'd Attorney General of the United States v. Irish Northern Aid Committee,* 668 F.2d 159 (2d Cir. 1982).

15. Irish Northern Aid, Inc., mission statement, https://web.archive.org/web/20071022052300/http::inac.org:80/mission.

16. John Courtney, *It Was Murder! Murders and Kidnappings in Ireland: The Inside Story* (Dublin: Blackwater, 1996), 56–62.

17. "Ireland: The Canny Copter Caper," *Time,* November 12, 1973.

18. Sean O'Callaghan, *The Informer: The Real Life Story of One Man's War against Terrorism* (London:, Corgi, 1999), 193–95.

19. A. J. Davidson, *Kidnapped: True Stories of Twelve Irish Hostages* (Dublin: Gill & Macmillan, 2003), 74–75.

20. Ann Hagedorn Auerbach, *Ransom: The Untold Story of International Kidnapping* (New York: Henry Holt, 1998), 214.

21. Peter Murtagh, "Dark Ending to Kidnap Nightmare," *Irish Times,* June 27, 2008. For more information on the spate of IRA kidnappings, see Paul Howard, *Hostage: Notorious Irish Kidnappings,* (Dublin: O'Brien, 2004).

22. The Weston family business, international food giant Associated British Food, is credited with introducing sliced bread to Great Britain during the 1930s. Howard, *Hostage,* 226.

23. "Attempt to Abduct Rich Businessman in Ireland Is Foiled," *New York Times,* August 8, 1983; O'Callaghan, *The Informer,* 217–18.

24. Courtney, *It Was Murder!* 92–102.

25. Howard, *Hostage,* 251.

## 8. A "Rough Patch" for the Garda

1. The declassified memorandum, tagged "Troubled Times for the Garda," was obtained from the US Department of State through a Freedom of Information Act request filed by the author on October 27, 2015. The "rough patch" in the title of this chapter was taken from that memorandum and is a comment on a challenging year for An Garda Síochána in 1983.

2. This account of Shergar's theft is based on contemporaneous press coverage; a comprehensive report on the theft from the committee representing the Shergar syndicate; a written statement from Garda chief superintendent Sean Feely that, to the author's knowledge, has never been previously published; and interviews with several individuals who have knowledge of the theft. Specific citations are provided when necessary for clarity. Particularly informative was Richard Baerlein, *Shergar and the Aga Khan's Thoroughbred Empire* (London: Michael Joseph, 1984).

3. Julian Lloyd, conversation with the author, London, May 5, 2015.

4. Information about the M7 can be found here: http://www.irishmotorwayinfo.com/inex/roads/m7/m7.html.

5. Fionola Meredith, "Life Goes on at the Most Bombed Hotel in the World," *Irish Times,* January 6, 2017. Between 1970 and 1994, the Europa was bombed a total of thirty-three times. It remains in operation today.

6. Derek Thompson, *Tommo: Too Busy to Die* (Compton, UK: Racing Post Books, Kindle ed., 2013), chapter 11.

7. Associated Press, "Callers Claim Shergar Was Killed," *Gettysburg Times,* February 11, 1983.

8. "Shergar May Now Be Dead," *Irish Press,* February 13, 1983; "Report of Syndicate Committee to Shareholders of Shergar Syndicate," February 3, 1984.

9. Quotations from Murphy are taken from a videotaped press conference

that formed part of *Who Kidnapped Shergar?* a program first broadcast by RTE (Ireland's seminational television/radio network) in March 2004.

10. John Courtney, telephone conversation with the author, January 27, 2017.

11. "Family of Groom Held by Gunmen," *Irish Press,* February 9, 1983.

12. The chronology of the calls was set out in the "Report of Syndicate Committee," "Contact with Kidnappers," sections 13–16, reproduced in appendix 3 herein. Full transcripts of the calls, along with an excellent account of the theft, can be found in Roy David, *The Shergar Mystery* (Melplash, UK: Trainers Record, 1986).

13. Liam Ryan, "Shergar Groom Is 'under Threat' from Kidnap Gang," *Irish Independent,* February 11, 1983.

14. Complete transcripts of the recordings are available in Roy David's excellent report of Shergar's theft, *The Shergar Mystery.*

15. "Shergar Search Moves South," *Irish Times,* February 12, 1983.

16. Liam Ryan, "Shergar's Thieves Led by Mystery Jockey," *Irish Independent,* February 14, 1983.

17. David, *The Shergar Mystery,* 105–7.

18. The Rosnaree Hotel should not be confused with the Rossnaree House, an upscale bed-and-breakfast in County Meath. The Rosnaree Hotel, where two members of the Irish National Liberation Army were shot to death in a January 1987 ambush, was demolished in 2010.

19. The use of Polaroid photographs as "proof" was repeated in an acknowledged IRA kidnapping later in 1983. During negotiations for the release of kidnap victim Don Tidey in December, the IRA provided a photograph that included a dated newspaper as proof that Tidey was alive. Tom Brady, "Provos Issue New Picture," *Irish Press,* December 15, 1983. Tidey was rescued after a shootout that left a Garda officer and a soldier dead. After the rescue, the Garda mounted a massive search for Shergar in the same area where Tidey was being held, thinking there might be a connection between the two crimes. The new search turned up nothing. "Link to Shergar Kidnappers," *Irish Independent,* December 15, 1983.

20. In October 1983, in the motion picture *Under Fire,* a photojournalist helped a rebel group in Nicaragua convince followers that the leader of the group still was alive by manufacturing a convincing photograph of the dead man. Perhaps art mirrors real life.

21. "No Photograph and No Trace of Shergar," *Irish Independent,* February 16, 1983.

22. David Ashforth, "'We've Got Shergar,' the Man on the Phone Said. 'If You Want Proof, We'll Send You His Ear,'" *Racing Post,* February 5, 2008.

23. Associated Press, "Shergar's Owners Still Hopeful," *Gettysburg Times,* October 8, 1983.

24. Joanne A. Fishman, "The Aga Khan Lifts Italy's Sails," *New York Times,* August 8, 1983.

25. "Report of Syndicate Committee," section 15.

26. Liam Ryan, "Gardai Will Act to Block Ransom Payment," *Irish Independent,* February 9, 1983.

27. "Shergar May Now Be Dead."

28. Associated Press, "Stolen Superstallion May Be Dead," *Greenwood (SC) Index-Journal,* February 14, 1983.

29. Ken Wharton, *Northern Ireland: An Agony Continued: The British Army and the Troubles, 1980–83* (Solihull, UK: Helion, 2015), 327, 397.

30. "Wife Angry at Concern for Shergar," *Irish Press,"* February 14, 1983.

31. Frank Khan, "Shergar: Fear of £4 Million Loss if Not Found Soon," *Irish Independent,* February 15, 1983.

32. "IFA Drafts Members in Shergar Search," *Irish Press,* February 15, 1983.

33. For information about the "stallion probes," an authorized attempt to locate Shergar or his remains through the use of remote viewing, see chapter 15.

34. Ryan, "Shergar's Thieves Led by Mystery Jockey."

35. In early February 1984, a year after Shergar went missing, Independent Newspapers Ltd. and *Independent* editor Vincent Doyle were fined a total of £400 in Dublin District Court for violation of the Official Secrets Act. The newspaper lost an appeal of the verdict a few months later.

36. "Radio Clue on Shergar," *Irish Press,* February 14, 1983.

37. "No Photograph and No Trace of Shergar."

## 9. The Man in the Trilby

1. David Remnick, "18 Months After Disappearance of Shergar, Questions Remain," *Washington Post,* August 26, 1984.

2. Martin Kelner, "Horsey and Detective Fields Stumped by Shergar," *Guardian,* March 21, 2004.

3. Richard Baerlein, *Shergar and the Aga Khan's Thoroughbred Empire* (London: Michael Joseph, 1984), 152–53; Matthew Hart, *The Irish Game: A True Story of Crime and Art* (New York: Walker, 2004), 7–25; "Ireland: Renegade Debutante," *Time,* May 20, 1974.

4. John Courtney, *It was Murder! Murders and Kidnappings in Ireland: The Inside Story* (Dublin: Blackwater, 1996), 56–62.

5. For the story of Fanfreluche, see Mike DelNagro, "The Million-Dollar Horse Heist," *Sports Illustrated,* August 1, 1977; Billy Reed, "Worldwide Search for Mare Ends in Kentucky," *Louisville Courier-Journal,* December 9, 1977; Billy Reed, "Mare Got a Second Identify in Summer," *Louisville Courier-Journal,* December 10, 1977; Billy Reed, "The Toast of Tompkinsville," *Sports Illustrated,* December 19, 1977.

6. Dave Anderson, "On Looking for a Horse," *New York Times,* February 14, 1983.

7. Frances Karon, "Carnauba: A Captivating Tale," *Saratoga Special,* August 23, 2007.

8. Dorothy Weil, "The Kidnapped $500,000 Horse," *St. Louis Post-Dispatch,* November 13, 1977.

9. "The Shergar Hunt: 'Stage Irishman' Leaves Limelight," *Times* (London), February 17, 1983.

10. Liam Ryan, "Shergar Still in Ireland," *Irish Independent,* February 20, 1983.

11. "Search," *Irish Independent,* February 17, 1983.

12. James Keogh, conversation with the author at the Heirloom restaurant in Midway, Kentucky, on February 10, 2017. Keogh now lives in central Kentucky

13. "Interpol Joins Shergar Chase," *Irish Press,* February 17, 1983.

14. Associated Press, "Several Leads in Shergar Case," *Gettysburg Times,* February 19, 1983.

15. Liam Ryan, "Someone Is Holding Back Information about Shergar, Say Gardai," *Irish Independent,* February 17, 1983.

16. "Shergar Still in Ireland Gardai Believe," *Irish Press,* February 20, 1983.

17. Associated Press, "No Trace Yet of Shergar," *Pentagraph* (Bloomington, IL), February 23, 1983.

18. "Shergar Owners 'Kept in Dark.'" *Irish Press,* February 23, 1983.

19. "Report of Syndicate Committee to Shareholders of Shergar Syndicate," February 3, 1984.

20. Liam Ryan, "Shergar Jockeys Quizzed," *Irish Independent,* February 26, 1983.

21. "Shergar 'Not in Ireland'—Lord Derby," *Irish Independent,* March 1, 1983.

22. "Theft of Horsebox Link with Shergar," *Irish Independent,* March 6, 1983.

23. Liam Ryan, "Shergar Relations with Gardai Are 'Strained.' " *Irish Independent,* March 14, 1983.

24. "Denial That IRA Took Shergar," *Irish Independent,* April 2, 1983.

25. Associated Press, "Irish Police End Search for Missing Racehorse," *New York Times,* May 25, 1983.

26. Remnick, "18 Months After Disappearance of Shergar."

## 10. "Rugby" and the Captain

1. "Shergar Search Moves South," *Irish Times,* February 12, 1983.

2. "Gesture," *Irish Press,* February 11, 1983.

3. Associated Press, "Stolen Superstallion May Be Dead," *Greenwood (SC) Index-Journal,* February 14, 1983.

4. Donal O'Higgins, "An Owner of the Kidnapped Multi-Million Dollar Racehorse Shergar . . .," United Press International Archives, March 16, 1983, https://www.upi.com/Archives/1983/03/16/An-owner-of-the-kidnapped-multi-million-dollar-racehorse-Shergar/4543416638800/; "No Payments by

Syndicate," in "Report of Syndicate Committee to Shareholders of Shergar Syndicate," February 3, 1984, section 18.

5. Much of the information here about Captain Berry's role was taken from an unpublished summary of Berry's contemporaneous notes made during the weeks after Shergar was stolen and the author's in-person interviews with him in May 2016 and March 2017.

6. A Dominican lay brother, St. Martin de Porres is the patron saint for people of mixed race, innkeepers, barbers, and public-health workers. It also was said that he had an excellent relationship with animals, which may have been why Berry's caller requested a relic from the saint to be paced in Shergar's stall. His feast day is November 3.

7. The author met Captain Berry for the first time on a pleasant day in May 2015. The timing of the visit marked an odd and unexpected coincidence: we found ourselves talking about Shergar almost thirty-two years to the day after Berry took the last call from Rugby, thirty-two years after he was prepared to offer himself as a hostage in an effort to help secure the Shergar's recovery.

8. The story broke on November 11, 1983, in a front-page article in the *Irish Times:* Peter Murtagh, "£80,000 Paid for Shergar Missing, Say Garda Sources," *Irish Times,* November 11, 1983. Cosgrove, Kenirons, and Minogue were identified in subsequent articles: "Vet Admits That £80,000 Given to Shergar's Kidnappers," *Irish Independent,* February 7, 1984; "Shergar Case Garda May Be Disciplined," *Irish Press,* November 9, 1984.

9. "Gardai Aware of Shergar Ransom," *Irish Independent,* November 17, 1983.

10. Tony Smurthwaite, "Shergar Story Continuing," *Daily Racing Form,* November 10, 1994.

## 11. The Insurance Game

1. The underwriters' slip was reproduced in Antony Brown, *Hazard Unlimited: The Story of Lloyd's of London* (London: Peter Davies, 1973), photo section between pp. 146 and 147.

2. Ibid., 154.

3. Ibid., 4–5.

4. Information about insurance coverage for Shergar was provided by Terry Hall in email communications and in telephone conversations with the author, June 23, 2017, and July 10, 2017.

5. Julian Lloyd, conversation with the author, London, May 6, 2015.

6. "Interesting, Very Interesting," in "Scorecard," ed. Robert W. Creamer, *Sports Illustrated,* June 27, 1983.

7. Gareth Parry, "Lloyd's Agrees to Pay out £7m for Shergar's Loss," *Manchester Guardian,* June 24, 1983.

8. Financing for the syndication of Shergar is discussed in detail here: Roy David, *The Shergar Mystery* (Melplash, UK: Trainers Record, 1986), 124–26.

9. Paul McGrath, "Law Report: Shergar Insurance Claim Fails: *O'Brien and Others v Hughes-Gibb & Co Ltd and Another*—Chancery Division (Mr. Justice Rattee) 26 April 1994," *Lloyd's Insurance Reports* 1 (1995): 90.

10. Michael Payton, conversation with the author, London, March 13, 2017.

11. "Shergar Kidnapping Unique, Says Lanigan," *Racing Post,* March 16, 1994.

12. Insurance policies for Shergar and a large file of other related documents were compiled by David J. Horgan to assist Stan Cosgrove in his case against Norwich Union. Horgan provided his files to the author during a meeting in Dublin on March 11, 2017.

13. Pantheon Ltd. was identified as the "Assured" on both policies. Pantheon was a Dublin company set up by Cosgrove when his share in Shergar was purchased.

14. Correspondence between Norwich Union and James Cosgrove, Stan Cosgrove's son and an insurance man himself, was among the material compiled and shared with the author by David J. Horgan.

15. Feely's statement, like most of the documentation relating to Stan Cosgrove's claim against Norwich Union, was obtained by David Horgan and provided to the author in Dublin.

16. Sean O'Callaghan, *The Informer: The Real Life Story of One Man's War against Terrorism* (London: Corgi Books, 1999), 193–95.

17. Colin McIntyre, "Shergar Owners Ask Damages," *Daily Racing Form,* February 24, 1983.

18. Willy Clilgan, "Kildare Council to Fight £20m Shergar Claim," *Irish Times,* February 24, 1983.

19. Henry Bauress, "Shergar: 30 years Later £20m Claim Was Never Pursued—Council Spokesperson," *Leinster Leader,* February 8, 2013.

## 12. The Usual Suspects

1. Sean Berry, conversations with the author, Kildare, May 7, 2015, and March 10, 2017; Julian Lloyd, conversation with the author, London May 6, 2015.

2. Since at least 1932, when Arthur Gardner's novel *Tinker's Kitchen* was published, the term *grass* has been associated with an informer. In Northern Ireland specifically, a *supergrass* refers to a member of the IRA or some other paramilitary group who identifies his comrades in return for immunity from prosecution. The first use of the term in that context may have been associated with Christopher Black, an IRA man who informed on a number of other IRA members to avoid a prison sentence. Based on Black's testimony at a mass trial in 1983, twenty-two members of the IRA were sentenced to a total of more than four thousand years. "1983: IRA Members Jailed for 4,000 Years," BBC archive *On This Day,* http://news.bbc.co.uk/onthisday/hi/dates/stories/august/5/newsid_2527000/2527437.stm.

3. Harrison Smith, "Sean O'Callaghan, IRA Assassin Turned Informant, Dies at 62," *Washington Post,* August 25, 2017.

4. David Horgan's handwritten notes of his meeting with Sean O'Callaghan were provided by him to the author in Dublin on March 11, 2017. The account of Horgan's meeting with O'Callaghan is based on Horgan's notes and on a conversation he had with the author, also on March 11, 2017.

5. O'Callaghan, *The Informer,* 193–95.

6. Ibid., 378.

7. "Statement on the Shergar Case by Chief Superintendent Sean Feely," signed January 14, 2002, provided to the author by David Horgan on March 11, 2017. To the author's knowledge, Feely's statement is being made public for the first time here.

8. Letter from Michael O'Sullivan to Stan Cosgrove, dated February 20, 2002, provided by David Horgan to the author on March 11, 2017.

9. Jeremy Greenwood, comp., *Sefton: "The Horse of the Year"* (London: Quiller, 1983), 51–64.

10. Jonathan Irwin with Emily Hourican, *Jack & Jill: The Story of Jonathan Irwin* (Cork: Mercier, 2014), 98–99.

11. Gordon Raymer, "Michael Pedersen: A Broken Man Who Stabbed His Children to Death," *Telegraph,* October 1, 2012.

12. "Document No. W.S. 658," Bureau of Military History, 1913–21, archived here: http://www.bureauofmilitaryhistory.ie/reels/bmh/BMH.WS0658.pdf.

13. Toby Harnden, *"Bandit Country": The IRA and South Armagh* (London: Hodder & Stoughton, 2000), 130–31.

## 13. The French Connections

1. David Remnick, "18 Months After Disappearance of Shergar, Questions Remain," *Washington Post,* August 26, 1984, recounting a story from Captain Sean Berry, head of the Irish Thoroughbred Breeders Association.

2. "2 Theories Given in Race Horse Theft," *Galveston Daily News,"* February 10, 1983.

3. "Thieves May Have Shergar in 'Secret Love Nest,'" *Galveston Daily News,"* February 14, 1983.

4. Dick Francis, "The Ugly Nightmare in World Where Everyone Dreams of Golden Pay-off," *Irish Independent,* February 10, 1983.

5. John M. Flynn, head of Weatherby's Ireland Bloodtyping Laboratory, explained the procedures for verifying a horse's parentage available in the early 1980s in an email to the author on August 21, 2017: "Blood typing was the internationally accepted technology for equine parentage testing. Basically, it consisted of two technologies, red cell typing using specific immunogens and protein polymorphism in identifying allele variation using electrophoresis. Both systems combined to form the basis for an effective parentage testing with

a probability of detecting an incorrect parentage of up to 97 percent. This system was used internationally up to the turn of the century when it was superseded by new DNA technology."

6. John M. Flynn, email to the author, September 16, 2017.

7. Francis acknowledged as much in his dedication to *The Danger:* "Liberty Market Ltd. is fictional, though similar organizations exist. No one who has helped me with the background of this book wants to be mentioned, but my thanks to them just the same." Dick Francis, *The Danger* (New York: Berkley, 1984).

8. In a conversation with the author on May 5, 2015, in London, insurance executive Julian Lloyd, who was in Ireland monitoring the search for Shergar in the weeks after the horse was stolen, said that Control Risks was contacted by the kidnap and ransom division of Lloyd's of London. In an email to the author on February 1, 2017, however, Georgina Parkes from Control Risks said that she could not "discuss specific organizations, whether we have undertaken work on their behalf or not." Readers interested in more information about Control Risks are referred to Ann Hagedorn Auerbach, *Ransom: The Untold Story of International Kidnapping* (New York: Henry Holt, 1998).

9. "Racing Writer Fears for Shergar," *Irish Press,* October 7, 1983.

10. Julian Lloyd, conversation with the author, London, May 6, 2015.

11. Ed Moloney, *A Secret History of the IRA* (New York: Norton, 2002), 12–16.

12. This account of the death of Jean-Michel Gambet is based upon a review of the 250-page investigative file obtained from the Lexington (Kentucky) Police Department through an Open Records request; a January 13, 2017, interview conducted by the author with retired police lieutenant Drexel Neal, one of the lead investigators on the case; and various press reports.

13. The Gambet/Mafia/Aga Khan theory was floated in the press a few weeks after Shergar was stolen (see Ken Curran, "Death Link with Shergar Denied," *Independent,* March 28, 1983), but the speculation also had staying power. On the twenty-fifth anniversary of Shergar's theft, the *Racing Post* ran a lengthy retrospective that included several "wild theories": David Ashforth, "'We've Got Shergar,' the Man on the Phone Said. 'If You Want Proof, We'll Send You His Ear,'" *Racing Post,* February 5, 2008. The *Racing Post* article also addressed the Wayne Murty/Marcel Boussac theory discussed later in this chapter.

14. Nick Robinson, "Setting the Pace: Publisher's Comment; The Mystery Death of Gambet," *Pacemaker,* April 1983.

15. Curren, "Death Link with Shergar Denied."

16. David L. Heckerman, "The Importance of Paperwork," *Blood-Horse,* March 12, 1983, 1024–25.

17. David L. Heckerman, "Homicide Ruling," *Blood-Horse,* March 12, 1983, 1823–24.

18. Ibid.

19. Captain Phil Kitchen, Lexington-Fayette County Urban Division of Police memorandum, August 30, 1983.

20. "Lexington Police Close Case in Death of Horseman," *Louisville Courier-Journal,* September 1, 1983.

21. "Medical Examiner Disputes Ruling in Horseman's Death," *Louisville Courier-Journal,* September 25, 1983.

22. "Shergar 'No Link' with Dead Rider," *Montreal Gazette,* March 29, 1983. The headline writer obviously was unfamiliar with Gambet and with the difference between a bloodstock agent and a jockey.

23. Philip Jodidio, *A Racing and Breeding Tradition: The Horses of the Aga Khan,* 2nd ed. (London: Prestel, 2011), 169–70.

24. A report on *Singer v. The Jockey Club* can be found here: http://www.5rb.com/case/singer-v-the-jockey-club/.

25. Boussac was a contemporary of the Aga Khan III, both having come into racing around the end of World War I. Boussac was the leading owner in France nineteen times and the country's leading breeder on seventeen occasions. By the late 1950s, however, Boussac's star was beginning to dim, and in the late 1970s his business and Thoroughbred empires were in the throes of bankruptcy. Tony Morris, "Extraordinary Highs to Equally Remarkable Lows," *Racing Post,* October 29, 2012.

26. Richard Baerlein, *Shergar and the Aga Khan's Thoroughbred Empire* (London: Michael Joseph, 1984), 76–77.

27. Peter Willett, *Makers of the Modern Thoroughbred* (Lexington: University Press of Kentucky, 1986), 143–44.

28. James Brown, "The Boussac Transaction," *Blood-Horse,* July 2, 1979, 3070–71; "French Court Rules against Murty," *Blood-Horse,* November 24, 1979, 6503.

29. *Murty v. Aga Khan,* 92 F.R.D. 478 (E.D.N.Y. 1981), https://casetext.com/case/murty-v-aga-khan.

30. Neil Wallis and Frank Curran, "Well, That's That!" *Daily Star,* November 8, 1983.

31. Baerlein, *Shergar and the Aga Khan's Thoroughbred Empire,* 62–62. Baerlein said that both the Aga Khan and Michael Stoute "were stunned to learn that any responsible racing journalist" would believe the story about Shergar, Murty, and the Arlington Million.

32. Remnick, "18 Months After Disappearance of Shergar."

## 14. The Pathologist and the Skull

1. "IFA Drafts Members in Shergar Search," *Irish Press,* February 15, 1983.

2. Richard Ford, "Police Take Up Crystal Ball in Shergar Hunt," *Times* (London), February 16, 1983.

3. Michael Clower, "Is This the Head of Shergar? 'Skull with Bullet Holes' Found in Latest Twist to Kidnap Mystery," *Racing Post,* April 14, 2000.

4. "Shergar Skull Alert a 'False Alarm': Expert," *Telegraph,* April 14, 2000.

5. "Scientist Doubts if Shergar Case Is Drawing to a Close," *Independent,* April 4, 1996.

6. "Shergar's Remains Discovered?" *Thoroughbred Daily News,* April 4, 1996.

7. Sean O'Callaghan, *The Informer: The Real Story of One Man's War against Terrorism* (London: Corgi Books, 1999), 194.

8. Ford, "Police Take Up Crystal Ball in Shergar Hunt."

9. Associated Press, "Psychics Brought into Search," *Seguin (TX) Gazette-Enterprise,* February 15, 1983.

## 15. The Stallion Probes

This chapter lacks extensive notes for a simple reason. Nothing about the search for Shergar conducted by the Mobius Group in 1983–1984 has ever been published before. In fact, to the best of the author's knowledge, the research files had not been opened by anyone for almost thirty-five years, not until the author visited the home of Mobius founder Stephan A. Schwartz on March 1–3, 2017. The author was granted full access to the Mobius Group's voluminous research material—some five hundred pages—from the Shergar project, discussed here in print for the first time. The author also relied on extensive interviews with Schwartz conducted over that two-day period, a lengthy telephone interview with Randall J. De Mattei (executive director of Mobius) on July 25, 2017, and a conversation with attorney Michael Payton in London on March 13, 2017.

1. Not all insurance claims were paid. Insurance carrier Norwich Union refused payment to Stan Cosgrove. His long battle with Norwich Union is discussed in chapter 11.

2. For more information about Deep Quest, readers may be interested in a television documentary, *In Search of . . . Psychic Seahunt,* at https://www.youtube.com/watch?v=BZYVY5EmKuQ. The Alexandria expedition is discussed in great detail in Stephan A. Schwartz, *The Alexandria Project* (Lincoln, NE: iUniverse, 2001). Subsequent underwater archaeological successes included locating the brig *Leander* and eighteen other wrecks in waters off the coast of Catalina Island, a survey of St. Ann's Bay in Jamaica, and locating the cargo vessel *Dean Richmond* in Lake Erie. Curriculum vitae of Stephen A. Schwartz, https://www.stephanaschwartz.com/biography/.

3. In a somewhat different, but equally applicable, context, noted author and futurist Arthur C. Clarke said that "any sufficiently advanced technology is indistinguishable from magic." https://www.clarkefoundation.org/about-sir-arthur/sir-arthurs-quotations/.

4. Useful histories about the history of government-sponsored parapsychology research include Annie Jacobsen, *Phenomena: The Secret History of the U.S. Government's Investigation into Extrasensory Perception and Psychokinesis* (New York: Little, Brown, 2017); and Edwin C. May, Victor Rubel, Joseph W.

McMoneagle, and Loyd Auerbach, *ESP Wars: East & West* (Crossroad, Kindle ed., 2015). A timeline of forty years of both government and civilian remote viewing programs can be found here: http://www.irva.org/remote-viewing/timeline.html.

5. *The Case of E.S.P., Horizon,* BBC, first broadcast September 26, 1983, uncut version available here: https://www.youtube.com/watch?v=h2Gog3xMluA.

6. Martin Kelner, "Horsey and Detective Fields Stumped by Shergar," *Guardian,* March 21, 2004.

7. Terry Hall has no specific recollection of this discussion. Terry Hall, telephone conversations with the author, June 23, 2017, and July 10, 2017.

8. The Special Air Service (SAS) is the British Army's elite special forces unit. http://www.eliteukforces.info/special-air-service/.

9. To the author's knowledge, the Polaroid photograph is reproduced here for the first time. Although the author believes that the photograph is what it appears to be, an image taken after Shergar was stolen, Jeff Oliver could not be located to provide confirmation of the photograph's origin. The Garda at the time refused comment about the existence of such photographs. O'Higgins, "Kidnappers of the Aga Khan's Racehorse."

10. Jacobsen, *Phenomena,* 151–53.

11. The Mobius Group's itinerary in Ireland was re-created through the author's review of travel receipts, notes, individual maps produced by remote viewers, and the resulting composite map.

12. This account of the Mobius Group's reconnoiter of the stone bridge property is based on interviews with Schwartz and De Mattei. When their accounts differed, as happened regarding some details of a second-night excursion onto the property by De Mattei and Walker, preference was given to De Mattei's account because he was on site. The author's attempts to locate Walker were unsuccessful.

13. Michael Payton's recollection of David Walker being impressed with Hella Hammid's uncanny powers of prediction was confirmed, in part, by insurance underwriter Julian Lloyd, who recalled hearing similar stories about the remote viewer's abilities. Although Lloyd did not identify Walker, Hammid, or anyone else by name, he said that he had heard similar stories about a "soldier" riding around Ireland with a "psychic." Julian Lloyd, conversation with the author, London, May 5, 2015.

## Epilogue

1. Official handicappers from Great Britain, Ireland, and France assigned three-year-old Shergar a rating of 100—the "norm"—for 1981. By a wide margin it was the highest rating given any horse that year. The highest rated juvenile racing in 1981, Green Forest, was assigned an 88; the best four-year-old was Northjet, with a rating of 92. Phil Bull and Reg Griffin, eds., *Racehorses of 1981*

(Halifax, UK: Portway, 1982), 966–69. See also Tony Morris and John Randall, *Horse Racing: Records, Facts and Champions,* 3rd ed. (Enfield, UK: Guinness, 1990), 40, for a discussion of Shergar's Timeform designation as Horse of the Year with a rating of 140.

2. Marcus Armytage, "Worship with Church at the Derby Altar," *Daily Telegraph,* May 29, 2017.

3. Timeform ratings are an objective way to assess the relative merits of racehorses. Readers interested in more information should refer to "A Guide to Understanding Timeform," http://www.racepedia.co.uk/blog/betting-tips/a-guide-to-understanding-timeform/.

4. John Randall and Tony Morris, *A Century of Champions: Horse-Racing's Millennium Book* (Halifax, UK: Portway, 1999), 80.

5. Greg Wood, "Frankel Hailed as Greatest Ever After Royal Ascot Queen Anne Stakes Win," *Guardian,* June 19, 2012; "Racing's Superstar," http://frankel.juddmonte.com/.

6. Michael Church, email to author, June 23, 2017.

7. Jonathan Irwin, discussion with the author, May 11, 2015.

8. Statistical information for Shergar's only crop was obtained from www.equineline.com.

9. Valentine Lamb, "Shergar Foal Gets Film Star Treatment," *Irish Field,* November 19, 1983.

10. David Hedges, "Shergar Sale Topper," *Blood-Horse,* November 26, 1983, 8676. A report on the sale distributed by United Press International reported the sale prices differently. According to UPI, Authaal sold for $402,670 as a weanling; the final price for Galletto was reported as $619,500. Jeanette McDermott, "Son of Kidnapped Stallion Brings Record Price," UPI Archives, November 21, 1983, http://www.upi.com/Archives/1983/11/21/Son-of-kidnapped-stallion-brings-record-price/4925438238800/. The difference likely can be attributed to different conversion rates for Irish guineas.

11. Church, email to author.

12. Tony Morris, "Reasons behind Aga's Dominance: Employing Variety of Stallions Helped Sinndar's Breeder Bag Fourth Derby," *Racing Post,* June 13, 2000.

13. British Champion Series, http://britishchampionsseries.com/stars/trainers/sir-michael-stoute/.

14. Chris Cook, "Water Swinburn Obituary," *Guardian,* December 13, 2016.

15. Lee Mottershead, "Coroner Says Shergar Rider Died After Falling from Window," *Racing Post,* February 9, 2017.

16. Marcus Armytage, "Racing Mourns Walter Swinburn, Three-Time Derby-Winning Jockey," *Telegraph,* December 12, 2016.

17. Julian Wilson, *Julian Wilson's 100 Greatest Racehorses* (London: Queen Anne, 1987), 141–43.

18. Philip Jodidio, *A Racing and Breeding Tradition: The Horses of the Aga Khan,* 2nd ed. (London: Prestel, 2011), 171–72.

19. "Stoute Disappointed," *Irish Press,* December 5, 1990.

20. "Horse Racing; Aga Khan to Return to Racing in Britain," *New York Times,* December 16, 1994.

21. Greg Wood, "No Regrets as Fulke Takes Stock of 40 Years," *Guardian,* October 22, 2006.

22. Dick Francis, *Lester: The Official Biography* (London: Michael Joseph, 1986). A lengthy accounting of Piggott's wins can be found in the appendix, 231–325.

23. Susan Heller Anderson, "Chronicle," *New York Times,* July 27, 1991.

24. Although legal action apparently was never initiated against Drion, and restitution reportedly was paid to the Aga Khan, information about the allegations of fraud became public during litigation in Ireland's High Court involving Drion's longtime secretary Mary Charlton. She filed a lawsuit claiming that she was being made a "scapegoat" for the alleged fraud. Lawyers for the Aga Khan eventually conceded that Charlton had never been a beneficiary of the fraud. "Aga Khan Accepts That Secretary Was Not Part of Fraud," *Irish Times,* October 30, 1999.

25. An obituary for Drion can be found in Tom Kelly, "Recent Deaths," *Meath Chronicle,* December 8, 2007.

26. Sue Finley, "Everything's Coming Up Coulonces," *TDN Shared Content,* http://www.thoroughbreddailynews.com/everythings-coming-up-coulonces-shared-archive/.

27. Aviva Insurance Ltd. was among the insurers of Troy and of Shergar. The company's liability for the death of Troy and the loss of Shergar was reported as £66,000 and £144,000 respectively. Interestingly, unlike some other of Shergar's insurers, Aviva "presumed" that Shergar was dead by August 1983. Mentions of Troy and Shergar are included in Aviva's corporate history: https://heritage.aviva.com/our-history/companies/a/aviva-insurance-ltd/.

28. Alex Brummer, "Lord Weinstock," *Guardian,* July 24, 2002. Troy was bred at Weinstock's Ballymacoll Stud in County Meath, Ireland.

29. "Golden Fleece Is Dead," *Irish Independent,* March 18, 1984.

30. Colin McIntyre, "Shergar Snatch Source of Concern for Irish Breeders," *Daily Racing Form,* February 15, 1983, 5.

31. George Ennor, "Shergar Snatch," *Daily Racing Form,* February 21, 1983, 8.

32. "Shergar: 30 Years Later—Kidnap as Reported by the *Leinster Leader,*" *Leinster Leader,* February 8, 2013.

33. Donal O'Higgins, "Racehorse Kidnap 'Severe Setback' for Breeders," *UPI Archives,* February 20, 1983.

34. Ken Curran, "Ireland Stays Ahead in Horse-Breeding Stakes," *Irish Independent,* March 19, 1984.

35. BBC, *Epsom Derby: The Shergar Story*," transcript of program broadcast on June 1, 2011, available here: http://www.bbc.com/sport/horse-racing/13593356.

36. Numbers for 2016 were the most recent statistics available at the time of writing. The complete report, "2016 Thoroughbred Industry Statistics," can be found here: http://www.irishracing.com/news?prid=180273.

37. Letter from Geraldine Van Bueren, BBC Copyright Department, to Captain Berry, dated November 5, 1984. Courtesy of Captain Berry.

38. Jonathan Irwin, *Jack & Jill: The Story of Jonathan Irwin* (Cork: Mercier, 2014).

39. "Shergar 'Found' in Channel Islands," *Irish Press,* March 27, 1991.

40. Michael Dwyer, review of *Shergar, Irish Times,* June 10, 2000. The film is available on DVD.

41. Ed Moloney, "Sean O'Callaghan," *The Broken Elbow* (blog), August 24, 2017, https://thebrokenelbow.com/2017/08/24/sean-ocallaghan/.

42. Gary O'Shea, "Tell Us the Hoof," *Sun,* February 12, 2018.

43. Letter from C. E. Weatherby, deputy secretary to the Jockey Club, dated September 23, 1987. The letter was sent in response to an inquiry asking whether the Jockey Club had made any official statements about Shergar. Because Shergar was a classic winner, the letter noted, his name "remains protected and cannot therefore be registered again for any other horse under the Rules of Racing in this country in perpetuity."

# Bibliography

Amore, Anthony M., and Tom Mashberg. *Stealing Rembrandts: The Untold Story of Notorious Art Heists.* New York: Palgrave Macmillan, St. Martin's, 2011.

Auerbach, Ann Hagedorn. *Ransom: The Untold Story of International Kidnapping.* New York: Henry Holt, 1998.

Baerlein, Richard. *Shergar and The Aga Khan's Thoroughbred Empire.* London: Michael Joseph, 1984.

Bartlett, Thomas. *Ireland: A History.* Cambridge: Cambridge University Press, 2010.

Bauer, Conrad. *Shergar: A True Crime Story of Kidnapping, Racehorse, and Politics.* N.p.: Maplewood.

Boser, Ulrich. *The Gardner Heist: The True Story of the World's Largest Unsolved Art Theft.* New York: Harper Collins, 2009.

Bourke, Richard, and Ian McBride, eds. *The Princeton History of Modern Ireland.* Princeton: Princeton University Press, 2010.

Brown, Antony. *Hazard Unlimited: The Story of Lloyd's of London.* London: Peter Davies, 1973.

Bull, Phil, and Reg Griffin. *Racehorses of 1980.* Halifax, UK: Portway, 1981.

———. *Racehorses of 1981.* Halifax, UK: Portway, 1982.

Cassidy, Rebecca. *The Sport of Kings: Kinship, Class and Thoroughbred Breeding in Newmarket.* Cambridge: Cambridge University Press, 2002.

Clutterbuck, Richard. *Kidnap & Ransom: The Response.* London: Faber & Faber, 1978.

———. *Protest and the Urban Guerrilla.* London: Cassell, 1973.

Courtney, John. *It Was Murder! Murders and Kidnappings in Ireland: The Inside Story.* Dublin: Blackwater, 1996.

David, Roy. *The Shergar Mystery.* Bridport, UK: Trainers Record, 1986.

Davidson, A. J. *Kidnapped: True Stories of Twelve Irish Hostages.* Dublin: Gill & Macmillan, 2003.

Emerson, Steven, and Brian Duffy. *The Fall of Pan Am 103: Inside the Lockerbie Investigation.* New York: G. P. Putnam's Sons, 1990.

Francis, Dick. *Blood Sport.* New York: Berkley Books, 1967.

———. *The Danger.* New York: Berkley Books, 1984.

Gilbey, Quintin. *Fun Was My Living.* London: Hutchinson, 1970.

Greenwood, Jeremy. *Sefton: The Horse for Any Year.* London: Quiller, 1983.

Hagedorn, Ann. *The Invisible Soldiers: How America Outsourced Our Security.* New York: Simon & Schuster, 2014.

Halstead, Stephan. *Shergar: The IRA Back Story.* Toronto: Crystal Dreams, 2015.

Harnden, Toby. *Bandit Country: The IRA & South Armagh.* London: Hodder & Stoughton, 1999.

Hart, Matthew. *The Irish Game: A True Story of Crime and Art.* New York: Walker, 2004.

Hewitt, Abram S. *Sire Lines.* Rev. ed. Lexington, KY: Eclipse, 2006.

Holland, Jack. *The American Connection: U.S. Guns, Money, and Influence in Northern Ireland.* Niwot, CO: Roberts Rinehart, 1987.

Hough, Richard. *Mountbatten: Hero of Our Time.* London: Pan Books, 1981.

Howard, Paul. *Hostage: Notorious Irish Kidnappings.* Dublin: O'Brien, 2004.

Irwin, Jonathan. *Jack & Jill: The Story of Jonathan Irwin.* Cork: Mercier, 2014.

Jacobsen, Annie. *Phenomena: The Secret History of the U.S. Government's Investigation into Extrasensory Perception and Psychokinesis.* New York: Little, Brown, 2017.

Jodidio, Philip. *A Racing and Breeding Tradition: The Horses of the Aga Khan.* 2nd ed. London: Prestel, 2011.

Lyle, R. C. *The Aga Khan's Horses.* London: Putnam, 1938.

McKittrick, David, and David McVea. *Making Sense of the Troubles: The Story of the Conflict in Northern Ireland.* Chicago: New Amsterdam Books, 2002

Moloney, Ed. *A Secret History of the IRA.* New York: Norton, 2002.

Morris, Tony. *Thoroughbred Stallions.* Swindon, UK: Crowood, 1990.

Morris, Tony, and John Randall. *Horse Racing: Records, Facts and Champions,* 3rd ed. Enfield, UK: Guinness, 1990.

Nickell, Joe. *Unsolved History: Investigating Mysteries of the Past.* Lexington: University Press of Kentucky, 2005.

O'Brien, Brendan. *The Long War: The IRA and Sinn Féin.* 2nd ed. Syracuse: Syracuse University Press, 1999.

O'Callaghan, Sean. *The Informer: The Real Story of One Man's War against Terrorism.* London: Corgi Books, 1999.

Ours, Dorothy. *Battleship: A Daring Heiress, a Teenage Jockey, and America's Horse.* New York: St. Martin's, 2013.

Palmer, Charles A., and Robert J. Palmer. *The Little Book of Horse Racing Law.* Chicago: ABA, 2014.

Palmer, Joe H. *American Race Horses, 1950.* New York: A. S. Barnes, 1951.

Randall, John, and Tony Randall. *A Century of Champions: Horse Racing's Millennium Book.* Halifax, UK: Portway, 1999.

Schwartz, Stephan A. *The Alexandria Project,* Lincoln, NE: iUniverse, 2001.

Shah, Sultan Muhammad, the Third Aga Khan. *The Memoirs of Aga Khan: World Enough and Time.* New York: Simon & Schuster, 1954.

Sowers, Richard. *The Kentucky Derby, Preakness and Belmont Stakes: A Comprehensive History.* Jefferson, NC: McFarland, 2014.

Taleb, Nassim Nicholas. *The Black Swan: The Impact of the Highly Improbable.* New York: Random House 2010.

Taylor, Peter. *Provos: The IRA and Sinn Fein.* London: Bloomsbury, 1998.

Thompson, Derek. *Tommo: Too Busy to Die.* Compton, UK: Racing Post Books, Kindle ed., 2013.

Turner, Colin. *In Search of Shergar.* London: Sidgwick & Jackson, 1984.

Wilkes, Roger, ed. *The Mammoth Book of Unsolved Crimes.* New York: Carroll & Graf, 1999.

Willett, Peter. *Makers of the Modern Thoroughbred.* Lexington: University Press of Kentucky, 1986.

Wilson, Julian. *Julian Wilson's 100 Greatest Racehorses.* London: Queen Anne, 1987.

# Index

*Page numbers in italics refer to illustrations.*

Shergar's potential as a sire, 175; stand-in for Sean Berry, 119; timing of theft, 102
Isabella Stewart Gardner Museum, 3–4
Ismaili Muslims, 6–7

John, Stanley, 100
J. O. Tobin (horse), 57–58
Joyce, T. (Norwich Union official), 130–31

Keadeen Hotel, 86, 119
Kelly, Patrick, 110–11
Kenirons, Martin, 121
Keogh, James, 109
Khojas, 6
kidnapping for ransom: mixed results for IRA, 78, 83–85; ransom for weapons, 49
King George VI and Queen Elizabeth Diamond Stakes, *66, 69*
King Neptune, 91–94. *See also* code words
Kris Plate, 29

*Lady Writing a Letter with Her Maid* (painting), 106
Lambton, George, 5, 11
Lanigan, Bob, 127
Leadon, Des: evaluation of skull found by Tommy Foley, 153–54; physical evidence, 152–56; veterinary surgeon, clinical pathologist at Irish Equine Centre, 152
League of Nations, 7
Liberty Market Ltd., 142
Libya, 37, 48–49, 76, 78, 82, 84, 142, 223–24n3

Lime Kiln gallop, 67–68
Lines, Cliff: best horses, 57–58; head lad at Freemason Lodge, 55; in the United States with J. O. Tobin, 57–58; return to Newmarket, 58
Lloyd, Julian: extortion, 125; inside job discounted, 171; IRA involvement, 134; mid-level IRA members, 142; on-site in Ireland after theft, 87; underwriter for John Marsh Syndicate, 86
Lloyd's Bank, 20
Lloyd's of London, 122–25; £7-million payout for theft, 125; history and process, 123–24
Loch Ness monster, 122
Logan, Johnny, 97–98
long war, 36–37
Lord Derby, 110
Lorillard, Pierre IV, 13
love of horses, 37
Lydian (horse), 64

Mafia, 144
Maghaberry Prison, 135
Magnier, John: Coolmore Stud, 39; early success, 39–40; insurance claim, lawsuit, 126–28
Mahmoud (horse), 15–16
Malicious Injuries Act, 132–33, 170
Mallon, Kevin: implicated by Sean O'Callaghan, 135; implicated in Shergar theft, 37, 84–85; IRA roles, 83–84; quiet life, 185–86
mares at Ballymany Stud, 102
Maxwell, Jeremy, 93–94
Maxwell, Judy, 93–94
Maze Prison, 76

HORSES IN HISTORY

SERIES EDITOR: James C. Nicholson

For thousands of years, humans have utilized horses for transportation, recreation, war, agriculture, and sport. Arguably, no animal has had a greater influence on human history. Horses in History explores this special human-equine relationship, encompassing a broad range of topics, from ancient Chinese polo to modern Thoroughbred racing. From biographies of influential equestrians to studies of horses in literature, television, and film, this series profiles racehorses, warhorses, sport horses, and plow horses in novel and compelling ways.